Women's Movements and the Filipina
1986–2008

Women's Movements and the Filipina

1986–2008

Mina Roces

UNIVERSITY OF HAWAI'I PRESS HONOLULU

© 2012 University of Hawai'i Press
All rights reserved
Printed in the United States of America

17 16 15 14 13 12   6 5 4 3 2 1

Library of Congress Cataloging-in-Publication Data

Roces, Mina.
  Women's movements and the Filipina, 1986–2008 / Mina Roces.
    p. cm.
  Includes bibliographical references and index.
  ISBN 978-0-8248-3499-9 (hardcover : alk. paper)
  1. Feminism—Philippines—History. 2. Women—Philippines—
Social conditions. 3. Women—Legal status, laws, etc.—
Philippines. 4. Women political activists—Philippines. I. Title.
  HQ1236.5.P6R63 2012
  305.4209599—dc23
                                  2011039930

*University of Hawai'i Press books are printed on acid-free
paper and meet the guidelines for permanence and durability
of the Council on Library Resources.*

Designed by Julie Matsuo-Chun

For Mikey Roces and Martyn Lyons

Contents

Acknowledgments

I have incurred huge debts in the research and writing of this book and it is my pleasure to thank all those who have contributed in many ways to this complex project. A Faculty of Arts and Social Sciences grant for 2004 and two Goldstar Grants from the University of New South Wales in 2005–2006 funded the research on the feminist nuns and the research on GABRIELA, DAWN, and CATW-AP. I am grateful to the Australian Research Council for a Discovery Grant (2007–2009) that enabled me to travel in order to complete the research as well as hire research assistance to transcribe the more than seventy-five interviews conducted for this book. I'd like to acknowledge the help of Raina Anne Bernardez, who transcribed most of the interviews with incredible patience from 2006–2009. In addition, Stephanie Yao, Delia Galao, and Yvonne Galao transcribed interviews in 2004–2005. The International Institute of Asian Studies, University of Leiden, awarded me an affiliated fellowship in 2006 and 2010, giving me the opportunity to interview a women's organization in the Netherlands and giving me use of the KITLV library.

Fieldwork in the Philippines was critical, and I am grateful to Sylvia Roces Montilla and the late Mrs. Leonora Montinola for their hospitality. I thank Mrs. Caridad Pineda for providing transportation in the initial stage of the research in 2003. I am particularly fortunate that women activists perceived assisting my research as part of their advocacy and went out of their way to talk to me, allow me access to their archives, and provide much-needed published materials. I want to single out Anna Leah Sarabia for her generosity in locating and copying radio and television shows for me and for sharing her memories on women's activism with me over a series of meetings and interviews. Women Media Circle's Sinag de Leon also deserves special mention for locating and copying documents from the WMC, CLIC, and KALAKASAN archives for me. Feminist nuns Mary John Mananzan (OSB), Virginia Fabella (MM), and Mary Soledad Perpiñan (RGS) shared their precious time and resources with me. Patricia Licuanan, Josefa Francisco, and Aurora Javate de Dios of Miriam College (and WAGI) gave me valuable information on the women's movements and helped me contact other women's organizations. I am thankful that Sylvia Estrada-Claudio introduced me to the women's health activists and the women's health movements. Tess Galapon organized my interviews with GABRIELA.

I also wish to acknowledge the help of libraries and librarians: Mercy Servida and Elvie Iremedio of Lopez Museum Library; the Institute of Women's Studies (Nursia) library; the Library of IFRS; WAGI; the Center for Women's Resources, Kanlungan Migrant Center, GABRIELA, Amihan, CWERC in Baguio City, and KITLV in Leiden, the Netherlands. Sister Virginia Fabella gave me permission to use her personal complete collection of *In God's Image*.

Earlier versions of parts of Chapters 1 and 8 were published in "The Filipino Catholic Nun as Transnational Feminist," *Women's History Review* 17, no. 1 (2008): 57–78, and a version of Chapter 2 was published in "Prostitution, Women's Movements and the Victim Narrative in the Philippines," *Women's Studies International Forum* 32, no. 4 (2009): 270–280.

All translations from Tagalog are my own, except for the song on p. 25. I have provided the original quotations in some endnotes.

I extend my thanks to Pam Kelley, my editor at the University of Hawai'i Press; Ann Ludeman, Alison Hope, and Stuart Robson; Alan Walker for his work on the index; and two anonymous reviewers for their constructive comments. I am also grateful for the Center for Women's Resources, Philippines, and Alexander G. Umali for the jacket art, which appeared as a cover for the journal *Babaylan* and is the artist's visual representation of the pre-Hispanic priestess.

To all the women who were interviewed and who gave me their time and shared their memories with me, I thank you: *maraming salamat po.*

Introduction

WOMEN'S MOVEMENTS AND WOMANHOOD

Maria, Maria

Since the 1980s, feminist songs have been part of the repertoire of women's activism. These songs revealed a preoccupation with Maria (a metaphor for all Filipino women) especially with her roles, her character, and her stories. These songs implored "Maria" to reject traditional stereotypes and embrace new role models. For example, one song titled "Maria" advised women that they should not allow themselves to be treated as toys that could be discarded or as subjects confined to the kitchen and the bedroom, but instead should model themselves on past women revolutionaries.[1] The lyrics of another song, "Sabon" (Soap), compelled women to reject television's two stereotypes of themselves as either sublime helpers (maids), or decorative objects.[2] The words of the song "Babae" (Woman), condemned weak women who were preoccupied with finding a man, and suggested women be inspired by revolutionaries and political activists.[3] Finally, "Bangon, Maria" (Arise, Maria) demanded that women wake up and break their chains.[4]

Feminists from the 1980s made the task of theorizing the feminine a priority. Because it was important to them that traditional constructions of the feminine be unpacked and dismantled, defining the Filipina—what she *was,* what she *is,* and what she *will become*—was central to activist ideologies. Furthermore, discourses on the feminine were imperative in the struggle against patriarchy. Representations of the

1

feminine were used in strategies such as lobbying for legislative changes. At the same time, women activists also were engaged in the business of critiquing cultural constructions of the feminine for the purposes of altering stereotypical sex roles. In this sense, representations of the Filipino woman were crucial in the feminist reeducation campaign—in the overall plan to resocialize the populace to give symbolic capital (prestige) to its women vis-à-vis its men. Thus, the question of Maria's heritage and identity (past, present, and future) has been central to the agendas and ideologies of women's movements since the 1980s.

This book is about the feminist project and its interrogation of the Filipino woman in the period from about the mid-1980s until 2008: locating her in history, society, and politics; imagining her past, present, and future; representing her in advocacy; and identifying strategies that transform her. The focus is on how women's organizations imagined and refashioned the Filipina in their campaign to improve women's status in the legal and cultural contexts. The drive to alter women's situations included a political strategy (for lobbying, campaigning, and changing legislation) and a cultural strategy (to change social attitudes and women's own assessment of themselves). Intrinsic to the achievement of these goals was analysis of the status of women and a feminist critique of that status. Although it is true that the women's movements were focused on altering legislation, lobbying, research, political advocacy, and education (to alter cultural attitudes), all these activities made it necessary to invoke discourses about the Filipino woman. Representations of Filipino women were of critical importance to feminist advocacy. They were important in justifying demands for legislative changes, they were needed as ammunition for criticizing gender relations in society, and they were crucial in the campaign to refashion women as advocates. I am interested in the cultural side of the feminist agenda: how women's organizations critiqued womanhood and how they themselves engaged in fashioning an alternative woman. This cultural production has been identified by feminist scholar Delia Aguilar as the realm in which women have been the most energetic and passionate: "The publication of books and journals, staging of plays, music composition, the visual arts, performances on radio and TV—in these utilization of women's talent, imagination, creativity and resources has been both remarkable and inspiring."[5] This study examines the history of this feminist project.

In particular, this book addresses the following specific questions: How did women's activists theorize the Filipino woman and how did they use this analysis to lobby for pro-women's legislation or alter social attitudes? What sort of "new Filipinas" did they propose as alternative role models? How were these new ideas disseminated to the public? And finally, what cultural strategies did they deploy to gain a mass following? Although inevitably the discussion surveys the history of women's movements since the 1980s, the emphasis is on the ways the Filipina has been imagined as intrinsic to women's advocacy.

Discourses on the Filipino woman were necessary in the projects of representing women for particular advocacies (for example, on behalf of prostitutes, women workers, or indigenous women), and in fashioning women (in imbuing feminist consciousness, or in introducing new role models and feminist epistemologies, and in the feminist practices designed to transforming "survivors" into "advocates"). Given the very vibrant nature of the women's movements, it is not surprising that activists produced many discourses (some of them contradictory) about the Filipino woman as part of their overall agendas of deconstructing Filipino womanhood or improving women's status. There was never one single consistent narrative produced on this controversial topic; instead, each narrative was linked to a specific advocacy or activist agenda. Some of these narratives will be discussed in this book.

Despite the myriad types of discourses, women activists were united in the overall project of women's empowerment. At face value, this larger aim often conflicted with some of the representations of women as victims or modern-day slaves. I argue that feminists often adopted what I will call a double narrative, or the deployment of two contrasting discourses— a narrative of victimization and a narrative of activism. I suggest that a double narrative of victim/survivor and advocate was used by activists in their discourses about the Filipino woman. I prefer the term "double narrative" because these representations of women reflect two sides of the same coin; although they are contradictory, women's movements have tapped on both opposing discourses for feminist ends. I also imply that the lines between both narratives are fluid and not fixed, because it is acknowledged that victims could become advocates or that the label "victim" was not totally devoid of agency (which is why the women's movements often prefer the term "survivor" to "victim"). For example, women activists deployed the victim narrative to argue for the passage of the Anti-Trafficking in Persons Act of 2003 that decriminalized prostitutes (whether or not there was consent), but preferred to use the narrative of advocacy, agency, and empowerment when fashioning former prostitutes and survivors of trafficking into feminist activists. The latter was part of the overall feminist project of dismantling cultural constructions of the feminine as "suffering

3

martyr" and rejecting the cultural capital associated with this ideal. In feminist herstories published by women's organizations, the colonial period is blamed for taking away women's religious power and replacing it with the ideology of domesticity emerging from the colonizer's patriarchal ideology. But juxtaposed in this narrative are stories of women's resistance and activism throughout history. Whereas women workers were represented as the most oppressed and exploited of women or as modern-day slaves, they also were imagined to be the most militant of advocates who had the potential not just of being the mass followers, but also of being the leaders of the women's movements. In presenting these contradictory discourses as a double narrative, I do not see contradictory discourses as necessarily "bad" or "good," or even problematic. Indeed, the contradictions merely stress the complexities faced by activists while acknowledging their adroit skills and political savvy in representing and fashioning women to fulfill their agendas.

The word "victim" here refers to the experience of violation—a material reality. The term "victim narrative" refers to the discourse in which women's experiences were constructed in a history of continuing oppression and violation. Its opposite—the story of resistance and activism—describes the narrative of advocacy.[6] In this book, I adopt the view of hybrid agency to refer to the manner in which women activists adopt and adapt transnational notions of consent, and exercise choice both within and against cultural and political structures.[7]

In this book, the term "women's movements" referred to women's activism initiated by women's organizations for the purposes of improving women's status. Here I refer to the various agendas of a plethora of women's organizations collectively. This study is confined only to those who are feminist, and does not include organizations formed and led by women for purposes of philanthropy or civic organizations formed by wives or female kin of politicians that act as a support group for male politicians. Although some of these groups aimed to provide a livelihood for impoverished women (with some even claiming NGO status), they fall within the more traditional types of units not explicitly feminist in orientation.[8]

The term "feminist organization" refers to those organizations whose main aims are to critique women's inequality and whose activism centers on altering or changing structures in society in order to remove gender discrimination. Many of these organizations might address only issues of particular or specific (or even narrow) groups of women, but in doing so they challenge patriarchy from small to significant ways.

Certainly, not all women and not all sectors are represented by these organizations, but the reality is that only those women who organized themselves can demand to be heard. I am deliberately using a very broad definition of "feminism": many women activists are uncomfortable with the term because it has long been associated with bra-burning, man-hating, or with manly or unfeminine women.[9] These activists' qualms can be explained by their perception that feminism is a Western term. Even though they might quibble with whether they considered themselves to be feminists (with feminism still carrying negative connotations) however, they see themselves as part of the women's movements. Although a number of women activists and women's organizations are happy to carry the badge of "feminist," I have noticed that even those who are anxious about the term, by the end of my interview with them, would concede that, given a general definition of the term, yes, they could be classified as a feminist. All the organizations included in this study are at least feminist in orientation.

The labels of socialist feminists, liberal feminists, Marxist feminists, national-democratic feminists, and radical feminists and ecofeminists do not apply to Filipino women's organizations whose ideologies often straddle these categories. My interviews with leading feminists in the Philippines confirmed that it is not helpful to categorize women's organizations according to these classifications.[10] The women's movement is much divided, and hence it is more accurate to use the term "women's movements" (plural) than the term "women's movement" (singular) to describe feminist activism since the 1980s. Feminists remain divided over all the major issues and consequently any writing about women's activism in the contemporary era (including this book) will be controversial. Ideological differences, though present, have not usually been the major reason for organizations splitting up; conflict is usually over political tactics and strategies, and the politics of critical collaboration with the state.[11] Personality clashes were often cited as responsible for triggering the tendency to leave one organization and form a new one, and activists seem very comfortable with this regular splintering, although discussing it is still very much taboo.[12] Activists, if they were willing to elaborate on differences, preferred to keep the information "off the record": personal intrigues and disagreements over tactics often occur even within the same organization. Intergenerational challenges are beginning to enter the picture as the young generation—women who are no longer directly affected by the national-democratic struggle—begin to question the dominant feminist discourses and reject the victim/agency dichotomy.[13]

I will not be focusing on the disunity here (and it was difficult to find activists willing to talk about it) but will call attention to some of the major differences when they are pertinent to my arguments.

This book includes a discussion of how the mainstream nation-wide lowland Christian women's movements represented the indigenous women of the highlands. Cordillera women's political activism during the Marcos dictatorship (1972–1986) has been mythologized by women's movements. Since the Spaniards were unable to colonize the Cordillera, indigenous women were spared from Spanish Catholicism, identified by the women's movements as the most profound and enduring ideology that has shaped Filipino womanhood from the sixteenth century to the present. Chapter 4 focuses on indigenous women to illustrate how women's movements have interacted with indigenous women as the "other Filipina." Finally, the absence of a section on the Filipino Muslim women's movements points to an important gap not covered in this study. Muslim women's issues are different from the dominant Christian majority (for example, a fatwa, or Islamic ruling, exists on the issue of reproductive health). There is a vibrant group of Muslim feminists, including a number of Muslim feminist lawyers; they merit an entire study on their own.

Short History of the Women's Movements

The history of feminism in the Philippines begins with the suffrage movement that was led by the National Federation of Women's Clubs in the 1920s. The vote was won largely due to the organizational skills of the first generation of feminists who campaigned hard to win the franchise from a constitutional convention that was largely against women's suffrage.[14] But once suffrage was won in 1937 and women entered political office, feminists became practically inactive until the 1960s, at which time student activism injected new life into the dormant women's movement. In the early 1970s, the Free Movement of New Women (MAKIBAKA; Malayang Kilusan ng Bagong Kababaihan) was organized as an offshoot of the Nationalist Youth (Kabataan Makabayan), founded initially to mobilize women as part of the student activism of the late 1960s and early 1970s. These activists protested social injustices, the Vietnam War, U.S. influence on domestic affairs, oil prices, inflation, the Marcos government's fascist tendencies, and the wide disparity between the rich and the poor. Under the leadership of Lorena Barros, MAKIBAKA developed a feminist consciousness. But when martial law was declared in

September 1972 and the students were forced underground (and Lorena Barros was killed by the military), MAKIBAKA was prevented from mutating into a feminist movement with a nationalist orientation, or, alternatively, a nationalist movement with a feminist orientation. With the premature silencing of MAKIBAKA, the development of the women's movement experienced a second hiatus.

There were, however, some women in the Communist underground whose common experience of gender discrimination in the Communist Party brought them together. The bonding of this small group who began to question the left's treatment of women cadres resulted in the formation of the Organization of Women for Freedom (KALAYAAN; Katipunan ng Kababaihan Para sa Kalayaan) in 1983.[15] This clearly feminist organization tackled issues of rape, domestic violence, pornography, and abortion. Reminiscing on the rationale behind the formation of KALAYAAN, Aida Santos, Fe Mangahas, and Ana Maria "Princess" Nemenzo admitted that they were determined to have a feminist group that was autonomous but committed to two revolutions—one for national liberation and one for women's liberation.[16] Together with another organization, PILIPINA (formed in 1981 and composed of left-leaning activists, including a feminist Benedictine nun), these two groups revived feminist activism, insisting that women's issues be given equal priority in the struggle against the dictatorship. Scholar Leonora Angeles, who has written an excellent master's thesis on the history of the woman question in the Philippines, identified both KALAYAAN and PILIPINA as among the first to apply feminism to their analytical framework at a time when the word "feminist" was shunned due to its association with Western feminism and women's liberation.[17] This cohort of women members of KALAYAAN and PILIPINA became the first group of feminist leaders that inspired the newly revitalized women's movement in the first decade of the 1980s. They pioneered activism with a feminist perspective tackling issues such as sexism in the media, reproductive rights, prostitution, and violence against women.[18]

But just at the time when political activists against the Marcos regime were developing a feminist consciousness, Marcos' chief political opponent, Benigno Aquino Jr. was assassinated on August 21, 1983. This one political act launched a tidal wave of protests that culminated in the People Power 1 revolution, which ousted President Ferdinand Marcos in 1986. The urgent need to devote their energy on the antidictatorship struggle in 1983 meant that once again women's liberation had to be temporarily shelved in order to focus on the movement to oust the dictator.

From 1983 until the ouster of Marcos, a number of activist women's groups mushroomed. These women's organizations were dedicated to the mobilization of women as a gendered force to politicize them against the Marcos regime. In March 1984, a group of women's organizations coalesced to form GABRIELA (General Assembly Binding Women for Reforms, Integrity, Equality, Leadership and Action). At that time, there were about fifty organizations in Manila and thirty-eight in Mindanao affiliated with GABRIELA.[19] By 1992, 120 organizations were affiliated with GABRIELA.[20] At its inception, GABRIELA was interested in harnessing women's power for the anti-Marcos dictatorship movement rather than in advocating specific feminist or women's issues.

But it was only after democratic institutions were restored in 1986 that women's activism gained momentum, resulting in what Carolyn Sobritchea has labeled "a critical mass of highly motivated feminist advocates" and what interviewees referred to as the era of a "blossoming" of the women's movements.[21] There were organizations of women of various sectors (such as peasants, urban poor, Muslim women, Cordillera women, migrant women, women workers, and women in media, to name a few) and issue-oriented organizations (such as those specializing on women's health, domestic violence, prostitution, women's legal advocacy and services, and "comfort women," or victims of sexual slavery during the Japanese Occupation, for example).[22] The Women's Media Circle Foundation Inc. (WMC) used the potential of tri-media (radio, television, and print media) for the women's movements, whereas women's health advocates and feminist lawyers explored the possibilities of alliance building for advocacy. The spectacular growth and effectiveness of NGOs could be partially explained by the impacts of the international conferences on women and the United Nations conferences in particular, as well as the funding made available for NGOs in the developing world.[23] Although GABRIELA tended to receive the lion's share of media and international attention because of its visible presence at demonstrations and the formation of its own women's party in 2003 (see subsequent section in this introduction, Women and Formal Politics), by the 1990s the myriad group of women's organizations including hundreds of grassroots organizations, women NGOs, coalitions, and professional groups, underscored the point that one could no longer speak of a single women's movement.[24] Delia Aguilar was careful to point out that GABRIELA was no longer as central to the women's movement as it had been in the 1980s because of the many groups flourishing outside its alliance.[25] A direct consequence of the plural nature of women's

activism was disunity, but it could be argued that its very plurality legiti-
mated its claim to speak for the Filipina. Carolyn Sobritchea claims that
differences, instead of being counterproductive "served as a catalyst for
all to work harder and cover all fronts, so to speak in the struggle to advance women's rights in the Philippines."[26] Although disagreement is not
unusual for activist groups and may in fact enrich the women's projects,
we need to note its negative consequences (most evident in the failure of
women's parties to get politicians elected; see subsequent section in this
introduction, Women and Formal Politics).

The issues raised by women's movements covered almost the entire
gamut of women's experiences: health and reproductive rights, domestic
violence, sexual harassment, globalization and its effects, the plight of
women workers and peasant women, indigenous women, Muslim wom-
en, rape, incest, class, unemployment and the contractualization of the
labor force, "comfort women," militarization, prostitution, the impact
of Christianity on shaping feminine ideal role models, the media, and
education as socializing factors, sexuality including lesbianism, poverty,
environmental factors, foreign debt, and other national issues.[27] Divorce
and abortion have been much more controversial and thus public discussion on these issues has been muted (see Chapter 9). This book will
examine the discourses on the Filipino woman that emerged in the advocacy of some of these issues.

Women and Formal Politics

Women were still marginalized in formal politics, with a general average
of a mere 11 percent (from 1986 to 2006) elected to local and national
office.[28] Because of these grim statistics, the most common tactic used
by activists to ensure that pro-women legislative acts were proposed, discussed, and passed in the legislature was to draft legislation and then
convince their allies in the legislature to sponsor them. But women activists also were interested in claiming power themselves. The first women's
party, Women for the Mother Country (KAIBA; Kababaihan Para sa
Inang Bayan) was established in 1987; KAIBA won only one congressional seat (Dominique Anna "Nikki" Coseteng) in the 1987 election. This
congresswoman eventually joined a traditional party.[29] Angeles explains
KAIBA's failure in terms of women's relative isolation from patronage
politics.[30] Eventually KAIBA became moribund.

But in 1995 the passage of the Party-List System Act that classified
women as a sector enabled women's parties to compete on a more level

playing field. This legislation provided that 20 percent (at least fifty) of the House of Representatives (250) be reserved for representatives of labor, peasants, urban poor, indigenous peoples, youth, fisherfolk, elderly, veterans, women, and other marginalized sectors elected through a party list system.[31] A new system allowing sectors to compete for "reserved seats" meant that those parties who were deprived of the traditional patronage networks like women's groups would have a chance at making it in the lower house. A total of six women's parties offered candidates under the women sector although only one party Abanse! Pinay (made up of PILIPINA members) was able to get a congresswoman (Patricia Sarenas) elected. The other women's parties who fielded candidates but were unsuccessful in gaining a seat were The New Filipina (Ang Bagong Pilipina), Women (Babayi), the National Council of Women in the Philippines, Gloria's League of Women (GLOW), and Womenpower.[32] One must also include the rare number of feminists who were elected as members of other sectoral parties such as the Akbayan (Citizen's Action Party; this party has an affirmative action platform stipulating that one of the three candidates fielded must be a woman) and Country First (Bayan Muna). For example, Liza Largoza Maza, then secretary general of GABRIELA, ran under Bayan Muna and Etta Rosales with Akbayan. Both women were elected to Congress and were credited for proposing pro-women legislation during their term. Congresswoman Maza was responsible for filing fifteen out of the thirty-eight pro-women bills and resolutions filed under the thirteenth congress.[33] In July 2003, GABRIELA launched its own women's party. Liza Maza became the first GABRIELA women's party member to enter Congress when she won a seat in the 2004 elections. In 2007, Luzviminda Calolot "Luz" Ilagan became the second, and in 2010 Emerciana "Emmi" de Jesus became the third.

The poignant history of Abanse! Pinay could serve as a case study for the challenges faced by the feminists in formal politics. In a peculiar example of déjà vu, Abanse! Pinay shared the same fate as KAIBA and became moribund; PILIPINA is still active, however. The party failed to get a seat in 2004 and 2007, making it ineligible to run again in the party list unless it registered under a new name. Like KAIBA, Abanse! Pinay had a short life span. A candid interview with Patricia Sarenas provided some insights into the reasons for the party's decline. According to Sarenas, PILIPINA had always been divided over what strategies to use to increase the membership of the party.[34] These debates within the party itself were never resolved.[35] If one added to this potent mix the personal disputes between members resulting in some members leaving the organization or abandoning the party, the fragile unity of this organization no doubt contributed to its failure to survive in the long term.[36] Whereas such disputes are not unusual in the dynamics of Philippine political parties, there is no denying that the consequences for the women's movements were crippling, preventing them from surviving as viable parties in the long term. Although GABRIELA seems to be holding its ground (as of this writing in 2010), it is still too soon to tell its future.

Election campaigns could be used for feminist propaganda. In reality, however, this potential is yet to be realized. Josefa Francisco argued that in the 1998 elections parties did not use election campaigns as a forum for debating each other. According to Francisco, the result was that "not a ripple of debate was felt," even over top priority issues such as reproductive rights, sexual rights, and women's poverty. Instead, these issues were avoided during the election campaign. Perhaps this could be explained by the fear of reprisals from the Catholic Church in such controversial issues. The consequence of the silence was that the women's parties missed the opportunity of using election campaigns as a venue for feminist propaganda.[37] Maybe election campaigns by nature—the need to entice potential voters—were far from ideal as venues for challenging patriarchy.

On the other hand, the activist strategy of lobbying with legislators sympathetic to particular women's issues has been very effective.[38] This strategy has been deployed consistently (with a good track record) from 1986 onwards. So far, it has been the best method of ensuring that pro-women legislation is passed. Another area of successful collaboration with the state is the link with the government body—the National Commission on the Role of Filipino Women (NCRFW). The NCRFW was established on January 7, 1975, through Presidential Decree No. 633 as an advisory body to the president and the cabinet on policies and programs for the advancement of women; it was renamed the Philippine Commission on Women on August 14, 2009.[39] But active collaboration of NGOs and government began after the 1986 revolution, when President Corazon Aquino appointed Remmy Ricken from PILIPINA as executive director of NCRFW. Carolyn Sobritchea has acknowledged the role of the NCRFW in initiating links between the state or government and women's NGOs through the formation of alliances such as the GO-NGO network in 1993.[40] There are areas where collaboration with the government has been positive for the women's movements although the activists were fully aware of the limits of this alliance. Members of PILIPINA have been appointed to the NCRFW. This book, however, moves away from a focus on women's engagement with the state; a thorough examination of the politics of critical collaboration with the state remains a topic for future research.

Filipino Feminisms in the Local and International Contexts

Although there is no doubt that Filipino feminist theory was influenced by international literature on the topic, Western feminism was immediately targeted as alien by activists who were self-conscious about their nationalist-democratic roots (as leftists). A rejection of the imperial hold also implied a rejection of imperial mentalities, including feminism. Women activists claimed that Filipino feminist theories were homegrown, based on the analysis of the women's situation in the Philippine context, influenced by the experiences of women survivors of exploitation.[41]

The leaders of the women's movements from the 1980s were highly educated women from the middle class and a tiny group of religious women (feminist nuns). Although feminist nuns were marginalized in the history and leadership of American second-wave feminisms, they were in the vanguard of Filipino women's activism.[42] The high profile of Catholic nuns, some of whom were celebrities and role models, was archetypical, injecting a unique flavor to women's movements in the Philippines and problematizing the very notion of class. (A number of these nuns were actually from the upper classes who took a vow of poverty when they entered the convent and often lived with the poor; see Chapters 1 and 8.) Women activists also wore different hats as academics, leaders of women's organizations, and government appointees or advisers; they also served as Philippine representatives to transnational and international organizations that formulate policies on women in the developing world (see Chapter 8). These close ties with the "field" cast a legitimizing aura on their ability to speak for women of the lower classes and other sectors. Upper-class women, who were the prime movers of the suffrage movement in the 1920s, were rarely present in this next phase of women's activism. Perhaps this could be partly explained by the fact that these women had achieved their aims—the right to vote and run for office—and were now benefiting from this victory by becoming politicians themselves (or were marrying politicians).[43] Women's studies academics writing on Filipino feminist theory were involved in feminist praxis as leaders and activists in women's organizations.

Since the leaders of the women's movements were once political activists against the Marcos regime, the desire to build a mass following and claim the lower classes as their constituency was foremost in their agendas. In fact, the Philippine women's movement in their self-representations (and legitimizing discourses) consistently claimed to speak for the lower classes. Whether this self-representation was supported by reality, however, was difficult to assess; nonetheless, the activists must be credited with making a conscious and persistent effort to research on the impacts of particular issues on the lower classes and to include lower-class members in their organization. It is appropriate to claim that women's movements reflected alliances between the middle class and lower classes.

THE INTERNATIONAL CONTEXT

Responding to demographic trends since the 1970s, feminists theorized the Filipina as "servants of globalization," working for wealthier countries all over the world as domestic helpers, entertainers, professional workers, and live-in caregivers; they were also seen as migrants for marriage.[44] The women's movements responded quickly to this shifting movement across national borders by making sure that the organizations they founded were transnationally based. These organizations lobbied the Philippine government, as well as countries hosting Filipino women workers or migrants, and international bodies such as the United Nations. Some of the activists themselves, particularly the feminist nuns, were particularly effective precisely because they were transnational activists unmoored in space and place (see Chapter 8). Many of the organizations discussed in this book established branches overseas, and advocacy work was performed simultaneously across the seas. Linked through the Internet, the cell phone, and the more traditional print and audiovisual media, the entire world was staked as their public arena of protest.

Transnational locations were also shifting locations as organizations sprouted or closed down around the world, depending on necessity. Locally based organizations therefore looked outwards towards the outside world when they represented the Filipina. On the other hand, the international branches of these transnational organizations looked back towards the Philippines—all the way to the woman's cultural socialization in her home country—to understand the woman migrant's past, an essential strategy in their advocacy. This two-way process—looking away from and towards the Philippines—informed activists' feminist positions.

The international outlook embraced by activists was not merely a product of the need to address the Filipina as transnational subject brought on by globalization and the place of the Philippines in the global south. Despite the self-conscious representation of Filipino feminists as homegrown (a label that has some credibility), the international context is vital. I hesitate to subscribe to a division between Western feminists and feminists of the rest of the world, and prefer to see Filipino feminists participating in international feminist debates. After all, four Filipino women have chaired the United Nations Commission on the Status of Women (CSW), and three have acted as experts for the Commission on the Elimination of Discrimination Against Women (CEDAW).[45] Filipino activists were also members of international feminist organizations (and often office bearers of organizations) such as Coalition Against Trafficking in Women-International (CATW-International); Women's Commission of EATWOT (Ecumenical Association of Third World Theologians); International Lesbian and Gay Association (ILGA); and Asian Peasant Network, to name a few. In this sense, one could argue that Filipina activists contributed to the international musings on the "woman question," providing expertise on migration and trafficking, in particular. They were not merely at the receiving end of a Western feminist lecture, but were actually proactive in challenging the Atlantic-centered feminists at international conferences. Filipina activists of CATW-AP clashed with Dutch feminists over whether prostitution is violence against women or sex work, and Filipino feminist nuns contributed to feminist theological debates.

The histories of women's movements in the Philippines must be located in a transnational context despite the anxiety over feminism as a Western or foreign import. After all, since the fiery debates between women of all color at the United Nations' first world conference on women held in Mexico City in 1975, international feminists can no longer be seen as predominantly middle-class white. Although United Nations protocols and international shifts in feminist theories have an impact on the Philippines, Filipina activists have through their positions in the United Nations, United Nations Development Fund for Women, and NGOs also participated in the international conversation about the "woman question." At the same time, because funding for NGOs often came from overseas, United Nations priorities had an impact on the distribution of money intended for development.[46]

FILIPINO FEMINIST THEORIES/FILIPINO FEMINISMS

The fundamental question of how women's groups constructed the Fili-pina—and how this has affected women's movements has not yet been seriously posed by scholars writing on women's movements in the Philippines. There has been no comprehensive study on women's movements in the Philippines or on Filipino feminist theory that documents the activists' self-conscious enterprise of developing an indigenous brand of feminism.[47] It is in the second half of the 1980s that a "critical mass" of women's organizations adopting a feminist perspective and prioritizing feminist issues appeared, and it is also from 1985 onwards that activists officially lay the foundation for Filipino feminist theory in the process of designing teaching modules for women's studies courses at the tertiary level. It is also at the end of the 1980s that women's organizations decided to focus on grassroots women.

Mary John Mananzan (OSB) (Order of Saint Benedict), a Benedictine feminist nun, has been credited with running the first women's studies workshop in the Philippines in 1985 at St. Scholastica's College.[48] This group of eighteen activists was the first to design a syllabus for a Filipino women's studies module. Mananzan later founded Nursia in 1988. Nursia ran three-day women's orientation seminars six times a year for "grassroots women"; these seminars were held in the Center and in the provinces. Whereas St. Scholastica's College ran women's studies courses for women in higher education, Nursia offered these women orientation seminars (or abridged versions of these courses) to factory workers, peasant women, and urban poor women.[49]

The Center for Women's Resources (CWR) was another women's NGO whose forte was providing basic women's orientation workshops for all sorts of women's organizations. Founded in 1982, it excels in the publication of educational materials on Filipino women's issues, coordinates the Paaralang Lisa Balando (PLB; an education training school for grassroots women), and develops education modules and instructor's training seminars.[50]

The University of the Philippines was the first Philippine university to offer a graduate degree in women's studies.[51] It founded its own University Center for Women's Studies in 1988. Miriam College (formerly Maryknoll College), a women's college with a critical mass of women activists in its faculty, set up the WAGI in 1997, offering training and education workshops for the community.[52] The three women's studies centers complemented their research activities with advocacy, training, and outreach services to the community.[53] These outreach services were very important as evidence of the activists' stress on the community as their primary constituency and the lower classes as their priority.

What is Filipina feminist theory? Specifically, activists seek to answer questions such as, Who is the Filipina woman? What sorts of enduring grand narratives of the feminine have been reproduced over the centuries? Where is this "Filipina woman" located? How can activists empower her? And finally, What new Filipina or what alternative narratives of women should we propose and fashion? This book focuses on how activists have deconstructed Filipino womanhood, and how they hoped to fashion an alternative Filipino woman. The analysis of Filipino constructions of the feminine was absolutely critical as the foundation for Filipino feminist theory. In addition, feminists have operated from a theoretical framework that perceived the Filipina as deeply connected with the world, with the premise that the Filipina postcolonial condition placed her at the bottom rung of the global racial hierarchy, epitomized by the women factory workers (especially in the electronics industries), by peasant women, and by the plight of domestic helpers overseas. Basic women's orientation seminars run by CWR explain the exploitation suffered by women workers as the result of the feudal nature of Philippine society, and discuss the country's developing world status subject to the neo-imperialism of the rich northern countries and their transnational operations. Since the activist perspective was to locate the Filipino woman in both the international and local context, and because for practical reasons organizations chose to have branches overseas, Filipino feminist theory could not be critiqued for being inward-looking.

Inevitably, however, discourses on the Filipino woman also reveal the complex relationship between women's movements and the state as the government is identified as both the enemy (in the case of prostitution, for example, where the state is critiqued for tacitly endorsing it and is willing to sacrifice its women for remittances and tourist dollars), and as an ally (as some departments including the legislature work with women's organizations and some activists gain political power or government positions). The Catholic Church and traditional Filipino cultural attitudes (particularly the pressures from the kinship group) receive their fair share of criticism in the narratives of the feminist movements. The complexities of activism in the Philippine context are particularly obvious when discussing the perceptive power of the Catholic Church (often seen as even more powerful than politicians) and the fact that some feminist leaders are Catholic nuns working with the poorest and most marginalized of women.

Filipino activists since the 1980s could not be accused of ignoring the issue of "class" because the question of "Which Filipino woman do we claim to represent?" received star billing, front and center in the published literature of almost all organizations. Feminist discourses from the 1980s onwards were fond of the phrase "grassroots women" and practically every NGO that was woman-centered claimed to speak on behalf of lower-class women classified by women's organizations into sectors such as peasants, prostitutes, urban poor, migrants, entertainers, workers, youth, Muslim women, and indigenous women, to name a few. A book such as this one that examines how women's organizations represent women in various discourses to a large extent reproduces this great sectoral divide. That Filipino feminist theory cannot get away from a sectoral view of women is problematic, but it is understandable since the answer to the question of the extent to which the analysis of women can be "desectored" is difficult to answer. For some issues, especially those that cut across class or ethnicity lines such as violence against women or domestic violence, women's groups advocate for a quintessential Filipino woman who is not imagined to be a member of a particular sector. The reality, of course, is that most women's experiences blur the lines between "sectors." Indigenous women are also women workers and migrants for example. Although part of the feminist project has been to dismantle grand narratives on womanhood, activists also have fashioned new narratives that cut across all sectors of women. Feminists had an acute sense of history, and the feminist interpretation of women's history applied to all women regardless of sector.[54] This feminist interpretation of Philippine history was to become an important part of Filipino feminist theory.

The Double Narrative in the Historiography of the Women's Movements

In order to theorize the Filipino woman, activists found it necessary to place womanhood in its unique historical and cultural context. It was important to analyze how womanhood has been defined over time because contemporary beliefs about it were products of a particular historical experience. As the official GABRIELA history of women expressed it, "Our beliefs and our minds were shaped by our experiences, environment, and the culture of the society where we grew up."[55] Being attuned to the political uses of history activists produced a historiography that reproduced the double narrative of women's oppression and resistance.

Since women were largely invisible in the history textbooks published before the 1980s, placing women at the center of historical and scholarly inquiry became an important preoccupation of activists writing about the "woman question" from about the 1980s. Mary John Mananzan's (OSB) edited anthology *Essays on Women* was the first to examine women's experiences in various historical periods from the precolonial era to contemporary times.[56] The WMC produced a two-part documentary entitled "From Priestess to President: The Story of Women's Struggle in the Philippines." This documentary was shown in two episodes of the television show *Womanwatch* in 1987. GABRIELA published its own version of women's history in 1989.[57] Short histories of Filipino women appeared in the newsletters published by women's organizations. In the 1990s, radio programs like *Tinig ng Nursia* (The Voice of Nursia, hereafter *Tinig*) and *XYZone* devoted some episodes to the discussion of women in Philippine history. GABRIELA's radio program *Babae Ka, May Say Ka!* (You are a woman, you have a say, hereafter *Babae Ka*) had a regular segment on women in history. Although it might be prudent to underscore the differences between the histories produced by the academe and the women activists, the blurring of lines between academic and activist made it difficult to distinguish between the two bodies of work.[58] In addition, women's organizations referred to women's histories written by scholars (including historians, social scientists, and literature specialists) in their advocacy. Because this book focuses on women's movements, I will analyze the historiography produced by the women's organizations as well as activists linked to organizations (including feminist nuns), and refer to the scholarship on Filipino women's histories in context.

Given the deep divisions in the women's movements, the absence of serious controversy in the historiography of the Filipino woman is remarkable. The consensus that the Spanish colonial era destroyed the "golden age" of women's egalitarian status with men and shaped contemporary womanhood remained largely unchallenged as late as 2006. The American colonial period was not singled out as a major watershed in this periodization of women's history, although it was criticized for encouraging the exploitation of women in factories and for perpetuating the definition of woman as mother and queen of the home.[59] In GABRIELA's version of history, Spanish friars defined Filipino womanhood in the period 1521–1896.[60] An unpublished study by Carolyn Medel

Añonuevo (which scholar and women's health activist Sylvia Estrada-Claudio quoted) concluded that the present-day Filipina's self-concept could be attributed to the Spanish Catholic Church's evangelizing and colonizing influence.[61] A book on the history of Philippine feminist poetry observed that the poetic tradition endorsed the Spanish colonial narrative as womanhood became synonymous with virginity, purity, and chastity.[62]

The contrast between the precolonial era represented as the highest point in women's status and the Spanish period as its nemesis informed the discussion of the past. Histories produced by the women activists were unique from mainstream historiography not just because they introduced the women's perspective for the first time, but also because of the emphasis placed on the precolonial period, in itself an underresearched field. Even though sources for this period were from outsiders writing on the Philippines, activists read these sources from a feminist perspective and determined the status of the indigenous woman, described by Spanish explorers and friars at the point of contact in the sixteenth century. All the versions underscored the high status women enjoyed with their role as priestess, the epitome of their social value. This new women's history paralleled that of Filipino nationalists in the nineteenth century, particularly José Rizal who also imagined the precolonial past as a lost Eden destroyed by Spanish colonization.[63] Just as Filipino nationalists constructed the past to build Filipino identity, national pride, and self-esteem, feminists upheld the indigenous woman as an empowered woman whose religious, economic, social, and cultural power was crushed by the Spanish colonizer in the project of fashioning woman according to Iberian and Christian ideals.

Mananzan's pioneering essay (which became the standard history used by women's organizations) concluded that the Spanish period had negative consequences for the Filipino woman.[64] Using Spanish written sources, Mananzan argued that women had religious power as priestesses (*babaylan* or *catalonan,* which are female healers or shamans), inherited property, engaged in business along with husbands, and had control over their own fertility. This led her to conclude, "In summary, we see that the woman had an honored position in the family whether as a daughter or a wife."[65] But the Spanish colonial ruler introduced patriarchal values from Christianity and sixteenth-century Iberian values that introduced the cult of domesticity and proposed the Virgin Mary as the ideal. The result was revolutionary:

Whereas the young girl in the pre-Spanish society enjoyed educational opportunities and similar freedom of movement as the young boy, the young girl under the Spanish influence became a sheltered, over-protected, timid maiden who received an education confined to the church, kitchen and children. She who could transact business with anybody, look after the economic welfare of the family, who could bear the responsibility of being a pact holder and even a leader of her tribe was reduced to a helpless creature like Maria Clara who could never leave the house unaccompanied by an ever present Tia Isabel.[66]

In "From Priestess to President," produced by the WMC, hosts Cecile B. Garrucho and Lily Lim presented a script much like Mananzan's history and even included an interview with her. Women in precolonial times were represented as equals of men because they could own and inherit property, had economic freedom, exercised civic and political rights, were protected by native laws, and shared in the decision-making processes at home and in the community. According to this interpretation, in this era men and women shared the household and childrearing duties. In contrast, Spanish rule was depicted as placing women under the servility of men as women's roles became confined to the bedroom, the kitchen, and the church.[67] This same view of women's history was again delivered to audiences of the radio program *XYZone* by anchor Rina Jimenez David in an episode devoted to women trailblazers in history. The talk show featured an interview with Dr. Alma Fernandez, a retired professor at the University of the Philippines who pointed out that the priestess' ability to connect the natural world to the spiritual world was a sign of her high status complemented by women's rights to property, abortion, and divorce.[68] Historians also endorsed this view. Milagros Guerrero's research on the pre-Hispanic priestess in the Spanish records concluded that the Spanish "assault on the functions of the *babaylan* did have one enduring consequence: the all too real diminution of the status of women in colonial Philippines."[69]

This interpretation of women's history had political uses: it claimed that the activists were immersed in a movement to recover rights lost to colonialism. In this sense, feminists could not be seen to be radical because they were merely demanding what was traditional. At the same time, this interpretation deflected criticisms that they were embracing a foreign or Western feminist viewpoint that was incompatible with Filipino culture (instead, Filipino women were nationalistic!). This same strategy also was used by the suffragists in an effort to blunt censure that they were "Americanitas," mimicking American women who wanted the right to vote and run for political office.[70] The arguments could be effective only if the historiography of a "lost Eden" of women's rights was endorsed, however. Hence, there has been little interest from activists in writing a more nuanced feminist history.

THE VIRGIN MARY AS IDEAL WOMAN

According to Mananzan, the Spanish friars imposed "the impossible model" of the Virgin Mary as the ideal woman.[71] GABRIELA's history referred to this construction of the feminine role model as the Virgin Mother. The norm for woman was conflated with "wife and mother," and the cult of domesticity enforced in order to protect women's virginity before marriage—now seen as a marker of a woman's worth and family honor. In addition, women's sexuality was denied because women were supposed to be incapable of sexual desire, remaining innocent or ignorant of the pleasures of the body, which were deemed as sinful.[72] According to Carol Añonuevo, the Filipina had only two models: "the virginal martyr and mother role of Mary or the evil women that the seductress Magdalene was portrayed to be."[73] Ideal women were required to be "virginal until married, fertile when married, and long suffering until death."[74] According to Añonuevo, this requirement resulted in the "non-complaining and silenced Filipina. A complex culture of martyrdom and silence molded young women into believing that they have to accept all the trials and hardships without question."[75] This image of Mary focused on the obedient Mary of the Anunciation or the Mater Dolorosa (suffering mother) and endorsed the belief that "enduring is necessary" (pagtitiis ang kailangan) or worse, that "forbearance and patience" (pagtitiis at pasensya) were the solution to the problem of domestic violence or a philandering husband.[76] According to KALAYAAN member Aida Santos Maranan, "Religion then became the women's overwhelming concern and sole refuge, inspiring their lives with the martyrdom of saints and patronesses, cultivating in women an infinite capacity for forbearance, suffering and forgiveness of all menial, mortal and male sins, obscuring in the process their capacity for greater involvement in things other than the hearth, home and heaven."[77] This symbolic capital given to "the woman as martyr" was one value the women activists were keen on dismantling.

Three female characters in the novels of José Rizal (the two novels that inspired the formation of the Filipino nation and later revolution against Spain) were fictional representations of this ideal. Sisa, in *Noli Me Tangere* (The social cancer), epitomized the suffering mother.[78] She represented the women of the working class who sacrificed everything for her two boys. Her husband not only neglected to support his wife, but also periodically took her wages to support his vices, which included drinking and gambling. Though her husband showed no concern for his wife and children and was guilty of domestic violence, Sisa never complained. Sisa's nature, consistently portrayed as quiet, hardworking, self-sacrificing, and submissive, appeared heroic and admirable even though her son's death at the hands of a Spanish friar drove her to madness.

The character of Juli represented the peasant woman who had to go into domestic service in order to clear her father's debts. Her life story epitomized the cultural belief system (see also the section on peasant women in Chapter 3), that peasant women were literally repayment of debt (*pambayad ng utang*).[79] Maria Clara, the beautiful, virginal heroine and a product of convent school education, represented the upper-class woman. She was an obedient daughter, shy, modest, quiet, and unobtrusive. Maria Clara's traits also epitomized the perfect woman described in the various rulebooks published in the Spanish colonial period regulating female conduct. In these books, women were meant to be virtuous; their sphere was the home.[80] The lives of saints became the role models for women of the early religious congregations.[81] Women were expected to behave like saints—devoted to prayer and good charitable works (Maria Clara donates her locket to a leper).[82] A study of the magazines published by elite women in the nineteenth century showed that women derived their lessons from catechisms, novenas, and the lives of saints. This literature conveyed the same instructions: women were to be obedient, submissive to authority, and meek.[83] That the character of Maria Clara acquired iconic status from the nineteenth century until the closing decades of the twentieth century, whether or not Rizal intended for this to happen, attested to the enduring success of the Spanish colonial construction of woman. In Rizal's novels, Maria Clara chose to enter the convent rather than a loveless marriage. Her tragic life ended in madness and early death. Scholar Lilia Quindoza Santiago argues that it was "a serious misreading" of Rizal's women's characters that led to Sisa becoming the model of the ideal mother, and the veneration of Maria Clara as the "icon of Filipino womanhood—modest, demure, and *mestisa*."[84]

Because society chose to adopt her as the iconic Filipino woman, Maria Clara has been the target of feminists from the suffragists of the

1920s up until the end of the twentieth century. In the 1920s, the lines between pro- and antisuffrage (at the male Constitutional Convention) were divided according to whether or not one wanted Maria Clara to be the template for the Filipino woman. Those who were against suffrage framed their discussion in terms of a nostalgic plea for the return of Maria Clara to the pedestal, while those who were for suffrage (particularly the women suffragists) denounced her as a character of fiction who did not resemble the Filipino women who fought in the revolution and who wanted to contribute to nation-building.[85] As late as the 1960s, journalist Carmen Guerrero Nakpil wrote that the idealization of Maria Clara was the greatest tragedy experienced by the Filipino woman in the last hundred years.[86]

To summarize, the histories of women's movements blamed the Spanish colonial period for shaping contemporary womanhood. The Spanish succeeded in destroying the power of the *babaylans* and replacing her with Maria Clara, who was domestic, obedient, meek, docile, religious, beautiful, and charitable, and who lived a saintly life accepting and enduring suffering. This idealization of the woman as martyr—an idealization that was a product of the colonial project—cut across class lines. In addition, this submissive woman was not expected to resist colonial rule or the power of the Catholic Church. Despite the fact that the Spanish colonizer departed in 1898, the cultural power of the Catholic Church remained and to this day continues to be a great challenge for women's movements, though church and state were separated in the early twentieth century. A lingering colonial legacy, the ideal woman touted by Maria Clara, Sisa, and Juli, continued to haunt dominant discourses on the Filipino woman. Though they succeeded in winning the vote, the suffragists were unable to exorcise this ideal. Consequently, women activists from the 1980s were committed to demolishing this enduring colonial role model.

ALTERNATIVE ROLE MODELS

Since women activists hoped to alter the definition of the Filipino woman inherited from a colonial past, the alternative histories they produced did not merely reproduce a history of women's subordination and oppression. Writing in 1985 as one of the pioneers on theorizing Filipina feminists, KALAYAAN's Aida Santos Maranan reflected on the "woman question" in the Philippines, focusing on the contrast between the woman in the domestic sphere and the "exemplary revolutionary heroines who

INTRODUCTION

transcended their times."[87] Juxtaposed between narratives of women's compliance with the Spanish domesticated religious ideal were stories of women's resistance. In the GABRIELA official history book *Si Maria, Nena, Gabriela Atbp* (Maria, Nena, Gabriela and others), heroines proposed as the new alternative models for women were given a space of their own highlighted in a separate "box" or section in the book's pages.[88] Included in this list of exceptional women were Gabriela Silang, Teresa Magbanua, Salud Algabre, and Consolacion Chiva.[89] All these women were revolutionaries who fought against the Spanish, the American, and the Japanese regimes. Gabriela Silang is the official role model for GABRIELA: in fact, the organization was named after her. The wife of Diego Silang, an Ilocano rebel who led a revolt against the Spaniards in the seventeenth century, Gabriela took over the leadership of her husband's revolt when he was killed until she herself was caught and hung in Vigan on September 20, 1763.[90] Exceptional women in the arts also were given a special feature in the GABRIELA history. This included Leona Florentino, a nineteenth-century poet who was described as unlike the demure, obedient Maria Clara, and Atang de la Rama, a celebrated artist of the musical theater during the American colonial era.[91]

Among the most famous of these feminist icons was Lorena Barros (who founded MAKIBAKA), Liza Balando (a factory worker who was killed during a demonstration demanding higher wages in 1971; note that the CWR school is named after her), and Liliosa Hilao, a religious woman who helped victims of illegal detention.[92] Lorena Barros lived a short life because she was killed at the age of twenty-six during a military encounter in Lucban, Quezon. Described as "now a symbol of poet, warrior, lover, woman. . . . Her life has become the subject matter for many poems, plays and stories."[93] Fe Mangahas, one of the original members of KALAYAAN, produced a play about Lorena Barros when she chaired the first Women's Desk at the Cultural Center of the Philippines. Entitled *Lorena,* the monologue was performed in Tagalog around 1987–1988 at the Cultural Center and was subsequently translated into English and performed overseas in Australia and Japan. Its success inspired the production of another monologue or play about Leona Florentino and the theme of domestic violence during the Spanish period.[94] The choice to publicize the biographies of these exceptional women dovetailed with the women's movements agenda of promoting herstories/histories of women's resistance proposing exceptional women in history as alternative role models to Maria Clara, Juli, and Sisa.

One song regularly performed by the artistic groups of women's organizations blatantly endorsed women revolutionaries and the three more contemporary activists (Lorena Barros, Liza Balando, and Liliosa Hilao) as alternative role models to Maria Clara, Sisa, and Juli. Although the song entitled "Babae" (Woman), was written by a male (Ramon Ayco), it was often sung during rituals, demonstrations, and events held by women's organizations. The lyrics echoed the women's movements critique of the Iberian-created stereotypes and offered their own alternative role models from women revolutionaries and activists.

> Are you a Maria Clara,
> A Huli and a Sisa
> Who does not know how to fight
> Why do you cry at your oppression
> Women, are you innately weak
> Are you a Cinderella
> Whose only hope is a man
> Are you a Nena
> Who earns a living as a whore?
> Women, are you only good in bed?
>
> Let us open our minds
> And study our society
> How your thought has been shaped
> And accept that you are just playthings
> Women, is this your fate?
> Why then are there Gabriela
> Teresa and Tandang Sora
> Who did not depend
> On pity and tears.
> They strove, weapon in hand
> Women who aimed to be free
> Why is there a Liza,
> A Liliosa and Lorena
> Who were not afraid to fight
> You now have many comrades
> Women, with weapons in hand.[95]

The words of this song captured the essence of the women's movements rejection of Hispanicized ideal characters. They opposed the view that women needed men to affirm their selfhood while praising three heroines of the resistance against Spain: Gabriela Silang (who led the revolt against the Spaniards in the seventeenth century and was the inspiration for the GABRIELA organization), Teresa Magbanua (who fought in the revolution against Spain as a soldier, reaching the rank of general), and Tandang Sora (the elderly woman in her eighties who nursed and cared for the soldiers in the same revolution). Whereas the seventeenth- to nineteenth-century role models were all women involved in the revolution against the colonial power (interestingly, the song mentions only the revolution against Spain; it does not allude to the Filipino-American War of 1899–1902), the three twentieth-century women offered as role models were all political activists against the Marcos dictatorship between 1972 and 1986. In this sense, one might be tempted to critique the women's movements for complying with the male yardstick for bravery or heroism.[96] But as will be shown in this book, feminists also attempted to redefine heroines to include survivors of rape, abuse, trafficking, and exploitation; and the experience of motherhood itself because it risked human life. But the song captured the essence of the "double narrative" in feminist historiographies as histories of women's oppression were juxtaposed with histories of women's resistance. It also reproduced the periodization of this feminist historiography—the American colonial period is given much less emphasis (in this case, that period is not mentioned in the song above) than the Spanish period and the contemporary context.

The television and radio programs produced by the WMC preferred to celebrate women's resistance and therefore expended longer sound bites of their historical segments to portray heroines. The *XYZone* history episode that focused on women trailblazers and the television documentary "From Priestess to President" both had short segments on the Spanish influence on women's status, and focused on women revolutionaries against Spain, and women's activism from the suffrage movement (which is still an underresearched field not just in the Philippines, but also in Asia generally), women guerrillas, and women activists.[97]

THE *BABAYLAN* AS MUSE

The *babaylan* became the mythological role model for feminists (including those in the diaspora), who redefined themselves as modern *babaylans*.[98] For example, the organization of Filipino women in Europe is called Babaylan, with branches such as Babaylan-France. The Filipino-American Women's Network ran Babaylan workshops, and Eileen Tabios, a Filipino-American poet, editor, and critic, had a regular online column with the byline "*Babaylan* Speaks," and referred to herself as a twentieth-century *babaylan.*[99] Claiming that the spirit of the *babaylan* was preserved in their "dangerous collective memory," feminists constructed a genealogical link with these mysterious women.[100] Women's movements interpreted their contemporary struggles as a continuation or reincarnation of the *babaylan* spirit who was remembered as an "old rebel." A poem by Mila Aguilar captured this image very well. Its first and last lines were

First line: You have aged, are you still a rebel?
Last line: "You have aged. Are you trying to say you are still a rebel?"[101]

Aguilar's representation of the *babaylan* as "old rebel" had historical basis in the documented *babaylan*'s resistance to the Spanish colonization and Christian conversion in the sixteenth century.[102] The Spanish quickly identified these priestesses as their main rivals in their task of Christian conversion and deliberately targeted them as "witches" and "devils." Spaniards also recorded evidence of steadfast and prolonged resistance to Spanish evangelization and colonialism; indeed, it could be argued that *babaylans* were perhaps among the last to accept the new religion.[103] To this day, there is no comprehensive scholarly study on the history of the *babaylan* in the precolonial era, although the closest is a monograph on the period of contact by historian Carolyn Brewer, some essays by Zeus Salazar, a chapter by Milagros Guerrero, and a small number of short publications by Fe Mangahas.[104] Most of what is known about pre-Hispanic Philippines, including the history of the *babaylan,* is based on Spanish accounts. The consensus reached by the above scholars who have critically evaluated these fragmentary sources is that the *babaylan* was a religious leader who presided not only over rituals of the rites of passage, but also over the rites of the agricultural cycle. Along with the chief, the blacksmith responsible for making weapons, and the warrior, the *babaylan* was among the most important figures of authority in pre-Hispanic Philippines.[105] Although the other three figures were more likely to be male, the *babaylan* was normally female, and men who aspired to that role were required to dress as women.[106] The *babaylan* were wise women past childbearing age who mediated between the spirit world and the community: "They were counsel to ruler and ruled, propitiators to the gods and spirits, atoners of people's sins, interpreters and diviners of nature's demands upon the community and healers of soul and body."[107]

Spanish accounts reveal that the *babaylan* possessed specialized knowledge of religion, commerce, and the cosmos.[108]

The feminist fascination for the *babaylan* motivated them to search for living *babaylans* in the foothills of Mount Banahaw where a unique Filipino Christian sect called the Ciudad Mistica de Dios was led by a woman who held the title of Suprema Isabel.[109] Despite the fact that in an interview the *suprema* herself rejected the suggestion that she was a *babaylan,* activists continue to be fascinated by this sect.[110] The *babaylan*'s "spirit" also was evoked in feminist rituals and conferences. In one of the plenary papers given in the international conference sponsored by GABRIELA in 1991, Ninotchka Rosca from GABRIELA-USA (the GABRIELA branch in the United States) ended her lecture on the culture of colonial domination with, "May the *babaylans* protect us from a situation like this."[111] Perhaps in keeping with this sentiment, the welcome ritual at the first day of that conference included the offering of oil to the Great Spirit by a contemporary *babaylan* where participants rubbed the oil in their palms to symbolize their unity with the spirit of the pre-Hispanic priestess.[112]

In 2005, to accompany the commemoration of the first centennial of the women's movements, an anthology was published that was part tribute and part celebration of the *babaylan* spirit.[113] In this anthology (based on a symposium on the *babaylan* held in 2005), feminists from a variety of fields, including the performing arts, reveled in what Mary John Mananzan (OSB) has termed "the *babaylan* in me."[114] The prologue to the book, for example, acknowledged the assistance of Senator Leticia Shahani, referred to as their "beloved and esteemed babaylan."[115] The book itself coined the term "Babaylan Feminism" or "babaylanism"; although these terms were not defined in any detail, the book's editors referred to *babaylanismo* as an "enlightened female consciousness": "a homespun concept, rooted in the country's specific historical and cultural context. As such *babaylanism* is holistic, non-dualistic and transformative."[116] From this cryptic definition, it may be gleaned that *babaylan* feminism meant "Filipino feminisms"—signaling the women's movements self-conscious representation of their theories and perspectives as homegrown. The *babaylan* became the muse in the project of articulating Filipina feminisms in theory and in practice, a process that is ongoing as of this writing in 2010.

Of all the alternative role models proposed by activists, the *babaylan* remains the most powerful icon. This could be partly explained by the fact that she represents the indigenous Filipina untainted by the colonial past. Another reason could be that she is still a mystery because there is not much that is known about her. But perhaps the *babaylan* appeal could be traced to her age and wisdom: the *babaylan* is an older woman with specialized religious knowledge and religious power. She offered an alternative construction of the feminine distinct from the colonial definition (the beautiful, domestic, long-suffering woman), as well as the contemporary activist. The woman as intellectual or scholar has never been part of the grand narrative of the Filipino woman. The *babaylan* mystique—her imaginative power—could be traced to her unique subject position as mature, wise woman with religious power—three characteristics that have yet to be associated with the cultural constructions of the feminine in the Philippines.

❀   ❀   ❀

The chapters that follow divide women's discourses of the feminine into three parts:

Part I: Representations: Representing the Filipino Woman;
Part II: Practices: Fashioning the Filipino Woman; and
Part III: Spaces: Locating Women's Movements.

Part I discusses how different women's organizations and particular groups of feminists represent the Filipino woman in their specific advocacies. Chapter 1 isolates one unique group of feminists—feminist nuns. Though much neglected in the scholarship on women's studies internationally, they have been important leaders of the women's movement in the Philippines. The distinctive contribution of these nuns to Filipino feminist theorizing has been in identifying the religious roots of women's oppression in the Philippine context. Chapter 2 focuses on how the women's movements represented prostitutes in their campaign for the Anti-Trafficking in Persons Act of 2003. Chapter 3 examines how activists imagine women workers of the lower classes (including overseas contract workers [OCW] and women migrants) and define them as the potential mass following (read: militant activists) of the women's movements. Chapter 4 discusses how activists represent indigenous women of the Cordillera, and Chapter 5 tackles the women's health movements—a book-length topic on its own—and its own perception of the Filipino woman intrinsic to its advocacy for women's health, particularly the controversial issues of reproductive rights and sexuality. Discourses on the feminine were invoked in public debates over issues such as rape, domestic violence, reproductive health, and sexuality.

Part II is preoccupied with how women's organizations fashioned women through their practices. Chapter 6 concentrates on the use of media—radio and television in particular—to disseminate the new feminist epistemologies to a potential mass audience. It analyzes how radio and television transmitted women's studies courses "on the air" and offered ordinary women alternative role models. Chapter 7 is devoted to the activities that involve the participation and indoctrination of potential followers. Oral testimonies, theater as advocacy, demonstrations, songs, and special rituals are practices in which former survivors become advocates or activists. Identities with particular feminist organizations are developed through participation in these activities, which often include the wearing of a particular "uniform." As described in this chapter, dress is used to express visually one's identity as a feminist activist.

Finally, Part III contends that activists' decision to locate themselves in the interstices—between national borders, and in the liminal space between above and below ground—has been an effective strategy. Chapter 8 places women's movements in the transnational context while Chapter 9 considers the strategies of one radical women's health organization (Linangan ng Kababaihan or Likhaan; Linangan ng Kababaihan literally means a place for honing or developing women) to introduce a future discussion of abortion as a reproductive right. Since the latter topic is still very much taboo in the Philippines, it is important to explore how the organization maneuvers in liminal spaces. In Likhaan's advocacy of this sensitive issue, its members are also involved in fashioning the Filipino woman of the future.

I have used the case studies of a number of women's organizations to provide the empirical evidence for the arguments made here. The sheer number of women's organizations and NGOs make it impossible to include all of them and do them justice. In order to represent as many organizations with some credibility, I have chosen one to three organizations for each women's issue or topic. A list of all the organizations that have very generously allowed me to use their materials and practices for this book is also provided in a separate page.

Sources

Sources for this book included the standard archival materials, plus more than seventy-eight interviews with members of women's organizations (including feminist nuns, politicians, and women in media), and fieldwork. I am a Filipina historian based in Australia, and I spent more than six months in the Philippines (Metro-Manila and Baguio City) between 2003 and 2010 for research. In addition, I conducted interviews with Filipino women's organizations in The Netherlands, France, and Italy between 2006–2008. I have read the newsletters and listened to forty radio shows (from five programs), watched six television episodes of *Womanwatch,* and *XYZ* television (kindly copied for me by the WMC), and DVD productions of the Philippine Educational Theater Association. In addition, I participated in some activities run by some of the women's organizations discussed in this book, including demonstrations (discussed in Chapter 7). The archival data include publications of the women's organizations, including stories of survivors, feminist comics, CD-ROMs, and websites associated with particular advocacy groups, as well as the minutes of meetings, speeches, songs, journals, newsletters, the published and unpublished writings of feminist nuns, and theater scripts. Since I am interested in both Filipino feminist historiography and Filipino feminist theory, I also examined the writings of Filipina feminists (who were leaders of women's organizations) in search of their interpretations of the Filipino woman past, present, and future. And finally, the radical women's health organization Likhaan presented me with a unique source of six romance-style paperback books in the Tagalog language that they had commissioned to introduce the taboo concept of abortion as a reproductive right. Organizations were very willing to share their time and materials with me and invited me to participate in their activities. In a special research trip conducted in 2008, these organizations commented on my chapter drafts. This enthusiasm for my research was part of their advocacy and this book documents an important part of their struggles.

Representing Women

1

The Religious Roots of Women's Oppression

FEMINIST NUNS AND THE FILIPINO WOMAN

The Catholic Nun as Feminist

The idea of Catholic nuns as feminists is largely neglected in women's studies.[1] The patriarchal nature of the Catholic Church along with its generally conservative outlook hardly positions it at the forefront of advocating radical social change in the sphere of women and gender relations. At the same time, the nuns themselves are part of religious congregations with no specific religious congregations designated as "feminist religious congregations." Instead, the choice to become a feminist nun is made individually. Hence, this chapter's collective identification of Filipino Catholic feminist nuns as a specific group is merely a construct. A tiny minority within the larger community of Catholic nuns, this group of female activists were nevertheless important leaders in the women's movements from the late 1970s until the present writing (2010). Contrary to their sisters in America who, according to Rebecca Sullivan, were marginalized in the history of second-wave feminism there, these special nuns became formidable activists in women's movements in Filipino feminist theorizing, as women's studies teachers, and as leaders and members of transnational organizations.[2]

This chapter focuses on this unique group of feminists—all highly educated women, many with postgraduate qualifications earned overseas. I argue that the nuns' unique status as religious women made these women effective activists in the Philippine context where religious persons had symbolic capital. The nuns' unique contribution to the women's movement was their deconstruction of the religious roots of women's oppression. Criticisms of Catholicism's practices had a greater impact coming from the mouths of nuns who were theological experts. If a nun critiqued the church, then it must be okay to do so! At the same time, the nuns also earned their legitimacy through their own mission work with the poor. Almost all feminist nuns interviewed lived part-time in the convent and part-time with the poor. This gave them the credibility to speak on behalf of poor women.

Their links to educational institutions allowed them to introduce the first women's studies courses, and to conduct or support research on women's issues in the local context. As women "unattached to men" or to "families," nuns were able to devote their lives to their mission work, which included feminist advocacy. At the same time, nuns were subjected to patriarchy in the Catholic Church, experiencing daily in their own lives the effects of discrimination, which enabled them to empathize with the oppression of ordinary women. Nuns also were unique in that they occupied transnational spaces or lived in the interstices; this subject will be developed in Chapter 8.

The nuns' discovered their moral power during their experiences as political activists in the Marcos dictatorship, during which period they became veterans of the demonstrations, street marches, and other forms of underground activism. The knowledge and track record they gained as martial law activists was of critical importance when they themselves formed women's organizations to advocate for particular women's issues or sectors. Nuns tapped on this moral power when, as activists, they had to confront the state and traditional mores that discriminated against women.

The exceptional place of these nuns in Filipino cultural constructions of the feminine partly explained their unique status. Because the Filipino cultural construction of the feminine was wife and mother, the Catholic nun was an ambivalent woman—unattached to a man and living in women-only communities. Banned from ordination, many chose to go into the academe after postgraduate (including doctoral) work. Because congregations were transnational, access to higher education overseas was easy and a number of nuns took advantage of this remarkable opportunity. When they returned to the Philippines, their duties effectively made them professionals living extremely busy full lives, attending to the needs of others, but fulfilling their intellectual and personal potential. In this sense, nuns as highly educated women with careers became alternative role models for women who did not want to embrace the ideals of domesticity espoused by the grand narrative of woman as wife and mother.[3] Nuns, however, were never acknowledged publicly as women professionals, and therefore did not appear to threaten the status quo despite their high status as religious women.

But nuns also participated in the fashioning of women. Their discourses on the Filipina coming from the perspective of feminist theology and their missionary praxis produced the double narrative. Although they blamed Christianity for encouraging women to accept suffering as intrinsic to womanhood, they also sought to empower women by demystifying suffering, and resocializing women into rejecting the Catholic ideals that endorsed subservience to men.

This chapter will consider these points by exploring the work and writings of a number of feminist nuns from a spread of religious congregations: Benedictine (OSB), Maryknoll (MM), Good Shepherd (RGS), Missionary Sisters of the Immaculate Heart of Mary (ICM), Religious of the Sacred Heart of Jesus (RSCJ), and Franciscan Sisters of the Immaculate Conception (SFIC). These congregations were more open to feminism; I have also included nuns who self-described as feminist even though their feminism might be branded conservative—that is, they analyzed situations from a woman's perspective but were not necessarily committed to changing women's status. This last group included nuns from the Religious of the Assumption (RA), the Religious of the Virgin Mary (RVM), and the Cenacle Sisters. Some of the feminist nuns such as Mary John Mananzan (OSB), Virginia Fabella (MM), Soledad Perpiñan (RGS), Christine Tan (RGS), Amelia Vasquez (RSCJ), Nila Bermisa (MM), and Helen Graham (MM) were prominent nuns holding celebrity status in the Philippines from the mid-1970s until the present writing (2010).

Although there is a growing literature on nuns from the perspective of women's history, there are currently only two in-depth studies that focus on Filipino Catholic nuns in the latter half of the twentieth century.[4] In these pioneer studies, nuns were identified either as political activists or as feminists, but not as straddling both spheres. Coeli Barry's dissertation documents the participation of nuns in the anti-Marcos struggle, and Heather Claussen traces the development of feminist consciousness in one order of nuns—the Benedictines.[5] Neither study examines the role of nuns in the post-1980s women's movements in the Philippines. In this sense, this chapter fills a vacuum in the field of women's studies in the Philippines and on feminist nuns internationally.

Becoming a Feminist Nun Abroad and a
Political Activist at Home

The peculiar historical context of the 1970s was instrumental in the evolution of the Filipino feminist nun. The blending of three historical situations in this tumultuous decade prepared the ground for the emergence of a group of activist women who were nuns: (1) the requirement that nuns go overseas as part of their formation training and the greater percentage of nuns who, barred from ordination, chose to obtain higher academic degrees; (2) the declaration of martial law in the Philippines when President Ferdinand Marcos imposed a dictatorship that unleashed an unprecedented violation of human rights; and (3) the consequences of Vatican II, especially in the developing world, in which the religious were encouraged to live among the poor. The combination of (2) and (3) in Latin American countries gave birth to liberation theology and its Philippine version the theology of struggle.[6]

The nuns received a feminist education overseas, then returned home and lived with the poor. Witnessing firsthand the victimization of the disempowered class under the brutal force of the military, nuns experienced their "baptism of fire" (to use Mananzan's phrase) in the martial law period—joining the workers in the barricades striking for better wages (strikes were illegal), documenting the plight of political prisoners, participating in the indigenous people's fight for ancestral lands, and linking arms with the urban poor who faced bulldozers that threatened to demolish their makeshift homes.[7] These experiences turned them into political activists against martial law. Once democratic institutions were restored in 1986, the nuns combined their feminist education overseas with their political activism at home and founded transnational women's organizations with bases that traversed national borders, and, using their ties to the educational infrastructure, disseminated this new feminist activism through women's studies courses, workshops, and the like.

ACADEMICS WITH INTERNATIONAL OUTLOOKS

Part of the nuns' training required them to spend some time abroad in mission work or to acquire academic qualifications. In some congregations, the women were required to spend time overseas as part of their sister formation training.[8] These experiences were not only crucial to the nuns' development as religious, but also were important steps in their evolution as feminists. It was during their stint overseas that nuns were taught feminist theologies and were embroiled in mission work. (Bermisa [MM] worked with prostitutes in Jakarta, for example.)[9] They took higher degrees in Theology, Christology, Philosophy, Missiology, and Ecclesiology, for example. They joined international organizations such as the EATWOT and published articles in journals, including the feminist *In God's Image.*

Virginia Fabella, a Maryknoll sister, went to the United States to obtain higher degrees at the Maryknoll Sisters Mission Institute (circa 1971–1975); she studied with feminist theologians such as Rosemary Ruether and Mary Daly.[10] Mary John Mananzan (OSB) completed a doctorate degree in philosophy with a major in linguistic philosophy at the Pontifical Gregorian University in Rome, and a degree in missiology at the Wilhelmsuniversitaet in Muenster, Germany. She also took up fellowships overseas such as the Dorothy Cadbury Fellowship in 1994 in Birmingham and the Henry Luce Fellowship at the Union Theological Seminary in New York in 1995, as well as a fellowship as an Asian Public Intellectual in 2002, which was given to her by the Nippon Foundation.[11] Amelia Vasquez (RSCJ) finished both undergraduate and graduate studies in the United States. Her undergraduate degree in philosophy and theology was at Maryville College, and her graduate studies in history and religion (Christianity) were completed at Manhattanville College, Columbia University, Harvard University, and Weston School of Theology. In addition, she was a missionary in Korea.[12] When she undertook a second master's degree overseas, she took courses with feminist women professors.[13] Mary Soledad Perpiñan (RGS) completed a master's degree from Fordham University in New York.[14] She has done special studies in spirituality at the Gregorian University in Rome and in social analysis at INODEP (Ecumenical Institute for the Development of Peoples), which is affiliated with the Sorbonne in Paris. She has read the American feminist theologians and quoted them in her written lectures.[15] Emelina Villegas (ICM) did postgraduate work in sociology in Leuven, Belgium, at the university there, and Margaret Lacson (MM), spent her orientation years in Newburgh, New York, and worked as a missionary in Japan.[16] Although Rosario Battung (RGS) received her master's in women and religion from the Institute of Formation and Religious Studies in the Philippines, she later entered the Good Shepherd Convent in New Zealand.[17]

The years spent overseas ensured that these nuns gained an international perspective, and gave them an opportunity to establish international links and networks. When EATWOT was formed in 1976, Filipino nuns such as Mananzan, Fabella, and Battung were among the founding members. In the Delhi conference of 1981, women members of EATWOT proposed the formation of a Women's Commission "to promote a theology of liberation from the perspective of women in the developing world, a theology that springs from a critical awareness of women's subjugated position and a commitment to change it."[18] Filipino feminist nuns, particularly Fabella, Mananzan, Battung, and Bermisa, became active members of the Women's Commission. Mananzan and Fabella, in particular, have published extensively on feminist theology from the Philippine perspective. In fact, their work is included in the standard histories and readers on feminist theologies under the headings of developing world feminist theologies. They contributed to international conversations on Christology from a feminist perspective (read: that Christ was a man was incidental).[19] Hence, these nuns were considered important feminist theologists in the international arena.[20] In addition, Fabella edited a number of books on developing world theologies published outside the Philippines.[21] When the EATWOT Women's Commission in Asia founded their feminist journal *In God's Image* in 1982, Fabella was on the Editorial Board. Articles on the Philippines were plentiful in the more than twenty years history of the journal with at least two special issues prepared by women in the Philippines (perhaps also because the Philippines is the only Asian country which has a Christian majority).[22] Filipino feminist nuns such as Bermisa, Battung, Mananzan, Vasquez, Villegas, Lacson, Lydia Lascano (ICM), and Teresa Dagdag (MM) published articles not just on feminist theology from the Philippine perspective, but also on Filipino women's issues and the woman question.[23]

MARTIAL LAW POLITICAL ACTIVISM AND THE CHURCH OF THE POOR

Vatican II (which coincided with martial law in the Philippines) redefined the church as the "church of the poor" giving the nuns the opportunity for the first time to leave the convents and live with the poor at the time when the gap between rich and poor became more pronounced. Contact with grassroots women enabled them to see women's victimization and women's oppression firsthand. Listening to women's stories introduced them to the world of Filipino machismo, and patriarchy in everyday Filipino culture, while their own marginalization in the Church hierarchy was a constant reminder of the patriarchy of the Catholic Church.

In a study about the impact of Vatican II on women religious in the Philippines (sponsored by the Institute of Women's Studies), the most important change was identified as the orientation towards the poor and marginalized sectors of society.[24]

A small number of nuns chose to spend some time outside the convent living among the poor. From the 1970s onwards, these individual nuns lived life alternately in and out of the convent, with some days of the week devoted to "convent duties" and other days to their particular "mission." All feminist nuns I interviewed between 2003–2006 were extremely busy individuals with tight schedules who set aside a number of days each week to live with poor women. Fabella, Vasquez, and Villegas were based in Cavite province, spending only one or two days a week in Metro-Manila.[25] In Cavite, Villegas worked first with salesgirls, then with women who worked in factories in the export processing zones (EPZs), while Fabella worked with women of the urban poor.[26] Battung's interests oscillated between the urban poor in Tondo and the labor unions in Cavite province.[27] Vasquez lived in a little community in Montalban visiting Manila three days a week (because she was provincial superior of her own congregation, the RSCJ).[28] Perpiñan worked with prostitutes in Metro-Manila and in the provinces.[29] Mananzan as chairperson of GABRIELA ensured that she had the pulse of the women's social movements, from the urban poor to the peasants and indigenous women. When I interviewed the late Christine Tan (RGS) in 1995, she was living in Leverisa, the community of urban poor in the city of Manila.[30] Even the nuns who continued to live in the convents, particularly those in the provinces, were often asked by the "outside world" to help the victims of martial law, particularly during demonstrations and rallies, since the presence of nuns in their habits legitimized the resistance and at times prevented the military from extreme violence.

The martial law experience politicized the nuns who were rapidly drawn into the struggles of the poor and dispossessed. Nuns dominated the Task Force Detainees, which agitated for the release of political detainees (in fact a nun, Mariani Dimaranan [SFIC] was president of the TFD, the Task Force Detainees, the organization that helped political detainees), nuns "womanned" the barricades of laborers striking for better wages and conditions (when strikes were illegal), and supported the indigenous people's fight to protect their ancestral lands from government appropriation. They conducted "conscientization" seminars to make the religious around the country aware of the experiences of the victims (both political and economic) of the Marcos dictatorship. Nuns stood at the forefront of demonstrations confronting the military. The iconography of the People Power Revolution of 1986 that toppled the Marcos regime was replete with images of militant nuns facing the military in order to protect civilians from possible violence from armed soldiers sent to disperse or destroy them.

The image of the militant nun was immortalized in a 1984 movie entitled *Sister Stella L.* The plot of the movie involved a nun, Stella Legaspi, who was initially politically indifferent, but who eventually became sensitized to the plight of the strikers during a labor dispute in a depressed area. Exposed to the miserable lives of the strikers, she joined them on the picket line, only to witness the military assault and murder a labor leader. This experience strengthened her determination to fight against tyranny and oppression. It was at the climax of the film that she delivered her message, "If we do not act, who will? If not now, when else?[31] Written by José Lacaba, this slogan was one of the catchphrases of the activists of the 1970s. The fact that Lacaba purposely gave these lines to the character that was a militant nun was testimony to the visibility of the militant nun as representative of opposition to the Marcos dictatorship.

But the activism of the nuns also impacted on the nuns' own subjectivities. They discovered their moral power.[32] Their presence in the forefront of rallies, strikes, and demonstrations immediately catapulted them into prominent negotiators with the military who often hesitated to harm these symbols of religious legitimacy (though legitimacy was earned through their work with the poor, as well). Even First Lady Imelda Marcos was not unaware of their moral power when she summoned Tan to the presidential palace for a "discussion."[33] Helen Graham, an American Maryknoll nun who moved to the Philippines in 1967, boasted to me in an interview that she had made Imelda Marcos cry.[34] And yet they had little power in a church that denied them ordination. Priests and seminarians without higher education could give sermons and homilies, while nuns with master's degrees and doctorates in scripture were forbidden from doing so, though they were allowed to give "reflections."[35] It was the gap between the moral power they exercised even in the midst of a brutal dictatorship and the realization that, "on the other hand, in the church we have no voice," that crystallized their growing feminist consciousness—and motivated them to form transnational feminist organizations.[36]

The Religious Roots of Women's Oppression

The nuns' major contribution to feminist theorizing of the Filipina was their deconstruction of what Mananzan has termed "the religious roots of women's oppression."[37]

> Religion has likewise helped instill in women the consciousness of being subordinate. The creation story has somehow been interpreted as (1) woman is made from man—therefore, she is a derivative being; (2) woman is made for man—therefore, she is a subservient being; and (3) woman is guilty for the sin of Adam— therefore, she is a dangerous temptress who has to be controlled. The emphasis on passivity, long-suffering, and patience as the virtues of the ideal woman conditions her to develop a victim consciousness; thus, women become victims of violence. The idea that before marriage, her virginity is her identity, and after marriage, maternity is, has plunged women into despair and self-hatred; they lose their virginity even not through their own fault. Many prostituted women say their loss of virginity has been the precipitating factor in their becoming prostitutes. Women are made to feel it is their sole responsibility to nurture children and to keep the marriage intact. That is why battered wives remain in their marriages despite imminent threats to their lives.[38]

This critical analysis here epitomized by an excerpt of Mananzan's essay (the theme that Christianity was the reason Filipino women accepted their subordinate status vis-à-vis men reproduced repeatedly in her published essays, oral lectures, addresses, personal papers, and radio talks), was a composite result of the nuns' transnational activities. Participation in the Women's Commission of EATWOT allowed these unusual women a space to critique patriarchy in the Catholic Church in the good company of other feminist nuns from the developing countries. In the 1994 EATWOT convention, the feminist contingent denounced the image of "God as a father who demanded the sacrifice of his only son as atonement for sins" as a "harmful image of God" that was used to "legitimize child abuse" and foster a "victim attitude" among women.[39] For these Asian feminist theologians, "The image of Jesus as a sacrificial lamb has likewise induced women to follow the path of 'innocent victimhood.'"[40] The pages of *In God's Image* were replete with examples of how this Christian construction of "woman" has been multiplied many times over in the developing world context; Filipino feminist nuns participated in these discussions with examples from the Philippines. An essay on "Women and Christianity in the Philippines," where the author acknowledged input from Fabella and Tan, blamed Christianity for commanding women to obey their husbands and exalting males as superior, while women were defined by the men in their lives.[41] The author lamented the attitudes that endorsed "Redemption for woman lay in self-rejection" and "This world was a vale of tears whose reward was eternal life in the next world; and suffering was glorified as a peculiarly female lot."[42]

But the nuns did not simply accept this feminist theological position taken from the Women's Commission of EATWOT and graft it uncritically onto the Philippine context. On the contrary, nuns analyzed the Filipino variants of Catholicism in order to discover how religion fostered what Mananzan termed the "victim consciousness" among women. In their publications, both Virginia Fabella and Mary John Mananzan identified specific traits of Filipino Catholicism that have been responsible for Filipino women's acceptance of their subordinate status vis-à-vis men: (1) the emphasis on the passion of Christ rather than on His resurrection, and (2) the popularity of two images—Christ as the Christ child or Sto Niño, and the Virgin Mary as Mater Dolorosa, or the suffering mother. According to Fabella, the brand of religiosity from popular Spanish tradition focused on tragedy epitomized by the Spanish image of Christ: "a tragic, agonizing, victim Christ or a dead Christ. Unlike the Christ of the Gospels, it is said that the Christ of Spanish folk tradition was either an infant or a corpse. The natives thus assimilated the Spanish devotion, not only to the *Santo Niño* (Holy child) and the *Santo Entierro* (Christ entombed), but to the Virgin Mary and patron saints."[43] This emphasis on Christ's suffering rather than Christ as liberator had an enormous impact on women who internalized the "suffering Christ" as a role model. Fabella was able to isolate this peculiar image of Christ that dominated the Philippine variant of Catholicism:

> In the course of time and movement across cultures, the
> positive meanings of Jesus' death became lost or distorted. In
> the Philippines, we have developed (or inherited) a dead-end
> theology of the cross with no resurrection or salvation in sight.
> Most of the women who sing the "pasyon" [passion of Christ]
> during Holy Week look upon the passion and death of Jesus
> as ends in themselves and actually relish being victims. This
> attitude is not uncommon among other women outside the

"pasyon" singers, and it is not helped when priests reinforce
the attitude through their homilies. One of them said not long
ago that he does not preach the resurrection as "the people are
not prepared for it."[44]

She communicated this insight to the international feminist theologists: "In my own culture, however, not many women would be familiar
with the figure of a liberating or liberated Jesus. They know him as the
suffering or crucified Jesus who understands their own suffering which
they passively or resignedly endure."[45]

Writing on Christology from an Asian feminist theological perspective, Mananzan likewise traced the Filipino preoccupation with
the "suffering Christ" to the Spanish Christ (the infant Jesus suddenly
transformed into the crucified Christ) transposed to the Philippines during the colonization. During this era, the image of the suffering Christ
was emphasized in festivals associated with Holy Week. In her view, the
festivities that highlighted the reading of the passion of Christ, and the
reenactment of his death, dramatized Good Friday and not Easter as the
climax of Holy Week. This particular version of the Christian message
disseminated in the Philippines by the Spanish friars legitimized Spanish
colonialism because the interpretation advanced was that Christ's suffering and defeat promised salvation in another world.[46] In this sense, the
colonized subjects were asked to embrace their suffering because it was
the key to a better afterlife.

The answer to the puzzling question of *why* it is that women but
not men were more likely to identify with the passion of Christ, has not
been a central focus of the theoretical reflections of these feminists who
were more interested in the women's perspective. Nuns claimed that the
idealization of the Virgin Mary as Mater Dolorosa (suffering mother)
complemented the crucified Christ as role model for women: "Mary has
been depicted as silent, sweet, self-effacing, docile, passive, submissive,
Mater Dolorosa. Actually this portrayal of Mary is a masculine perception of idealized femininity which has been inflicted on us and which
many of us in turn have tried hard to internalize."[47] The twin models
of the suffering mother and the tormented Christ entrenched cultural
beliefs that the ideal woman should endure the trials that came with her
social subordination in silence.

These nuns contributed to theological debates from the perspective
of developing countries and the Philippines in particular, or were teaching these radical ideas to the next generation of religious. They applied

this feminist theorizing to the Philippine situation while using local praxis to articulate how Christianity has negatively affected women's lives. The transnational and transcultural approach to the woman question in the Philippines pointed to the cultural predilection for glorifying suffering as a woman's role as one primary reason why women accepted their subordinate roles. Nuns who were continuously approached as "advisers" heard many stories of women who saw their trials in a positive light because it meant that, like Jesus Christ, they were given a cross that they had to carry all the way to Calvary. Suffering became a metaphor for one's experience of Calvary; a prerequisite for winning redemption in the next life. This interpretation was validated by my own personal experiences in the field. My aunt and cousin confided to me "my husband is my cross." These women were not merely resigned to a life of suffering: such suffering was perceived to be a "blessing"—an opportunity to show one deserved eternal salvation. Like my relatives, many Filipinas interpreted their suffering as an earthly test necessary to gain entry to paradise. The nuns had discovered the template that gave the woman as martyr her symbolic capital.

Feminist nuns therefore knew that it was necessary to demythologize "suffering," to remove the status assigned to the woman as martyr. When Emelina Villegas (ICM) was subjected to countless stories of women factory workers in Cavite province who experienced philandering husbands or partners who abandoned them, she gave them all the same counsel: "they should not suffer unnecessarily, I call that 'useless suffering.' I tell them 'useless suffering.' And then I always tell them—what about your children, do you want your children to experience this?" Villegas empathized with the huge burden and the pain these women faced every day so her strategy was to confront them directly with the question: Is it useful or is that useless? [laugh]. Useless suffering. It is not worth it, it is a waste of tears."[48] By labeling certain suffering as useless and wasteful, this nun hoped to demystify it. Mananzan wrote, "the long-suffering doormat model of a 'goodwife' is no longer tenable."[49] This particular strategy and approach to feminist theorizing of the Filipina was a product of the feminist clergy. Demystifying suffering destroyed what Mananzan has termed the "negative idol."[50]

Once the negative idol was destroyed, however, it became necessary to propose alternative role models for women. Since these were religious women, the suggested alternatives were Christ as liberator and Mary as woman.[51] The oppression of women was publicly declared to be "sinful."[52]

Feminist Nuns Fashion Women

Aware that the Filipino woman they talked about was a product of socialization, reeducation of women became a priority. This was accomplished with several strategies: formal education in schools and gender workshops or seminars, and women's organizing and advocacy. Nuns who already were plugged in to the educational sector if their congregations ran colleges of higher education began to spread their new ideas in the classroom. The martial law period had introduced the possibilities of "traveling classrooms," wherein nuns and laity offered "conscientization seminars" throughout the Philippines. By the post-Marcos era (post-1986), nuns built on this experience and began to run "gender sensitizing" workshops across class boundaries and across national borders. Nuns taught women's studies courses at St. Scholastica's College, at Miriam College (formerly Maryknoll), and at the Institute and Formation of Religious Studies. From the feminist attack on Christianity, nuns extended their critiques to include socialization in the family, education in school, the media, and other aspects of cultural mores that perpetuated women's subordination or women's silences.[53] Socialization in the family reaffirmed woman's role as inferior to and subservient to men. Whereas boys were indulged while young, girls were taught to care for younger siblings, to do the household chores, and to look after the men. Mananzan speculated that a majority of marital conflicts in the Philippines might be due to the immaturity of the Filipino husband and the wife's loss of respect when she discovered the man she married turned out to be a boy. Since she believed she alone was responsible for the success or failure of her marriage, she was likely to endure an unhappy or abusive domestic life "for the sake of the children."[54]

Although nuns could not administer the sacrament of the Holy Mass or give homilies, they were allowed to give reflections. Nuns were proactive in using this small space in the liturgy to introduce their ideas. This was done creatively—through reflections, songs, prayers, and the sharing of stories of women's experiences of prostitution and exploitation. In these special rituals, the songs and prayers required women to assert themselves and demand that their voices be recognized. In everyday ritual and prayer women were told not to tolerate violence against them and were informed about women's rights and women's choices.[55]

Since each of these nuns worked part-time with the poor, some of them chose to focus on particular sectors of women—that is, urban poor, salesgirls, factory workers, women migrants, prostitutes, indigenous women, and so on. Eventually some of these nuns were drawn in as either leaders or spokespersons for particular women's organizations. Mananzan was one of the founders of GABRIELA; she served as its chair for more than two decades. She also was one of the original founders of PILIPINA and the CWR. In addition, she founded the Center for Migrant Workers in Spain and initiated the Citizen's Alliance for Consumer Protection.[56] She has been a prime mover in the development of Women's Studies Education in the Philippines and inspired the first women's studies institute in the country. Soledad Perpiñan (RGS) founded the Third World Movement Against the Exploitation of Women (TW-MAE-W) to address the issue of prostitution (discussed in more detail in the next chapter), and Teresa Dagdag (MM) was a founder and executive director of Igorota Foundation, focusing on the highland women of the Cordillera region.[57] Aurora R. Sambranco (ICM) was named as president of DAWN (the organization that helps Filipina migrants to Japan and their Japanese-Filipino children; see Chapter 2).[58] In their writings, lectures, and speeches—some of them published in the newsletters of women's organizations and in *In God's Image*—the nuns publicly articulated the problems of women—prostitution, domestic violence, rape, and incest. In many of these issues, these religious women have had the privilege to speak on behalf of Filipino women to local and international audiences.

These nuns, who were trained as academics, combined their field experiences with empirical research when they wrote and spoke about women's issues. Together with the lay leaders of women's organizations, they had a significant impact on feminist activism. Their work with the poor and the marginalized sectors ensured that lower-class women's issues were given high priority. Their status as religious persons gave legitimacy and moral capital to their advocacy so that these organizations benefited from the participation and leadership (and even fundraising talents) of the nuns.

On the other hand, their identity as religious persons hindered their activism since they could not officially go against the Catholic Church. Nuns could not publicly indicate support for certain issues such as divorce, abortion, and reproductive rights (natural family planning is the only contraception endorsed by the Catholic Church). Some nuns like Perpiñan have publicly declared their opposition to abortion, but because she worked with prostitutes she had "no qualms" about advocating the use of condoms. On the issue of divorce, her experiences "handling marital cases" convinced her "that some—there are no more marriages

in a lot of cases." But although she personally might believe that in these cases divorce would be appropriate, she said, "But I would not be advocating that, you know."[59]

Some nuns such as Mananzan claimed that divorce was a middle-class issue: lower-class couples usually separate or have de facto relationships because they are not able to afford to pay for lawyer's fees to formalize a legal separation, whereas elite women could afford to get an annulment from the church and a legal separation from the state. Given this interpretation, Mananzan rationalized that, since her focus was on the lower classes, divorce as an issue was not a priority in her advocacy. (Some women's activists who are not religious women, such as Sylvia Estrada-Claudio, disagreed with this: their own work with poor women revealed that it was important to these women to be able to acquire a divorce.)[60] Other nuns believed that abandonment was the prevalent experience of poor women making abandonment a more pressing issue for poor women than divorce.[61] Given these restrictions, the nuns assessed their situation and decided it was best to channel their energies in the spaces where they believed they had more chances of success. As Soledad Perpiñan put it in an interview, "I choose my battles."[62]

❀ ❀ ❀

A challenge to the definition of woman as "suffering martyr" is a radical concept in a country where Catholicism and Filipino men have by and large defined "what a woman is." Thus, being a feminist nun was classified as "dangerous" by no less than Mary John Mananzan (OSB), the most prominent feminist nun in the country.[63] This is not just because the oppressed and exploited appealed to them for help and they were expected to risk their lives to help them, but also because they had to face the strong arm of the state and the ire of the Catholic male hierarchy all the way to the papacy. When Nila Bermisa led the investigation into sexual abuse within the Catholic Church, she confessed that it was a "tough job because again you have to think about the bishops and the superiors of the religious congregations telling them, hey, your priest is like this!"[64]

But this small group of nuns working within these limitations had a significant impact on the women's movement. Impacts ranged from feminist theorizing, where one of their unique contributions lay in placing the woman question in its religious context and demystifying women's suffering and victimization. But if indeed Filipino women embraced suffering because it was the road to redemption, the nuns' campaign to

replace the martyred Christ with the liberated Christ and to replace the Mater Dolorosa with Mary the woman had the potential to alter most profoundly the construction of "the Filipina." Raising issues during classes, radio shows, or as daily advisers on topics considered taboo lifted the cultural ban on them (after all, if a nun could talk about it, it must be okay; see Chapter 6), and gave victims of rape, violence, and sexual harassment the courage to share their stories and seek help. In addition, the nuns gave women information about their bodies, especially about their health, sexuality, and reproductive health. They also founded feminist organizations with transnational moorings and a transnational perspective, seeking to foster feminist identities cross-culturally and across nation-states. At the same time, they encouraged women to reject a life of suffering. For these nuns, the victim narrative was a "negative idol."

Although feminist nuns supported ordination for women, when asked whether they would personally choose to be ordained, the answer was a surprising and unanimous "no." The reason they gave was that the present hierarchal system meant that priests were subject to more rigorous rules than the nuns were, and were required to spend all their time administering the sacraments. Nuns, monitored only by their local superiors, had more freedom to pursue their individual mission or advocacy.[65] Thus, despite their unequal standing with priests, the nuns capitalized on a small window of opportunity—the freedom to traverse spaces and cross borders of class, locality, nation, and ideologies—a lifestyle denied to ordained priests.[66]

The fact that some of these nuns were Manila celebrities was evidence of their prominence and impact as role models and feminist icons. Mananzan, Fabella, the late Tan (who became a member of the 1986 Constitutional Convention), Perpiñan, and the late Mariani were famous women at home and abroad among feminist theologians and at the United Nations. Nila Bermisa mentioned that the feminist nuns' research into sexual abuse in the Catholic Church had made nuns famous, and referred to herself as the "infamous nun."[67] The militant nun as activist effigy first appeared in the film *Sister Stella L.* and was elevated to iconic status in the photographic accounts of the People Power 1 revolution that toppled the Marcos regime. Since 1986, this group of activist nuns have been more closely associated with the women's movements—an activism just as dangerous as the fight against a brutal dictatorship, because here they must confront the formidable power of the Catholic Church. As religious women, they epitomized the fraught nature of women's activism. Although their status as religious persons was the

source of their symbolic capital as activists giving their cause an aura of legitimacy, their identity as Catholic nuns limited their activism in areas that directly challenged the Catholic Church's position (in reproductive health and divorce, for example). Nuns such as Christine Tan (RGS), for example, have been threatened with excommunication.[68] Like guerrillas, these women had to choose their battles and know when to attack and when to retreat, when to protest loudly, or when to whisper quietly to those women who sought their personal advice.

2

Prostitution, Women's Movements, and the Victim Narrative

In the international context, the activism over prostitution as a feminist issue has the protagonists divided over the interpretation of whether prostitution is violence against women (VAW) or sex work. The former defines prostitutes as victims of male violence and patriarchy while the latter sees prostitution as a kind of work making it a labor issue.[1] I am not going to revisit these arguments here; my intention instead is to note the international context of this fiery debate that continues to haunt the specter of international feminists everywhere.

Although the supporters for either camp could be found among Filipina activists, the prevailing position has been the view that prostitution is VAW. Feminists have cited the peculiar conditions of the Philippines as a developing country—especially the acute and continuing problems of poverty and unemployment, the historical presence of American bases, and the lack of social protection for families—as reasons for opposing the legitimization of prostitution as a profession, because in their opinion women's choices were severely constrained.[2]

In this book I use the term "prostitute" rather than "sex worker" (which implies prostitution as work), or "prostituted women" (which implies prostitution as VAW) to make the point that I am not taking the position of either camp in the international feminist debate on prostitution. The word "entertainer" is used to refer to the Filipina OCWs in Japan who may or may not be involved in prostitution.

My reading of the Philippine context is that existing cultural constructions of the feminine that idealized the woman as martyr introduced another complexity to those grappling with prostitution as a feminist issue. Feminists hoped to alter constructions of the feminine to remove the symbolic capital given to the woman as martyr, but this strategy contradicted the position that prostitutes were victims of violence. How feminists negotiated this conundrum is one of the major themes of this book. The activism over prostitution as a feminist issue captured much of the experiences and complex challenges encountered by activists. On the one hand, deployment of the victim narrative was successful in advocating laws on behalf of prostitutes; on the other hand, feminists were not keen on encouraging women to wear the badge of "victim" permanently in everyday practice. This chapter focuses on one side of the double narrative the use of the victim narrative in the battle to decriminalize prostitution and shift the discursive blame onto the traffickers, pimps, and clients. Representing prostitutes as victims has largely been a successful effort, winning the passage of progressive legislation such as the Anti-Trafficking in Persons Act of 2003. But since activists wanted to fashion women into advocates and empowered agents, and not victims, they also directed their attention to the transformation of women's consciousness and self-esteem. The latter project will be discussed in more detail in Part II of this book (Practices: Fashioning Women) in Chapter 7. Empirical data for the arguments made above will be taken from the materials of three women's organizations that focus on prostitution as a feminist issue.

Three Women's Organizations

The Development Action for Women Network (DAWN) is an NGO "devoted to assisting Filipino women migrants in Japan and their Japanese Filipino children in the promotion and protection of their human rights and welfare."[3] Formed in 1996, it focused on the lives of the women who went to Japan to entertain Japanese men in bars, but who all too often ended up in prostitution.[4] A number of them return to the Philippines pregnant and abandoned by their Japanese customers-turned-partners. DAWN not only gave them the opportunities for an alternative livelihood through their Sikhay business (weaving and sewing clothes for export to Japan), but it also helped the Filipino-Japanese children by locating their fathers and pressuring those men to send financial support to their children. DAWN brought these women and their children together as a new "family" through activities such as socials, theater, dance, and seminars on human rights. DAWN is superbly organized; it has published two books and has produced a quarterly newsletter (*Sinag,* literally translated as Dawn or Daybreak) since January 1997.[5] In addition, DAWN has transnational links with DAWN-Japan run by Japanese women who sell Sikhay products in Japan and assist in the task of locating the Japanese fathers of the Filipino-Japanese children.

The Third World Movement Against Trafficking in Women (TW-MAE-W) is an organization founded on Human Rights Day December 10, 1980, by Good Shepherd nun Soledad Perpiñan, an activist during the martial law regime of President Marcos. It was the sex tourism in the 1970s and military prostitution that inspired her to work with prostitutes in Metro-Manila and to build shelters for them, while giving them the training for alternative employment. Due to its prominence, it was given consultative status in the United Nations Economic and Social Council in 1985. TW-MAE-W built "drop-in centers" called "Belens" where prostitutes were given counseling, and training for alternative employment that included leading gender-sensitizing workshops. TW-MAE-W has since expanded its scope to include issues on the sexual exploitation of women, marriage brokers (the so-called "mail-order bride" phenomenon), migrant workers, ethnic rights, child prostitution, and the religious oppression of women.[6]

Coalition Against Trafficking in Women, Asia-Pacific (CATW-AP) was formed in May 1993 in Manila as part of the Vienna World Conference on Human Rights. It focuses on trafficking and prostitution, framing these issues in the context of human rights and VAW.[7] A branch of the international organization founded by Kathleen Barry (Coalition Against Trafficking in Women, International; CATW-International) in 1988, CATW-AP's perspectives dovetailed with its parent organization, whose goals included "to challenge acceptance of the sex industry, normalization of prostitution as work, and to deromanticize legalization initiatives in various countries."[8] In the Philippines, CATW-AP campaigned for more than eight years for the passage of the Anti-Trafficking in Persons Act of 2003 that decriminalized prostitutes and punished the traffickers and syndicates.[9]

Prostitution in the Philippine National and Transnational Context

Prostitution is a huge dollar-earning industry in the Philippines. Not only does it bring in tourist dollars, some OCWs who become prostitutes sent remittances to the Philippines; the income they sent formed part of the PHP110 billion pesos (US$12.8 billion) total of all money sent home by OCWs (including domestic helpers, and so on) in 2003.[10] In the 1970s, during the authoritarian regime of President Ferdinand Marcos, international tourism was promoted heavily, making it the forerunner of the Philippine economy as Manila developed a reputation as an "international sex city" or as the "sex capital of Asia."[11] One consequence of this campaign was the commodification of the Filipino woman—often marketed as one of the country's main tourist attractions.[12] When international tourism dropped to fourth place in foreign exchange earnings in the 1990s, a continuing male bias in foreign tourist compositions persisted as 83 percent of visitors traveling for pleasure (on holiday).[13] Even though prostitution is illegal, the government had a history of unofficially promoting rather than discouraging the industry by encouraging representations of the Philippines as peopled by beautiful women available to foreigners, and by granting visas to overseas-bound entertainers (some of whom became drawn into prostitution) and calling them overseas performing artists (OPAs). In this sense, the government was a major adversary of the women's movement who saw it as willing to "sacrifice" its women for economic gain. In addition, women activists blamed the presence of U.S. military bases and regular visits of the American Seventh Fleet as responsible for the growth of the prostitution industry.[14]

Prostitution conflated the Filipina with "sex object" and reinforced Orientalist imaginings of the Filipina Other as exotic and erotic sex slave, a commodity that could be purchased cheaply by the men of the First World. American-based feminist scholar Neferti Xina M. Tadiar showed acute insight when she identified prostitution and prostituted Filipinas as synecdoche for the prostitution of the country to global capital.[15] The Philippines sent around forty thousand women to Japan as entertainers every six months. For example, in 2002 there were 69,989 women OPAs in Japan.[16] The ubiquitous presence of the Filipina as prostitute partly explained why the issue of prostitution has such high priority in the agenda of the women's movements.

Prostitution as VAW, Prostituted Women as Victims

Women's movements in the Philippines are by no means united over the issue of prostitution, but the dominant narrative is that prostitution is identified as VAW and not sex work.[17] In the words of the CATW-AP, "prostitution is unwanted sex for women and therefore 'paid rape.'"[18] Introducing an anthology of life stories of trafficked women, Aida F. Santos declared, "the sex that often is found in prostitution and other forms of sexual exploitation is basically torture, except that one is 'paid' to endure it."[19] Furthermore, "a place rife with violence and exploitation ought not to be considered a 'workplace.'"[20] In the issue on prostitution in *Piglas Diwa,* the journal of CWR, this NGO argued that Article 138 of the Labor Code's indirect classification of prostitution as work made "the selling of flesh socially acceptable." From their perspective, the view that prostitution was "sex work" denied that it was a form of VAW, and this denial "abuses, exploits and ruins the dignity of women."[21] Activists believed the use of the term "commercial sex worker" glamorized prostitution and decontextualized it from the violence, abuse, and exploitation while exempting the perpetuators from responsibility.[22] According to Perpiñan (RGS), speaking for TW-MAE-W, prostitutes were "victims and survivors of a social evil which has been allowed to grow and thrive."[23]

Hence, activists claimed that the right term was "prostituted women" to emphasize their victimization. In radio talk show program *XY-Zone*'s episode on the Anti-Trafficking in Persons Act of 2003, a program presented soon after the law's passage, resource person and CATW-AP chair Aurora Javate de Dios corrected anchor Lily Malasa's use of the term "sex work." In response to the query, "What can you say about sex work?," de Dios answered, "We don't use the term 'sex work'" because the use of that term gave dignity to the type of work that victimized women. When Malasa asked, "What is the right term?," de Dios replied, "prostituted women" (a term introduced by Raquel Tiglao), because poverty forced women to become involved in a transaction in which they were clearly the victims.[24] In another radio talk show, *Okay Ka, Mare!* (You are okay, sister!, hereafter *Okay Ka*) the resource person from the CWR also told audiences that the correct word was "prostituted women," to emphasize their victimization and lack of choice.[25]

In this discourse, prostitutes are not just victims of male violence and male desire, but also victims of poverty. Here, the Philippine government was blamed because it was unable to provide them with adequate or alternative employment. According to CATW-AP, "Prostitution is not a choice. . . . It is an attempt to survive."[26] In a developing country, women who do not have educational qualifications only had the limited options of factory worker, domestic helper, or prostitute. Of those three poor choices, prostitution was the most lucrative. According to Aida F. Santos, speaking of trafficked women, "choice was never really a part of their lives."[27]

Prostitutes also have been represented as social victims of a culture that glorified women's suffering for the family as "dutiful daughters" and "self-sacrificing mothers" who put their kinship group above personal fulfillment. Quoting from Dr. Christina Gates, psychologist and secretary general of the Centre for Restorative Justice in Asia (CRJA), DAWN referred to the Filipina entertainers in Japan as "sacrificial lambs" who denied their own personal needs for the benefit of their families.[28] The testimonies of the entertainers disclosed that many sent their earnings back to their families.[29] In sum, feminists represented prostitutes as victims—as women who were pushed towards a life of prostitution through no fault of their own by the country's poverty and the government's inability to provide adequate job choices, and by social norms that idealized the woman as martyr and dutiful daughter.

Prostitutes also were represented by the women's organizations discussed in this chapter as duped women, lured into the profession by unscrupulous agents. Published accounts of the stories of trafficked women used in feminist advocacy replicated the narrative of naïve women tricked or trapped into prostitution by friends and acquaintances who promised them jobs as servers or entertainers overseas, but who found themselves imprisoned in brothels. Accounts of trafficked women exposed the cruel, dark, seedy, inhumane side of the agents who thrived on women's naïvete, taking women as far away as Cyprus, Nigeria, and Japan.[30]

Some of the testimonies themselves contradicted this representation as innocent victims. *Moving On,* an anthology of stories of former Filipina entertainers in Japan published by DAWN as part of their research advocacy, exposed how women went to Japan expecting to work as entertainers, but ended up having sex with customers. Many of these women had their passports confiscated and were later forced to deliver a weekly quota of "dates" with customers or risk paying a hefty fine, or worse—being left outside in the cold without adequate clothing.[31] One strategy for coping with these unrealistic demands for "dates" was for women to choose one man to become their "boyfriend." Inevitably, the "boyfriend" would expect the women to have sex with him, blurring the lines between "entertainer," "prostitute," or "lover."[32] Many of the women did not see themselves as selling sex, but rather as falling in love with "boyfriends." Indeed, DAWN's statistics reveal that 51 percent of these women ended up marrying or having children with former customers.[33] Some of the women who sought refuge with DAWN were pregnant women abandoned by their Japanese lovers who had been compelled to return home. By the time the woman accessed DAWN's services, she was quite desperate, suffering discrimination from a family who was happy to take her earnings but not to endure the shame associated with having an unmarried, single mother among them, with a child who was subjected to teasing in school for being fatherless and for being a Japanese-Filipino child of a "Japayuki."[34] The poignant tale of the women's experiences of eventual prostitution and rejection brought home the message that these women were tragic heroines.

But when I read the stories, I was also struck by another recurring theme. Despite the original experience of exploitation and prostitution, almost all the women returned to Japan six or seven times to fulfill six-month contracts at different clubs. Did this not make their representation as victims problematic? After all, the first time they signed up for a Japan stint one could argue that they were innocent victims, but the next time they presumably knew what sort of job they were getting into. Why would women return to a situation where they knew they could once again be dehumanized, exploited, and abused?

DAWN's answer to this puzzling and complex question was that these patterns of renewing contracts to Japan was further evidence of women's commodification (in this case, self-commodification), because they measured their value only as breadwinners:

> The impact of the local economy on the lives of the poor is more evident when the OPAs return and in spite of the indignities and disappointments they suffered in Japan, many OPAs opt to return to their jobs there.
>
> Dr. Gates refers to this as the "commodification" of OPAs. Those who decide to return to Japan have become commodified, equating themselves to the money they are able to earn.
>
> In their struggle for survival, the women also go through a process of depersonalization. They forget their own needs and become *sacrificial lambs* for the benefit of their families. . . .
>
> Thus, the women respondents measure their success in terms of the investments they are able to make from their earnings and not their negative experiences as OPAs in Japan. (emphasis added)[35]

Activists therefore treated this tendency to return to the source of their abuse as another evidence of victimization. This time, women were victims of a society that measured their worth in terms of how they could provide for their family's financial difficulties despite the dehumanized conditions of work. To "correct" this tendency to see themselves only as breadwinners, DAWN director Carmelita Nuqui stressed that DAWN's orientation included a lecture on their rights as human beings and a "values" seminar, where the women were told that the amount of money earned was not the only form of symbolic capital, if earning it was at the cost of suffering personal indignities and human rights violations.[36]

As I will illustrate in the next section of this chapter, the activists' use of the victim narrative had a definite purpose for their advocacy. But such a narrative elided the possibility that the women might have *chosen* to return to Japan. Activists focused on the women who sought the service of the NGOs. But despite the horror stories sensationalized in the press involving the torture, rape, and violence inflicted on Filipino entertainers in Japan, interviews with the entertainers themselves conducted by one researcher revealed that they were reluctant to support a government ban against overseas deployment of female entertainers.[37] In fact, several thousand of these entertainers demonstrated against the ban in 1991. This group of women (labeled "winners" or *panalo* by this one study) felt a sense of achievement because they contributed to the family's financial improvement. Though holding low status in Japan, they acquired some new status as returnees because they came back with material trappings of success: televisions, video recorders, Walkmans, jewelry, CD recorders, electrical appliances, iPods, money, and other "gifts."[38] They had simply sublimated how their new status or income was earned.

Granted that the accomplishments of entertainers came at a huge price, reading entertainers and prostitutes as "victims" and "sacrificial lambs" effaced their agency, not just in terms of the women's negotiation for better financial status, but also in the realm of social independence. Not all Filipina feminists advocated the above position on prostitution. As mentioned in endnote 17 of this chapter, Nelia Sancho is one of the few Filipina activists who uses the term "sex worker."[39] Other feminists point to the ways in which prostitutes act as negotiators or to how prostitution enables women to escape from the oppressive ties of the kinship group. Neferti Tadiar's analysis of feminist fiction writer Fanny Garcia's short story "Pina, Pina, Where Are You Going?" interprets Pina's sojourn into the world of prostitution as both a pressure to fulfill kinship obligations of *kapwa* (defined by her as women's "syncretic sociability," or what I would see as fulfilling the construction of woman as dutiful support system of the kinship group) and the desire to escape from family and community.[40] A study of streetwalkers in Cubao (Metro-Manila) focused on how they negotiated with customers, police, NGO staff, and families,

thereby mapping the prostitute as negotiator. Although the study concluded that, despite short-term gains, they were "real losers in the long
haul" remaining "in an oppressed, exploited and dehumanized state"),
they were discussed as active agents in their stories.[41] The story of Pina
(short for Pinay, slang for Filipina) illustrates the complexities and am-
bivalences that prostitution offers to women—linking them to families
and also enabling them to escape from the overpowering kinship group.

Finally, the possibility that prostitutes were "selling sex" was conspicuously absent in this discursive narrative; instead, the discourse was
that women were being "bought" or "sold," not that women were "selling sex." This discourse that effaces women's agency (read: prostitutes
are being bought or sold but are not actively selling sex) was a direct
consequence of the victim narrative where the prostitute was an object
of male desire but whose own sexuality or sexual expression was denied or at least submerged. This perhaps reflects the history of Filipino
feminisms in which women's sexual desire (including lesbianism) was
discussed only very recently—beginning in about the mid-1990s (see
Chapter 5).[42] At the same time, this particular discourse also locates the
position of Filipina feminists as clearly within the "prostitution is VAW"
camp in the great feminist divide.

Lobbying for the Anti-Trafficking in Persons Act of 2003

The victim narrative was crucial to the feminist lobby for the passage of
the Anti-Trafficking in Persons Act of 2003. If prostitutes were victims,
they could not possibly exude sexuality; instead they were victims of male
desire. This interpretation is in sharp contrast to the tourist or First World
representations of them as sex objects. As a result, prostitution became
a human rights issue, and women's groups demanded that, rather than
focus on prostitutes as the "problem," society shift the blame on male desire—and society's notion that women can be bought.[43] This was the theoretical position that underlined the campaign to decriminalize prostitutes
and punish the perpetuators (the clients, the pimps, the syndicates). If
prostitutes were victims, then they should not be treated as criminals since
the real criminals were the men who wanted to buy sex. This theoretical
position was not unique to the Philippines: it also was embedded in both
CATW-International's primary goals and the United Nations Protocol on
Trafficking (hereafter Palermo Protocol) that took effect in 2000.[44]

Here, women's movements accomplished a coup d'état by presenting an alternative to the patriarchal perspective. Although studies on prostitution focused on the reasons why women were "pushed" into the profession through poverty and family obligations, by the 1990s feminists shifted the analysis to a fundamental criticism of male sexual demand for prostitution or male accountability, which was identified as the culprit perpetuating the subordinate status of women.[45] "As has been often pointed out, 'sex work' only exists because of the demand from men. And that male demand has remained unquestioned and unaddressed in national policies or laws or even in public discussions."[46]

When the Anti-Trafficking in Persons Act was passed in 2003 it became a subject for discussion on radio talk shows where resource persons and anchors from various women's organizations linked prostitution to the cultural socialization that made it acceptable for men to treat women like commodities so much so that, *"natural iyon sa lalaki na bumili sa babae"* (it is natural for men to buy women).[47] CATW-AP Chairperson Aurora Javate de Dios discussed the campaign to "break the cycle of prostitution" by unpacking and critiquing society's acceptance of the male prerogative to "buy" women. She explained that the new law that punished clients and traffickers (the Anti-Trafficking in Persons Act of 2003, also known as Republic Act [RA] 9208) hoped to send the message that men should alter their perceptions that women were commodities that could be bought.[48] In 2006, CAT-W launched the slogans "women are not for sale" and "real men do not buy women."[49] It was this particular message (that women should not be bought and that real men did not buy women) that women activists wanted to disseminate through a nationwide information campaign.[50] The *Tinig* radio program, produced by the Institute of Women's Studies of St. Scholastica's College, agreed with this position when host Arche Ligo pointed out that there would be no prostitutes if there were no men wanting sex, just as there would be no bars if there were no drinkers.[51] TW-MAE-W echoed this with a position paper that declared, "[W]ithout the demand provided by men, prostitution will most likely cease to exist, and yet men are not considered, except by feminists, as the problem to be solved."[52]

It was this reasoning that lay behind the controversial definition of the Anti-Trafficking in Persons Act of 2003 that defined trafficking as

> The recruitment, transportation, transfer or harbouring, or receipt of persons *with or without the victim's consent or knowledge,* within or across national borders by means of threat or use of force, or other forms of coercion, abduction, fraud, deception,

abuse of power or of position, taking advantage of the vulnerability of the person, or, the giving or receiving of payments
or benefits to achieve the consent of a person having control
over another person for the purpose of exploitation which
includes at a minimum, the exploitation or the prostitution of
others or other forms of sexual exploitation, forced labour or
services, slavery, servitude or the removal and sale of organs.[53]
(emphasis added).

Intrinsic to this definition was the notion of "consent." The premise that women's consent was immaterial was inexorably linked to the
construction of the prostituted woman as victim. The passing of the bill
with this rider was lauded as one of CATW-AP's greatest achievements
(because the campaign was led by CATW-AP and its allies and the final
bill that was passed into law was drafted by CATW-AP).[54] Senator Luisa Ejercito, who was responsible for taking the bill to the Senate, was
advised by CATW-AP.[55] Considering that the majority of the senators
(most of whom are men) were not empathetic to this issue and the notion of consent was controversial, the passage of this act was a huge
triumph for the women's movements. This victory could be attributed to
the vigorous campaign of CATW-AP and its allies. CATW-AP and its
allies used several strategies in the almost decade-long campaign to get
this legislation passed. These included disseminating their positions in
the media, networking with politicians and legislators (as well as with
their allies in the women's movements), and the use of public protest.
Jean Enriquez gave credit to the alliance with government bodies such
as the National Commission on the Role of Filipino Women, individual
politicians such as Senators Loren Legarda and Luisa Ejercito, and the
senate legislative staff, who recognized CATW-AP as "experts" on the
issue. In the end, the alliances with women politicians (particularly Senators Luisa Ejercito and Loren Legarda) served them well, and the bill
finally became law in 2003 more or less as CATW-AP had drafted it.[56]

Because trafficking is with or without the consent of the "trafficked,"
the Anti-Trafficking in Persons Act of 2003 absolved the prostitutes of
criminal acts and criminalized the perpetuators. Women who sued traffickers were to be given anonymity and protection by the government
and other organizations, whereas clients were to be punished with fines
and jail terms.[57] Since the survivors were women and children and the
perpetuators were men (including the customers), the campaign for the
passage of this bill educated other women about their rights and the need

to shift the discussion on prostitution from the prostitutes to the men who were the pimps and customers. The victim narrative ("all prostitutes were victims whether or not they consented to it") used in the campaign was responsible for the shift in perspective from the perception of prostitutes from women who sold sex for money to women who were victims of violence and male patriarchal attempts to transform them into sex objects. The victim narrative was therefore a very powerful narrative that could be tapped to win feminist victories. Unfortunately, though, it had reaffirmed traditional constructions of the woman as martyr or dutiful woman, the very idealization the women's movement had hoped to erase. Hence, although it was a discourse that suited the campaigns of the women's movement at one level—for legislative change, for example—women's organizations also used alternative strategies aimed at transforming survivors into advocates (see Chapter 7).

Assessing the Victim Narrative

The deployment of the victim narrative had some positive impacts on cultural attitudes. It has drawn public attention to the plight of prostitutes (now seen as victims or sacrificial lambs). The fact that there was a great deal of support for the Anti-Trafficking in Persons Act of 2003 revealed that society was rethinking the category "prostitute." That consent was immaterial—that is, that prostitutes were victims whether they consented to prostitution or not—effectively favored women, who were absolved of crimes, vis-à-vis men, who were clients and pimps. At face value, it would appear that such a victim narrative denied women agency, but Filipino feminists succeeded in empowering the term "victim" without requiring the women to be "ideal victims" (i.e., *only* those who were duped or abducted). Japanese feminist theoretician Chizuko Ueno, for instance, has argued that one flaw in the feminist position that turned the "comfort women" from prostitutes to victims of rape was the demand that women conform to a category of "model victim" (only those who were duped).[58] By declaring that consent was immaterial, Filipino feminists were able to escape from the pitfall wherein women would have to prove that they were duped in order to be considered a victim of trafficking.

Second, raising the issue of prostitution in the public sphere lifted the cultural ban on what was previously a taboo topic. Rape, sex, sexuality, domestic violence, AIDS/HIV, STDs, incest, and prostitution were included in the list of subjects hidden behind the veil of silence. Women's activism removed some of the shame attached to women victimized as trafficked women, telling them that it was okay to come out and tell their stories. Labeling them "victims" removed the shame and attempted to restore dignity to these women.

The narrative that entertainers have been social victims affixed blame not only on the perpetuators of violence, rape, or sexual desire, but also on society either for commodifying women (as DAWN argued in the case of entertainers) or for ostracizing them. This narrative compelled audiences to examine their complicity in the continuing trauma and victimization of these women.

Achieving the larger goals of all organizations, however, seem elusive. CATW-AP and TW-MAE-W both aimed for "a world without prostitution" and "an end to prostitution and trafficking."[59] The Japanese-Filipino children dreamt of being reunited with their Japanese fathers. Although DAWN was often successful in contacting the Japanese father to pressure him to provide financial support for the children, the support inevitably trickled down to nothing after a couple of years, making victory temporary.[60]

If audiences refused to engage with the victim narrative or chose to ignore it, activists could find themselves in a dead-end situation. At this point, the mission to refashion women into advocates became more important. If feminists were unable to change governments or cultural attitudes, they could still transform women followers. In addition, the fundamental project of empowering women implied the renunciation of their representation as victims as well as the symbolic capital associated with the woman as martyr. Hence, feminist women's organizations have been proactive in forging alliances with the former prostitutes and giving them a feminist education through participation in gender workshops and by co-opting them in some activist campaigns. In fact, one could argue that the organizations discussed here could not carry out their advocacy without the direct participation of former prostitutes who are essential subjects in the project of increasing public awareness through strategies using oral testimonies and theater as advocacy. The co-optation of former prostitutes into the women's movements reveals the genuine desire of activists to have a mass following while legitimizing their organization's claim to speak for prostitutes. In fact survivors' groups in the Philippines formed a national network that initiated its own programs. Buklod in Olongapo City, Bagong Kamalayan in Quezon City, and Lawig Bubai in Davao City for example, organized their own services and livelihood programs, revealing not only the diversity, but also the national and geographical scope of the survivor's activist bases.[61]

3
The Woman as Worker

Although constructions of the feminine defined woman as "wife and mother," for the majority of lower-class women the reality was that these wives and mothers were also, simultaneously, workers. The majority of Filipinos are from the working classes and the income brought in by the women of the family, whether primary or supplementary in nature, was crucial to the survival of the kinship group. The feminization of the labor force (including global labor) from the 1970s onwards has further increased the value of women's work. The spectacular rise in the number of women OCWs, for example, has made housewives into breadwinners to the point of challenging or "remaking" Filipino masculinities in the Ilocos region, where men were transformed into househusbands overnight.[1]

It is thus not surprising that women's organizations were most preoccupied with the woman as worker in the many areas women contributed to the workforce—as peasants, factory workers, vendors, and migrant workers, especially domestic helpers, abroad. The fact that women's movements classified women into sectors that identified their working roles—with particular organizations representing each sector; for example—testified to the intrinsic connection, at least in the minds of activists, that women's identities and issues were linked to their occupations.

This chapter will focus on how women workers have been represented by the women's movements, in particular focusing on some of GABRIELA's sectoral affiliates such as the Movement of Women Workers (KMK; Kilusan ng Manggagawang Kababaihan), Amihan, GABRIELA-Youth, SAMAKANA (see below, this chapter), the CWR, and the Kanlungan Migrant Center (the feminist NGO for migrant workers). My reading of the evidence is that women's organizations represented the woman as worker as being the most exploited and oppressed of humanity—as modern-day slaves.[2] At the same time, women workers also were identified as the women's movements most likely followers, and were clearly imagined to be potential radicals. In the words of the women's department of the most formidable labor union, the May 1st Movement (KMU; Kilusang Mayo Uno), "The most exploited and oppressed are the most reliable in the struggle" (this applied to men too, though).[3] In unpacking the grand narratives of the woman as worker, the image of the woman as slave—subject to her male supervisors or boss, subject to her husband and children—was accompanied by the woman as militant activist. In this sense, discourses on the woman as worker also reproduced the double narrative.

Feminist theorizing perceived the Filipina to be deeply connected to the world, with the premise that the Filipina postcolonial condition placed her at the bottom rung of the global racial hierarchy as a "servant of globalization," to borrow a term from Rhacel Parreñas.[4] Basic women's orientation workshops run by GABRIELA and CWR explained the exploitation suffered by women workers as a result of the feudal nature of Philippine society, and the country's developing world condition in which it is vulnerable to the neo-imperialism of the rich northern countries and their transnational corporations. Though this analysis reflected GABRIELA's links with the Philippine Left and the national democratic ideology of this militant women's organization, it also underscored the point that women workers were vulnerable to global markets and local political dynamics. The status of workers and peasants was linked to the larger process of globalization and the liberalization of the economy, and the place of the Philippines in the global South. Given this theoretical perspective, it should come as no surprise that GABRIELA was against globalization. It protested against the GATT, the WTO, APEC, and President Fidel Ramos' Medium-Term Development Plan, which was more popularly known by its nickname, "Philippines 2000." New projects proposed in the name of development were immediately suspect, particularly if development meant the alienation of land from the peasantry, the loss of existing jobs, or the pollution of the environment. Hence, activists confronted the global and local capitalist classes. Since the women's movement's legitimizing discourse was that it was a grass-roots movement, it took the side of the working-class woman against the local and global capitalist classes. That globalization was targeted as the *bête noire* of working women was clear from the number of times conferences or special issues of newsletters were devoted to this theme.

Although women workers were represented as modern-day slaves, the implication was that it was precisely because they were enslaved that they needed to organize themselves as a militant group to negotiate for better conditions. Women workers were urged to join organizations pertinent to their sectors, attend gender workshops, and participate in demonstrations, pickets, and lobbying activities in order to make their demands heard and to pressure governments and businesses to concede to these proposals for change. GABRIELA's leaders were women peasants, workers, urban poor, and factory workers. Women workers spoke for themselves in media, including radio and television programs (see Chapter 6), and at demonstrations. In these platforms, women workers appeared as confident, intelligent, and expert legitimate leaders of their organizations. The pages of GABRIELA's newsletter (*GABRIELA Women's Update*) were replete with stories of women workers participating in demonstrations and rallies. The message was clear: women must involve themselves in organized protest in order to improve their lives.

Women Factory Workers

Women's labor has tended to concentrate on specific industries: the service sectors; handicrafts, electronics (in 1981, 90 percent of electronics workers were women, increasing to 95 percent in 1996), garments and textiles, food and beverage, ceramics (also 95 percent in 1996), semiconductors (electronics equipment), retail/department stores, and food processing.[5] The EPZs, or industrial zones, employed huge numbers of women factory workers; and it is in these zones where women's organizations are the most active. Women were first involved in the overall labor union movement before forming women's organizations of workers. They participated in union-wide advocacies for workers rights, the right to strike, and to have collective bargaining agreements, as well as for better pay and conditions. KMU was the most radical union; before 1983 it had women followers, but very few women leaders. Even in workplaces that employed a majority of women workers, union leadership remained in the hands of men. It was the realization that union activism needed a gendered lens coupled with women's exclusion from the overall leadership of the union movement that inspired the formation of exclusive women's organizations. The KMK identified women factory workers as the leading force of the women's movements; its history revealed its close links with the KMU since some of its leaders were also KMU members.[6]

The KMK traced its beginnings with the establishment of the Women's Industrial Workers Alliance (WIWA) in 1983, although some sources claimed it was founded in 1981.[7] It was dedicated to addressing women's concerns in the manufacturing sector, agriculture, and other industries.[8] It described itself as an organization of women formed by the women's committee inside unions but it did not claim to be a federation, nor was it a women's committee of the KMU.[9] Once it had affiliated with GABRIELA around September 1984, it had access to the very pulse of the women's movements at that time. By 1986, it had 168 chapters.[10] KMK membership fluctuated over time, influenced by the domestic economy and the history of the Philippine Left. In 1993, it claimed twenty thousand members nationally, reaching its peak in 1998 when it boasted forty thousand members; these members were from the national capital region as well as Bulacan, Bataan, Baguio, Cebu, Bacolod and Mindanao.[11] The Left split between the "reaffirmists" (RAs) and the "rejectionists" (RJs) in 1992–1993 was identified as responsible for the decline in numbers after 1998.[12] This split had a massive effect on GABRIELA itself: when it aligned itself with the RAs, those who identified with the RJs left the organization.[13]

The issues that KMK brought to the forefront of the women's struggle changed over the years from its birth to 2006. Although sexual harassment and maternity leave benefits received priority from the 1980s until the mid-1990s, the contractualization of women's labor took center stage from the mid-1990s onwards until the present writing (2010). Part of this shift in emphasis was due to some of the victories of the movement, such as the passing of the Anti-Sexual Harassment Act of 1995. On the other hand, the trend towards the increasing contractualization of women's labor in the late 1990s threatened to erode the major gains of the women's labor movement (particularly security of tenure and the benefits associated with that, including overtime pay).[14]

SEXUAL HARASSMENT

The campaign against sexual harassment was the signature crusade of this sector of the women's movements. It was women workers in factories who were most vulnerable and most likely to encounter this sexist practice in the workplace, and it was they who provided testimonies as part of the legislative lobby for a law against sexual harassment. The KMK was at the forefront of the educational campaign that defined sexual harassment in the local context of factory work. The effect was that the women's movements' campaign against sexual harassment was very much influenced by the experience of women factory workers.

In order to begin a campaign against sexual harassment it was necessary to define and contextualize it. Feminists were therefore compelled to examine the entire gamut of women's objectification in the workplace from job advertisements to career promotions. Analysis of the advertisements for jobs for women revealed a common denominator: they wanted to hire women with "attractive and pleasing personality, and single status," whether or not the job required such traits.[15] Sometimes, apart from a pleasing personality, they were required to be at least 5 foot 2 inches tall.[16] Sometimes the decision to hire a woman depended on what she was wearing that day.[17] Nanette Miranda, who became secretary general of KMK, recounted how she and fellow applicants were required to lift their skirts and show their legs to the male supervisor before they were hired as salesclerks.[18] This was confirmed by research conducted by the CWR, where applicants for salesgirls in Shoemart Department Stores were asked to show that their legs and thighs were free of scars and their skins satin-smooth.[19] In some cases, women were required to pass pregnancy tests or virginity tests before they were hired.[20] These requirements validated the traditional metanarrative that objectified women as beautiful as opposed to intelligent, which was the criterion for men to be hired. Women workers were expected to conform to the stereotype of single and attractive. An editorial of the KMK newsletter *Ugnay-Kababaihan* summed up this image of the woman worker based on job advertisements: "Wanted female operator *Wanted male supervisor *Wanted Attractive Waitress/A go-go Dancer/Singer with Pleasing Personality *Wanted Attractive and Sexy Salesladies *Wanted Domestic Helper *Wanted Attractive Receptionist/Secretary."[21] The author lamented the process in which the image of women as sex objects bound to the domestic sphere was merely transposed to the workforce where women were expected to be slaves or decorative objects: "If at home we are only housewives or sex objects, at work we are identical to slaves or items of decoration."[22]

Furthermore, the social assumption was that women were best suited to jobs that required dexterity and infinite patience. Hence, it was axiomatic that they be given the tedious, repetitive tasks in factory work because these jobs were feminine. This explained the numbers of women employed in the electronics industry and the preference for women workers in the banana industry, where the chores of packing and weighing bananas were considered a delicate assignment.[23] The woman as worker was expected to be attractive but not intelligent, and to be suited to repetitive, tedious, and meticulous tasks rather than managerial tasks that required leadership qualities. The activists critiqued this grand narrative and demanded the dismantling of assumptions that women workers be decorative, docile, and submissive.

Sexual harassment became even more acute once women were actually hired in the factories. Factory workers alluded to the informal "lay down or lay off" policy of male supervisors who asked for sexual favors in exchange for job security or promotion. If women did not comply, they risked losing their jobs.[24] The institutionalization of this practice was such that in some factories male supervisors were known to have several mistresses. Nanette Miranda, who worked in the electronics industry, observed that one supervisor had three mistresses—one per shift![25] The benefits accrued by these women who were dubbed "favorites" included better salaries; for example, in one company instead of a salary of P113 the woman received P118.[26] Even in foreign-owned companies such as Korean Sang Woo, the Korean supervisors have been known to touch private parts of women workers.[27] In addition, supervisors stole kisses from tired women workers while janitors found ways to discover the color of women's panties by observing them from below while they climbed up and down wooden staircases. In one incident, the ceiling of the female bathroom gave way because the janitors were peeping at the women through a hole in the ceiling.[28] Even the security guards were guilty of sexual harassment when they deliberately overstepped physical boundaries and touched women's breasts during body searches.[29] Policemen sent to confront women workers on strike deliberately deployed sexual harassment as a technique to break the picket line. Because women strikers faced the police with arms linked, police tried to force them to break ranks by touching their breasts, nipples, and genitalia [30]

KMK and its allies in the women's movement were proactive in the campaign against sexual harassment in the workforce by presenting their testimonies as part of the advocacy for the Anti-Sexual Harassment Act (passed in 1995).[31] Women's NGOs, including KMK, GABRIELA, and the CWR, also published educational materials—sometimes in the form of Tagalog comics—defining sexual harassment and advising victims of their rights. Basic women's orientation workshops run by the women's committees of unions also discussed this problem. At the same time, KMK worked with their allies in the legislature. Sexual harassment was also a priority issue for women students at universities and colleges. GABRIELA-Youth exposed the practice where professors demand sex in exchange for passing or higher grades, and introduced the concept of peer harassment as well (from classmates, for example) by holding public forums on campus.[32]

By repudiating the representation of women workers as beautiful sex objects employed to please men or supervisors, the KMK/GABRIELA began the process of altering patriarchal discourses on the woman worker. At the very least, it underscored the point that this behavioral practice was VAW and was no longer to be tolerated or tacitly accepted as normal.

CONTRACTUALIZATION OF LABOR

The increasing trend towards the contractualization of labor made it *the* priority issue of the KMK from about 2000 to the present writing (2010). From the perspective of the workers, this phenomenon, considered as a result of the globalization of capital and the outsourcing of the labor force, threatened to erase all the rights won by the labor movement. It removed security of tenure, making the women workers much more vulnerable to exploitation by the business owners and sexual harassment by managers.[33] The contractualization of labor or labor flexibilization was defined as the hiring of workers for a short term only, using the following labels: trainees, helpers, apprentices, floaters, piece raters, casuals, seasonal, daily workers, or contractual workers.[34] In the research conducted and published by the CWR, they noted that, from 1990 to 2000, one in five employed were contract workers. They argued that the figures become even more significant if one chose to use case studies of specific companies and their employment statistics. The data revealed the following percentage of contract workers in several businesses: Shoemart Department Stores: 90 percent of the salespersons (most of them women); VASSAR (a plastics factory): 78 percent; LAWS (garments): 88 percent; MODE (garments, an industry that relies on piece raters and daily workers): 100 percent; and CELEBES (canning sardines): 96 percent.[35] Hence, for some particular companies, labor contractualization was the norm rather than the exception. Companies operating in designated EPZs were also notorious for hiring workers on contract only.[36] Since there was a "no strike" policy in the EPZ areas, women workers became even more vulnerable to exploitation (and were paid less than the minimum wage) and sexual harassment (because the supervisors could make promises of extended contracts, for example). Since the women had to incur expenses in the application process for employment, the pressure to toe the line was paramount and inhibited women from complaining, let alone asserting themselves.

Activists were concerned with the impact of labor contractualization on the women. Interviews with contract workers pointed to the lowering of self-esteem and the creation of a culture of docility.[37] The life of a contract worker was depicted as a life without human rights and without security.[38] In addition, the jobs assigned to women were seen as extensions of women's domestic responsibilities such as serving clients, arranging and selling products, cleaning, caring, teaching, or doing laundry; the jobs were often in the garments industry where it is assumed that the duties did not require physical strength.[39] The word "slave" (*alipin*) was used prominently to describe the way employers treated the women, and the word "endure" (*tiis*) was used to underscore the women's response to the harsh working conditions and insecurity of tenure. In fact, women's enslavement in the home was aggravated by contractualization of the labor force since women doing piecework at home had to do the job while doing domestic chores; they often relied on the labor of their own children to fulfill quotas.[40] The low self-esteem was caused by the low value placed on women's work and the insecurity of tenure. Representations of the contract worker in the comics genre depicted a woman plagued by self-doubt. The woman was haunted by several negative questions: (1) Is her college degree worthless? (2) Will she be out of work by the age of thirty (since youth and beauty are preferred attributes)? (3) Will she be required to forfeit marriage (since single women are the norm)? and (4) With no future prospects in sight, will she forever be a burden to her family?[41]

But alongside representations of the contract worker as a slave who lacked self-esteem were the recommendations that contract workers needed to organize against globalization. Contract workers were generally reluctant to join unions for fear that they would either lose their jobs or not have their contracts renewed. Furthermore, contract work was not conducive to the formation of unions because workers expected to be employed for such a short time there was no motivation or time to organize for the future. Logistics added yet another obstacle: contract workers were scattered over several industries spanning different geographical locations.[42] And yet, the message transmitted was unequivocal: workers needed to unite and organize in a militant struggle to end the contractualization of labor and globalization. Contract workers also were encouraged to seek alliances with other workers and citizens to fight against contractualization.[43] CWR published two regular journals (*Piglas-Diwa* and *Marso 8*) and occasional books; in this body of work it was suggested that an organization of contract workers was necessary to lobby for the decrease in the number of contract workers per business.[44] The KMK has continued to lobby for the Security of Tenure Bill (House Bill 4461), and a coalition, the Coalition Against Contractualization, has been formed to represent the cause of contract laborers. Women's orientation workshops run by KMK or the CWR introduced the feminist perspective to ordinary women workers, with CWR publications used as teaching modules.[45]

The message that workers must help themselves applied to all workers, whether tenured or contractual. In the regular reports published by GABRIELA and the CWR, victories achieved by the KMK, for instance, were attributed to its militant labor activism in specific business locations or companies. In 1999, the KMK succeeded in affirming a ban on labor-only contracting at Samsung. In addition, they were able to negotiate for the establishment of a health and safety committee and cooperative system in the canteen, and an increase in wages and meal allowances.[46] Women's organizations fundamentally believed in the power of labor union organizing; their strategy included working with male unions, such as the KMU.[47] Techniques employed by the KMK mirrored KMU or other union modes of protest and pressure such as forums, pageants (such as a Santacruzan with women parading with sashes naming their demands), chanting their complaints during their breaks, and concerts. The strike was used only as a last resort, and only when the union believed they had the majority support of its members, the workers.[48]

Peasant Women

Since the foremost issue raised by peasants has been genuine land reform, and because it has been difficult to pressure elite landowners to redistribute land to the peasantry, the nature of activism has had to be combative. Ligaya Lindio-McGovern's study of KAMMI's (a branch of Amihan, the organization of peasant women affiliated with GABRIELA; see history below) politics of resistance in Mindoro examined the strategies deployed by peasant women (and men as well) involving land occupation, or "the process of collectively occupying idle lands (*lupang tiwangwang*) and making them productive."[49] These "idle lands" were actually owned by absentee landlords or corporations. A radical form of protest, "land occupation" had major repercussions as powerful landlords retaliated with violence, and often were supported by the military.[50] This punitive reaction, termed "militarization" of the provinces, has had gendered implications, with military men guilty of the sexual harassment and rape of peasant women. Peasants were the biggest victims of militarization since the army has not just been used as an instrument to enforce landlord interests, but it also has been deployed to check the growth of the NPA (New People's Army, the military arm of the Communist Party) in the provinces. McGovern's study documented specific cases where KAMMI's successful attempts at land occupation were ephemeral because militarization eventually drove them out, such as by burning their houses or crops.[51] Remaining one of Amihan's strongest bastions, community organizations in Mindoro could boast of small achievements such as the launch of some pharmacies in the smallest political units (*barangays*) and the provision of herbal medicines.[52]

Apart from land reform and militarization, unique issues that emerged from the peasant women's activism included the problems of debt and usury, day care, pesticides, reproductive health (such as contraception and abortion), domestic violence, lack of services such as education (literacy rates are lower for peasant women compared to urban women), wages, the double burden—where women had to work for a wage and also do domestic duties at home with no help from their husbands—and gender discrimination, with land titles only in men's names. The trend towards converting agricultural lands to grazing, aquaculture, or tourist development sites (including golf courses) in order to exempt landholdings from land reform also had an adverse effect on peasants, both male and female. Apart from shrinking the availability of land that potentially could be redistributed to peasants, land conversion also deprived peasants of wage work, since these lands were formerly worked by them even if they could not own them.[53] Health, reproductive health, abortion and domestic violence will be discussed in Chapters 6 and 10. I will focus here on the issues of land reform and militarization using the case study of Amihan, the national feminist organization of peasant women that is affiliated with GABRIELA.

Amihan (a word that means harvest wind), also known as the National Federation of Peasant Women, was founded in 1986 as part of the peasant women's struggle for genuine land reform. Amihan's feminist slant could be seen in its emphasis on "women's rights to own land, priority to widows and single mothers in land distribution programs, just wages for women agricultural workers, protection from sexual harassment, and the extension of maternity benefits and day care services."[54] In addition, it campaigned for the "democratization of the family," defining that as "equal division of labor within the household, equal rights in decision-making and control of family resources, and the right of the women to participate in activities outside the family and home."[55] Furthermore, they endorsed the view that marriage and the family were not private matters, particularly with regard to issues of domestic violence.[56]

GABRIELA's newsletter reported that in 1988 eleven organizations based in twenty provinces (out of seventy) formed Amihan, comprising a total membership of eight thousand, most of them peasants with little formal education.[57] Judy Taguiwalo, one of the original founding members of Amihan confirmed in an interview that the actual founding date was 1986 while 2008 Amihan Deputy Secretary General Tess Vistro claimed that the original membership was five thousand not eight thousand.[58] During the Corazon Aquino presidency (1986–1992), militarization kept membership numbers down, but from 1988 onwards it grew to ten to twelve thousand. By 2003, Congress membership reached twenty thousand, though membership was always fluid with some provinces such as Mindoro more active than others.[59]

Though the word "slave" was conspicuously absent from the narratives of peasant women's status, descriptions of their experiences underscored society's view of them as second-class citizens whose interests could be dismissed for the sake of the family. If parents did not have enough financial resources to send all their children to school, boys were prioritized over girls. Former Amihan Secretary General Judy Taguiwalo described the attitude towards peasant women as debt payment (*pambayad ng utang*), since families sent their daughters away to become domestic helpers to pay off debts.[60] This construction has been traced to historical roots; the character of Juli in José Rizal's novel discussed in the introduction is an example.[61] Although women performed all types of farmwork except plowing, they received lower wages than did men. Since women were responsible for the family budget, they were pressured to engage in entrepreneurial activities in order to stretch the family budget. The financial stress often led to quarrels between couples that often resulted in domestic violence.[62]

In this sense, peasants were "society's coping mechanism," whose lives and labor could be sacrificed to enable the family's survival.[63] But they were also encouraged to organize themselves and be proactive in advocating for change. The position of the peasantry as part of the lower classes meant that they lacked the political connections for legislative changes in their favor. One major reason for the failure of genuine land reform in the Philippines was that the legislature was still dominated by the upper classes who, as landlords or with ties to the landlord classes, were reluctant to abide by the peasant demand for free land distribution, whereas the introduction of exemptions to the legislation meant that landowners could claim on technical grounds that their lands were in that category. Thus, activists were aware that any legislative changes or real changes had to come "from below," through relentless, vigilant, and sustained organized advocacy. Globalization and the conversion of the lands into cash crops has been identified as the peasants' "biggest problem" in the past ten years. CWR through its publication *Piglas Diwa* therefore advised women peasants to use collective action as a primary strategy to combat the economic pressures on their farming practices.[64]

Organizations focused on training women to become militant. The *Piglas-Diwa* publication on women victims of militarization tracked the making of an activist in comics genre. The main character, a teenage girl from Metro-Manila named Annie, visits her relatives in the provinces, only to witness the military steal the family's food, farm animals, and belongings, and sexually harass the women. Accused of conspiring with the NPA, two people are killed and the town forced to evacuate to a shelter. While she is in the shelter, Annie meets a nun who convinces her to present her testimony to the Human Rights Commission. The story ends with Annie's metamorphosis into an activist with GABRIELA, and the last scene shows her giving speeches at rallies.[65] Annie's story is interesting because she not a peasant woman but a teenage student studying in Manila who becomes transformed into an activist because she witnesses military abuse of the peasantry. She represents the GABRIELA ideal woman, able to be a spokesperson for oppressed women.

I'm Always at Rallies (*Rally ako ng rally!*)

Women workers and women peasants were the most visible sector of women at demonstrations, rallies, and other public spectacles of protest. It was the women peasants and workers that made up the army of regular collective public protesters in the streets. McGovern recounted that there was a rally almost every day during her fieldwork in the early 1990s; an Amihan national leader cited an average of three demonstrations a week taking place in Manila, though that was not as much as took place in Mindoro.[66] Cathy Estavillo confirmed that Amihan joined demonstrations that went beyond local issues participating in the rallies against globalization and against militarization, and the regular GABRI-ELA protest during the president's annual state of the nation address, during which time opposition groups held their alternative state of the nation address.[67] On June 6, 1996, Amihan led a national demonstration in Manila to inspire peasant women to continue the struggle for true agrarian reform and to criticize President Fidel Ramos' Philippines 2000 program.[68] Peasants traveled all the way from the provinces to Quezon City in Metro-Manila to present their demands.[69] Some demonstrations became camp-outs, such as the Amihan and Mabuhay Farmers protest in front of the Department of Agriculture in 1998 to call attention to their demands about disputed land in San Francisco, Quezon province.[70] Metro-Manila became the regular site for demonstrations and rallies merely because it housed the buildings of the Philippine legislature, the presidential palace, major government agencies, and the United States Embassy, the usual targets of organized protests.[71]

In these demonstrations, peasant women become spokespersons— delivering speeches, carrying placards, and chanting slogans. They also developed solidarity with all other protesters when they linked arms to face the police.[72] Here, demonstrations became one essential aspect of the women's movement's process of fashioning the new Filipino woman as militant activist. Demonstrations featured more prominently in Amihan's history during the 1990s than they did after 2000. During the times of increasing militarization, women had the added burden of having to run peasant organizations when their men were forced to evacuate to avoid the repercussions of being labeled by government as part of the NPA.[73]

Land occupation required even more committed protest: the presence of soldiers, security guards, police or armed vigilantes sent to disperse the activists carried the threat of violence. McGovern's fieldwork in Mindoro revealed how in some instances the military burned houses, imprisoned or executed protesters, and stole belongings.[74]

Not only were women activists more vulnerable than men to militarization because they were targeted for rape and sexual harassment, but also they often had to deal with irate husbands who disapproved of their wives' participation in women's activism. Women's involvement in Amihan, for example, became a source of conflict for couples whose husbands resented the time wives spent away from home (read: unable to do housework). At the same time, men feared that feminist education would result in their loss of power at home. Women had to negotiate with husbands so that they could join protest activities.[75]

The axiom that women must be proactive in organizing themselves was endorsed by many of the NGOs under GABRIELA's wings. For example, the primer for SAMAKANA, the NGO for urban poor women, not only underscored the need for an organized and united front, but also gave out handy hints for forming organizations in their localities.[76] Urban poor women had synergies with peasant women since their primary issue—demolition of their houses—was congruent with peasant demands for land. Women of the urban poor often were classified as squatters and lived in makeshift houses in the city close to their place of employment.[77] When the land they occupied was needed for conversion into new building works (such as shopping malls, for example), they faced eviction. Women organized for alternative low-income housing (and land) and to prevent demolition of their homes. Much like "land occupation," the urban poor protests required militancy because activists staged pickets and camp-outs, usually in front of the National Housing Authority.[78] They also participated in the demonstrations on March 8 (International Working Women's Day; IWWD) and in the annual state of the nation address protests.[79]

The iconic image of the woman worker as a militant activist protesting in the streets had some truth in practice. Nanette Miranda, secretary general of KMK, spent so much of her life participating in demonstrations, rallies, and strikes that she often slept in the streets in the picket lines. She summed up her lifestyle in an interview with the phrase: "I am always at the rallies" (*rally ako ng rally*). Miranda's schedule of demonstrations, rallies, and pickets was not unusual for activists representing the sectors. SAMAKANA's Nerissa Guerrero regularly camped out in front of the National Housing Authority to protest the demolition of squatter settlements.[80] The diary of activities posted in GABRIELA's office blackboard in 2003, for example, disclosed that demonstrations and rallies were a prominent part of their schedule each week. The role of demonstrations in fashioning feminist identities will be discussed in Chapter 7. After all, radical demands required a militant façade and a deportment that delivered the serious message in unequivocal terms. This was GABRIELA's forte.

GABRIELA led its peers as the organization that mobilized large numbers of women workers of the lower classes to take their causes to the public domain. Whereas the membership of GABRIELA ebbed and flowed depending on the political context of the time, over two decades (from 1985 to 2005) between 120 and 200 women's organizations were affiliated with it. In 2006, it had fifty thousand members.[81] Their visibility in radical protest projected far beyond their numbers. Almost every demonstration and strike that impacted on women had GABRIELA's empathy, moral support, and physical presence. It is therefore not surprising that the GABRIELA street protester had captured both the national and international imagination as the quintessential Filipina feminist.

Women Workers Abroad

In 1995 the death of Flor Contemplacion, the maid who was hung in Singapore after having been convicted of killing her fellow Filipina maid Delia Maga and the son of Maga's employer, attracted worldwide attention to the plight of Filipina domestic helpers abroad. Although the Philippine government has been sending contract labor overseas since the 1970s, by the end of the twentieth century the Philippine labor diaspora had become possibly the largest in the world with 8 million citizens abroad (10 percent of the population).[82] From 1993 to 1998, women comprised 57 percent of the aggregate number of new hires in land-based overseas employment.[83] The increasing feminization of this global labor force extended the notion of women's work outside the home to its maximum potential (overseas). Flor Contemplacion's story touched many Filipinos and became the metaphor for the Filipino nation victimized by more-affluent countries. Not only was she a victim of powerful (read: imperial) Singapore, who ignored President Fidel Ramos' plea to stop her execution, but she also was a victim of her own country's negligence because the Philippine Embassy ignored the situation of a "mere maid." Thus, the irony of the Filipino situation became palpable: though the remittances sent by OCWs were so significant (US$10 billion in 2005) that they were crucial to the Philippine economy, the Philippine government has in turn been callous towards the perils faced by these migrants who are vulnerable to abuse and human rights violations.[84] Instead, the government continues, as of this writing, to see OCWs as the solution to the economic morass of the country (particularly chronic unemployment). Hence, instead of coming to their rescue in cases of abuse or maltreatment, the government is worried about the impact that activism might have on the future demand for Filipino overseas workers. Scholar Neferti Tadiar embellished the metaphor when she depicted Flor Contemplacion/the Filipino nation as a colonized body. Flor's life story epitomized the experiences of a colonized subject: she performed a job that was compared to modern slavery and she was powerless against the strong arm of Singapore's political state.[85] The public outrage that erupted as a consequence of the Flor Contemplacion case could also be explained by the feeling of helplessness that accompanied the realization of the Filipino postcolonial condition as "servants of globalization."[86] Though subsequently these overseas contract workers have been reinvented officially as "Bagong Bayani" (new heroes/heroines) because their remittances were essential to the Philippine domestic economy, this has not rehabilitated the status or perception of the Filipino overseas worker as modern-day slaves. One seafarer (a seaman, part of the global shipping industry that hired more than 255,000 mostly male Filipinos, the largest national group) modified the label and said they should be called "Gagong Bayani" (stupid heroes), "because even if we contribute significantly to the country, the government fails to help unemployed sea men . . . I pity my fellow seafarers."[87]

Filipina OCWs comprised 55 percent of the overseas workforce, mostly in the areas of domestic service, live-in caregivers,[88] and nurses,[89] as entertainers to Japan (see Chapter 3), construction workers,[90] hostesses,[91] and seafarers.[92] The large numbers of domestic helpers in Hong Kong, Singapore, Saudi Arabia, Rome, Greece, and in other parts of Europe and the Middle East encouraged foreigners to conflate "Filipina" with "domestic helper" or "maid."[93] The entry for "Filipineza" in one Greek dictionary conflated "Filipina" with domestic worker, and in Italy and Spain domestic helpers were often referred to affectionately as "mia Filipina."[94] Their large numbers and visibility (occupying the malls and public spaces during their "days off" in Liberty Plaza in Hong Kong, Lucky Plaza in Singapore, and Stazione Termini in Rome) call attention to their presence as a labor force. There is a robust scholarly literature on Filipino women as OCWs, particularly as domestic helpers and I do not intend to duplicate or summarize them here.[95] The scholarship, most of it excellent, has consciously avoided representing women workers as mere victims and has explored the wide gamut of women's experiences, including transnational mothering and its limitations. Whereas studies emphasized the social costs of migration, they also pointed out that migration often liberated women from the constraints of the control of the kinship group.[96] There has been less interest in analyzing activists who worked on behalf of women overseas domestic helpers, although the recent interest in the study of transnational activism will soon address this obvious gap.[97] In this chapter, I will shift the analytical lens to an exploration of how women activists represented women OCW in their advocacy; I will use Kanlungan as an example. As advocates, activists were not expected to be impartial and an analysis of their discourses revealed a different "Filipina" from that produced by the scholarship on the topic. Since the Philippine government has been very slow to act on behalf of these migrants (in fact, the government wants to encourage more of them to leave without putting resources on protecting the rights of these workers), it is the NGOs who have stepped into the vacuum to help those victimized by abusive employers or dubious or illegal agencies and contractors. Superbly organized across national borders, these transnational activists (mostly women), rallied together across the globe to support victims of injustice. Interviews with the Center for Migrant Advocacy, for example, revealed that the Philippine embassies around the world relied on their help and their overseas networks to help specific cases of abuse.[98]

Kanlungan Center Foundation Inc. was established on July 17, 1989, as an NGO crisis intervention center working "towards the attainment of redress, justice and empowerment for Filipino/a migrant workers, and a policy environment in the Philippines and abroad that respects and protects the rights of migrant workers, especially women."[99] The services they offered included legal assistance; counseling; education and training; information and advocacy; and welfare assistance, including a temporary shelter for women.[100] They have an office in Quezon City in Metro-Manila and one in the province of La Union.[101] They published an occasional newsletter called *T.N.T.*, a pun on several phrases. *T.N.T.*, officially defined as *Trends, News and Tidbits,* also referred to *tago-ng-tago* (TnT), or the perennial hiding that undocumented migrant workers had to do to avoid deportation.[102] *T.N.T.* also alluded to the explosive, and was a metaphor for the NGOs activist positions.[103] Kanlungan produced a two-hour radio show that aired only for a month that provided counseling on the air, warning phone callers about the perils of migration.[104] Another special newsletter (*Kanlungan ng Migrante*) showcased the organization's research output. *T.N.T.* was published in English, Tagalog, and Taglish, whereas *Kanlungan ng Migrante* reported in Tagalog language only. A close read of the two newsletters revealed the organization's preoccupation with the many court cases they undertook on behalf of victimized migrants. They detailed the cases where Kanlungan intervened on behalf of a migrant and trotted out statistics on the number of cases they took.[105] A special section "case update" was devoted to the description of the specific cases by different authors who sometimes were identified only by their first names (presumably Kanlungan staff members).

An examination of the Kanlungan website revealed the same pattern. A separate link took the browser to "case updates," the section of the website that had the most voluminous material detailing the many experiences of exploitation encountered by Filipino migrant workers overseas and Kanlungan's fight to find justice for the victims.[106]

Activists represented the OCW (read: domestic helper or entertainer in most cases) as the epitome of the modern-day slave. A review published in GABRIELA's *Laya Feminist Quarterly* captured the sentiment with its title, "Of Aprons and Bikinis Filipinas: Modern Slaves of the World."[107] The everyday life of a domestic helper subject to the beck and call of her employer twenty-four hours a day, every day, who was vulnerable to physical and verbal abuse (including rape, sexual harassment, and injuries) or who was virtually imprisoned in the home and deprived of comfort, food, or communication, dominated the activist narrative. The poignant tale of the Filipina overseas domestic helper as lonely, depressed, and suffering low status and self-esteem (since many of them were college graduates who had been compelled to de-skill), laboring for the sake of the family (most sent remittances to support the family), dominated their discourses. The message the women's organizations sent to prospective women seeking jobs overseas was that "overseas employment is simply risky."[108] And indeed, the statistics of 2,654 reported cases per month or eighty-seven overseas Filipino workers suffering from human rights abuses *daily,* provided empirical evidence that many Filipinas were treated like slaves or less than human by their employers or employment agencies abroad.[109]

Overseas contract workers themselves complained that they were treated like slaves.[110] In a letter to President Ramos, Filipino migrant workers in Greece declared that they were not commodities but "human beings with basic rights who will not consent to be diminished by our status and work location."[111] They represented their lives as "pagtitiis" (forbearance) all in the name of the family back home who relied on their remittances.[112] The pages of *T.N.T.* were replete with accounts (and statistics) of the many cases of abuse of human rights they hoped to win on behalf of the migrant women. In fact, the newsletter was preoccupied with reportage on the number of cases pending, the number of cases won, and the many activities such as demonstrations and lobbying on behalf of OCWs. Testimonies of OCWs (needed as evidence in the various court cases) exposed the abuses endured and described the tale of escape from their tormentors and subsequent refuge in Kanlungan.[113]

Kanlungan literature represented women OCWs as modern-day

slaves and victims of abuse, trafficking, illegal recruiting, and employer mistreatment, including the nonpayment of salaries and physical and verbal abuse. The narratives emphasized the social costs of migration rather than its benefits. The official position was that migration was very risky and that the price paid for the chance to earn more money was far too great. Social costs of migration did not only include the trauma suffered by the victims, but also the impact of migration on the families left behind, particularly children left by their mothers who became domestic helpers abroad. There was a conspicuous absence of any success stories in the literature published. Positive stories were really tragedies that involved a successful rescue by Kanlungan or a court case where the OCW received compensation. Kanlungan was against globalization (the WTO and GATT Treaties) and the further deployment of OCWs.[114] The attitude of the phrase used by many OCWs to rationalize their decision to choose the hard life, "I will grasp the blade" (*kapit sa patalim*), was denounced as "a victim's psyche," and "a product of the dismal economic situation in the country that has driven many people to desperation."[115] Although the OCWs themselves might have interpreted the decision to grasp the blade as a sign of agency, activists believed that such a path only made them vulnerable to exploitation and abuse. Given these circumstances, the activist position against the deployment of women as OCWs placed them in direct conflict with the Philippine government who hoped to increase the numbers of Filipino overseas contract labor to one million a year.

The feminist position therefore was to prevent the government's use of women as commodities or as dispensable labor capital in order to save its own economy. Women were not to be sacrificed for the sake of the economy. In the words of Helen Dabu, of the Kanlungan Migrant Center, "our migrant workers have become money making machines."[116] Echoing the same lament as DAWN on behalf of the Overseas Performing Arts in Japan, Kanlungan objected to women's commodification as breadwinners who were appreciated only for the income they brought to the family while society turns a blind eye to the social and personal costs. There was a noticeable absence of any success stories of women who might have earned enough money to improve the family's status in the home country or to send their children to school. Of course, this reflects the fact that those who approached Kanlungan were usually those who were distressed victims of exploitation rather than those who might have had more positive experiences.[117] Scholarly studies of women and migration pointed out how the woman's role as breadwinner has given them some autonomy with regards to decision making in the family.[118] These narratives of agency were absent from Kanlungan's publications precisely because their aims were to dissuade women from contemplating the risks of going abroad. Current trends showing that women continue to leave the country in ever-increasing numbers (more than one million in 2008), with the Philippines recognized as the world's largest exporter of migrant labor, mean that Kanlungan is embroiled in a losing battle although it has been successful as an NGO.[119] Although migrant advocacy groups such as Kanlungan informed workers of their human rights, provided feminist counseling, and were genuine in their attempts to secure justice for victims of exploitation, the practical difficulties of mobilizing OCWs as an active membership group (because they were scattered all over the world) meant that the organization had to focus on helping the families left behind.

The Woman as Worker Reconsidered

The title theme of GABRIELA's newsletter for January–March 1998, "Continuing the Tradition of Militance," best described that organization's self-representation as an activist group.[120] Women workers—peasants, factory workers, and urban poor—composed the bulk of the members and were the most proactive of activists in that umbrella organization. Situated among the lowest classes in the social hierarchy, their demands often clashed with the interests of the elite and with those who have political power. Along with those advocating for reproductive rights, they were perceived to be the most radical of activists. Radical demands required militant strategies; as the GABRIELA headline proclaimed, militancy has become a tradition intrinsic to the organization's identity. And indeed, GABRIELA's street protests and demonstrations were legendary, and GABRIELA women were imagined as the country's iconic feminist activists.

Perhaps militancy was an inevitable requirement: the very interests of the women peasants and workers were in direct opposition to government policies. GABRIELA was against President Fidel Ramos' Medium-Term Development Plan, the signing of the GATT, the militarization of the provinces, the Visiting Forces Agreement (where U.S. Special Forces would come and cooperate with Filipino troops), the establishment of EPZs (which were supposed to be strike free), the Comprehensive Land Reform Program (which was seen as not going far enough), the demolition of squatters' homes, the move to open pit mining, and globalization in general. Kanlungan Migrant Center's perspective that overseas employment is too risky opposed the government's policy of increasing the deployment of overseas workers to one million a year (from 2007 onwards).

The clash between government and women activists went beyond policy and politics to representations of women workers. Kanlungan Migrant Center and other organizations for migrant women (like the Center for Migrant Advocacy [CMC], Migrante, another NGO that focuses on migrants both male and female) made it a priority to inform migrants of their human rights so that they would be less vulnerable to abuse and exploitation. The government, on the other hand, preferred to project the opposite image. According to Steven McKay, the government-sponsored marketing of seafarers abroad used "particular narratives of *Filipinoness,* national heroism, and subordinate masculinity" with the result that "Filipino seafarers not only remain in subordinate positions, but there is a growing emphasis on their feminine and willingly subservient character."[121]

Has activism had an impact on redefining the woman as worker? GABRIELA's mobilization of women workers in protest activities and their public visibility has been influential in transforming the image of the woman worker as confident, strong, and feisty. They have been able to raise issues such as sexual harassment, maternity leave, day care, unhealthy working conditions, low wages, militarization, contractualization of labor, land reform, and other gendered forms of injustice. In this sense, the image of a docile women's workforce no longer dominates the narrative of the woman as worker in the Philippines.

But domestic tasks remained intrinsic to the domain of women, whether or not they were working outside the home. One OCW's synopsis of her life in Spain (once she was joined by her Filipino family) applied to most. She claimed, "I am a maid three times over: I am a maid to my employer, a maid to my husband, and a maid to my children."[122] Interestingly, activists have been less proactive about launching a reeducation campaign to introduce the concept of men performing household tasks, despite the testimonies from women workers that they had to face the double burden of work and housework. Although the problems of domestic helpers overseas were clearly targeted by a number of NGOs, there remains an uncomfortable silence on the issue of domestic helpers at home; in 2008, however, there was for the first time some discussion of legislation proposed for a higher monthly wage for them. One explanation for this neglect was that middle-class women activists who themselves relied on domestic helpers to enable their advocacy felt ambivalent if not uncomfortable with an issue that was so close to home. Thus, while there is a plethora of organizations dedicated to the advocacy of domestic helpers overseas, I have not been able to find one that specializes in domestic helpers within the Philippines.

The phenomenon of the OCW who is a domestic helper is a site of contradiction, irony, and ambivalence. Her decision to leave the Philippines, though fuelled by economic considerations, is modern in the sense that she extends the parameters of women's work outside the home to its maximum potential by accepting employment overseas. But her occupation sees her performing the same traditional tasks of mothering and domestic duties. Ironically, it is the salary from this domestic job overseas that transforms her position in the family at home to main breadwinner (bringing in more wages than her husband) that has had the greatest impact on social constructions of masculinity and femininity. Alicia Pinggol's study of the impact of the exodus of Ilocano women as domestic helpers overseas must be revisited here. Since the status of breadwinner was intrinsic to Ilocano notions of masculinity, the shift of breadwinner status from husband to wife has compelled men to rethink masculinity and redefine it in small but significant ways. Some men have adjusted to being househusbands while women's financial clout has given them more power to make decisions in the family and to have more status in the local community.[123] Rhacel Parreñas' book on transnational families also examined the impact of migration on gender roles. Her nuanced analysis proposed that migration produced a "gender paradox": women were able to embrace new roles as breadwinners but mothers were criticized for leaving their children. Thus, while female OCWs were able to extend definitions of the feminine to include "breadwinner," they were perceived to have failed to live up to cultural expectations of ideal motherhood, because they were seen to have abandoned their children.[124] The NGO representation of the migrant workers as vulnerable and exploited obscured the transformative power of women's new status as breadwinners on Filipino male identity and family dynamics. Thus, while women's organizations have been proactive in transforming the image of the woman as worker to militant activist, it was women's new roles as breadwinners that has compelled men to experience at last what it is like to be the less dominant person in a relationship.

4

Indigenous Women

WOMEN OF THE CORDILLERA

Indigenous women of the highlands have been the "Other" of the Christian lowland majority. Since the Cordillera escaped Spanish conquest, the women were not subjected to Christian constructions of the feminine. Spared from the influences of the Catholic Church and the Catholic religion, indigenous women were singled out as different. In addition, the traditional gender relationships between indigenous peoples in the highlands were considered (particularly in the economic sphere) to be more egalitarian than were lowland practices. Cordillera women also were very active in the region's resistance movements partly because successive Philippine governments coveted their ancestral lands in the name of "development"—for mining, logging, and the damming of rivers. Although this region has been identified as the most depressed and exploited in the Philippines, indigenous peoples, especially women, have been mythologized for their robust resistance struggles against oppressors, including the Spanish colonial regime, the Marcos dictatorship, and multinational corporations. Could the Cordillera women then be imagined as a potential alternative role model to the woman as suffering martyr?

This chapter will discuss the representation of indigenous women in the women's movements using sources from three organizations: Center for Women's Resources, Cordillera (CWERC); Innabuyog Philippines, which is allied with GABRIELA; and Igorota, founded by a feminist

Maryknoll nun. My reading of the evidence is that, while acknowledging that certain unique aspects distinguished indigenous women from the majority of Filipinas, activists focused on the similarities between highland women and their lowland counterparts. Indigenous women were classified as a sector of women in the sense that "women workers," "women peasants," and "urban poor women" were classified as specific categories of women. But in unpacking the categories of indigenous women, activists applied the same taxonomy as they did on lowland Filipinas of the lower classes. Indigenous women were further divided into "indigenous peasant women," "indigenous women workers," or "indigenous migrant women," and so on. In this sense, indigenous women's experiences were represented as similar to those of lowland women in the same category. For example, indigenous women who worked in the Baguio City EPZ were subjected to the same problems—such as sexual harassment and the contractualization of labor—as were women workers in other EPZs. Many Cordillera women joined the increasing numbers of OCWs, migrating to the Middle East and Hong Kong as domestic helpers. Indigenous women experienced the impacts of development and globalization along similar lines as the majority of lower-class women. The peculiar industries and conditions in the highlands such as mining and logging and the militarization of the provinces further compounded the precarious situation of women, who, like their lowland sisters, were subjected to the evils of globalization from abroad and patriarchy at home. What distinguished them from the majority was that they were represented as the most depressed and exploited of women. And yet, I will argue, women's movements focused on "sameness" with lowland women rather than on difference. Perhaps a narrative that emphasized indigenous women's similarities with all Filipino women was an attempt to include them into the meta-history of the national lowland or mainstream women's movements. By emphasizing their sameness with lower-class Filipino women, however, indigenous women lost the chance to become alternative role models in the women's movements even though they were mythologized as resistance fighters.

Cordillera Resistance

The indigenous peoples of the Cordillera are collectively known as the Igorots. They belong to seven ethnolinguistic groups comprising the Isneg, Tinguian, Kalinga, Bontok, Kankanaey, Ibaloy, and Ifugao. Five smaller groups occupy the border areas: the Balangao, Amduntug,

Ikalahan, Apayao, and Gad-dang. Each of these groups has its own culture, language, and identity.[1] Geographically, the region is divided into the provinces of the Mountain Province, Kalinga-Apayao, Benguet, Ifugao, and Abra, and the city of Baguio.[2] Once the summer capital of the American colonial regime, the City of Baguio is one of the designated EPZs where multinational corporations are permitted to invest in industry such as factories, and where investors are protected by a no-union policy, thereby keeping wages low. The Baguio City EPZ sits on sixty-six hectares of prime land and includes seven companies, all of them totally foreign owned, whose products range from electronics and plastics, to garments such as leather gloves for export. Their privileges include tax holidays for five years and the imposition of a "no-union policy."[3] The entire highlands region itself is rich in natural resources, attracting companies interested in mining (for gold, in particular) and logging. Even in agriculture, the Cordillera, with less than 1.8 percent of the country's population, in 2006 produced more than 2 percent of the country's rice, sweet potato, coffee, and livestock, and 65–80 percent of the country's potatoes, cabbages, carrots, and other temperate clime vegetables in 2006.[4] The population of the Cordillera was 1.4 million in 2000, of which about 50 percent were women (around 750,000).[5]

The region's natural resources, including water for hydroelectric energy, enticed governments both colonial and national to exploit the area. Consequently, the history of the indigenous peoples could be read as a history of resistance to colonization from outsiders seeking to "tame" the population in the name of Christianity, education, progress, development, and globalization. The Igorots succeeded in repelling the Spaniards, thus escaping the Christianization of the Filipino. The American regime introduced public school education and initiated the industries, an exploitation that increased in intensity in the postwar years, reaching its apogee in the authoritarian regime of President Ferdinand Marcos (1972–1986).[6]

The ethnic minority groups were particularly victimized by the martial law regime. The fact that the press was censored made it difficult to expose human rights abuses, and the authoritarian regime meant that the minorities could not resort to democratic representation in the legislature. President Marcos wanted to build a series of four hydroelectric dams (Chico I, Chico II, Chico III, and Chico IV) in the Chico River. The dams would have deprived the Mountain Province groups, especially the Kalinga and the Bontok, of their ancestral lands.

It was this issue that rekindled Cordillera resistance and gave birth to the contemporary militant activism of the highlands. At first, villagers tore down the camps of exploration teams and, with the help of Catholic priests, sent petitions to President Marcos.[7] When the engineers and military returned and rebuilt their camps, the Kalingas continued their protest of tearing down the camps, enduring relentless arrest and detention. The protest galvanized the peoples of the Cordillera into making multilateral agreements with each other (traditionally, they only made bilateral agreements) initiating the formation of the Kalinga-Bontok Peace Pact Holders. But the protests in the 1970s were spontaneous protests with men and women going to the barricades only when they felt that everything else they had tried had failed.[8] Macliïng Dulag, their leader, went to visit President Marcos. It was alleged that attempts were made to bribe Dulag; he returned empty-handed and disillusioned. The conflict escalated when the military was called in to quell dissent and activists were arrested, detained, tortured, and "salvaged" (killed). At this point, the NPA became close allies of the activists.

Women participated in this militant protest in unique ways, thus contributing to its success. When the protest became particularly heated, women bared themselves, undressing in unison, and marching militantly forward to push the barriers erected by the "developers." This was a traditional form of Kalinga protest, only used as a last resort and only when in extremely serious situations to drive away intruders.[9] According to oral testimonies, the last time this protest had been used was when the Spanish conquistadores arrived in Benguet in the sixteenth century, attracted by the gold mines of Benguet.[10]

The victory of the Chico Dam protest transformed the Cordillera woman into "an icon of militancy in the Philippine women's movement."[11] GABRIELA National-Philippines Chairperson Mary John Mananzan (OSB) referred to this protest action as being "almost a legend among us."[12] The story of the Kalinga women's undressing to shame the military was reproduced in a children's book published by GABRIELA, whose text was based on the oral testimonies of the Kalinga protesters themselves.[13] This book placed women at the center of protest and mythologized the women's undress when the book's authors interpreted the act of undressing as the climax of the resistance movement.[14]

There is a marked discrepancy between the mythologizing of Cordillera women in the resistance by the national women's movements and the Cordillera people's collective memory of the resistance. The Cordillera version of the events, celebrated yearly as Cordillera Day, marked the death anniversary of Macliïng Dulag (April 24, 1984), who acquired iconic status among the indigenous peoples as the hero of the struggles in the 1970s and 1980s.[15] In 2002, the annual event included a workshop on the role of women in the Cordillera struggle; at that workshop, veterans took center stage and recounted their participation in the resistance against the Chico Dam.[16] The main events of the day were the speeches, Cordillera dances, and the rally—rituals affirming contemporary Cordillera resistance and celebrating Cordillera identity. A detailed account of how Cordillera Day was celebrated in 1996 by Dutch ethnographer Dorothea Hilhorst in her book *The Real World of NGOs* revealed that women activists (here represented by the Cordillera Women's Non-Governmental Organization [CWNGO]) although present in the audience, were not leading characters in the speeches, although women are represented in the solidarity night performances as one of the sectors.[17]

The celebrations marking Cordillera Day in 1996 conflated Cordillera identity with resistance to national governments, from Marcos to Ramos, who were portrayed as having designs on the natural resources of the Ifugao. They exposed the legitimizing discourses of "progress" and "development" as facades for exploitation, appropriating the national democratic discourse of the Philippine Left. But a day that paid tribute to the male hero Dulag as the spirit of Cordillera resistance gave women mere auxiliary roles. Although women's organizations often held special workshops as part of the program of events associated with celebrating Cordillera Day (in 2000, for example), women's issues did not take center stage.[18]

Outside the Cordillera, feminist activists co-opted the Kalinga women's bare-breasted protest into the heroic narrative of the women's movements. In the GABRIELA version of the Chico Dam protest, the role of the men was given less emphasis, while the women's valiant exposure of their naked bodies was identified as the strategy critical to the victory. Although the Kalinga undress protest was not specifically a feminist one, the Kalinga women's resistance has had a greater impact on women activists outside the Cordillera.

Women's Movements in the Cordillera

Women's movements in the Cordillera began after the Chico Dam struggles. Among the issues raised in the indigenous resistance movement was women's organizing and education. The founding of GABRIELA had an impact in the highlands. A visit by the GABRIELA national leadership inspired participation in the IWWD rally on March 8, 1984.[19] The first Cordillera Women's Congress was held March 6–8, 1987, and CWERC was formed, replacing the Baguio Benguet Women's Education and Resource Centre (BBWERC).[20] Around the same time (1987), Igorota Foundation was founded by a Catholic Maryknoll feminist nun, Teresa Dagdag.[21] In March 1990, Innabuyog, a regional federation of women's organizations, was formed.[22] By 1992, sixty women's organizations had joined, totaling eight thousand members.[23] Innabuyog was closely affiliated with GABRIELA, linking it closely with the national women's movements. In October 1991, BEGNAS, an alliance of nine women's organizations in Itogon, Benguet (a region in the Cordillera) was founded with a membership of one thousand. BEGNAS aimed to unite women in mining communities to protect women's rights in the mines, and to protect the life and health of women and children in mining communities.[24]

Although Cordillera women activists were closely allied to the mainstream lowland women's movements, the differences between traditional Cordillera culture and that of the lowland Christian majority presented new challenges to feminists. Cultural attitudes on marriage, divorce, sexuality, rape, and domestic violence were different. Though they escaped Christianity's religious roots of women's oppression, and although the general scholarly consensus was that traditional culture was more egalitarian in terms of gender relations, activists had to confront new challenges, including the impact of outsiders and the competition between national and regional interests.

Women's Activism and Cordillera Constructions of the Feminine

Anthropologists writing on traditional culture have remarked positively on the egalitarian relations between the sexes in the highlands. Regardless of whether they subscribed to models that argued for the complementary roles of the sexes or to the more popular view that the once-traditional complementary roles were being eroded by contact with the majority populations and encroaching modernities, the consensus that Cordillera gender relations were more egalitarian than the rest of the country remained unscathed.[25] In contrast, Bernadette Resurrección's approach in the study of Cordillera women represented them as interacting with modernity, globalization, and the majority culture, including Christianity.[26] This interpretation was compatible with women activists' interaction with Cordillera women. Feminists did not represent the Cordillera woman as moored in the past, nor did they imagine gender relations as static. Instead, they identified constant change as the epicenter of the Cordillera women's life. Cordillera women were besieged by so-called development, militarization, globalization, modernities, and ecological changes. Activism focused on monitoring the changes that have dramatically altered the lives of Cordillera women who had become transformed from agricultural workers to overseas domestic helpers overnight. Activism was an attempt to tame these massive changes from the women's perspective, not necessarily to restore imagined egalitarian roles. But before I discuss the national women's movements discourse on the Cordillera women, I will summarize the scholarly discussion of gender roles and division of labor in traditional highland culture, bearing in mind the caveat above.

Women were defined as the primary agriculturalists, and were conferred with the tasks of sowing, transplanting, and weeding the paddy fields, while men performed the heavier jobs such as plowing and transporting the harvest to the village.[27] The Cordillera region is famous for its magnificent rice terraces, and men were assigned the task of maintaining the infrastructure of these terraces (terrace walls, dikes, irrigation canals, and watersheds).[28] In areas that practiced swidden agriculture, men cleared the forest while women did the planting, harvesting, and transporting of produce. Although agricultural tasks were divided between men and women, child care was shared. Child rearing was not the sole responsibility of parents, but of the entire village. Traditionally, it was the women who worked in the farm while men stayed at home to cook and look after the children.[29] Ifugao custom did not discriminate between men and women on inheritance, and inherited property was kept separate from conjugal property.[30] This had parallels with Bontok society, where child care was considered a man's concern.[31] Divorce was allowed in traditional custom; since fertility was highly valued (even more than virginity), among the Bontok infertility provided sufficient grounds for divorce or separation.[32] Indeed, childlessness was the primary cause for the separation of couples.[33] Abortion and contraception were not common, perhaps due to the desire for many children.[34] The desire for many children meant that adequate health care rather than birth control was emphasized. VAW, particularly rape and domestic violence, was anathema. The traditional punishment was banishment from the community or ostracism. Among the Bontok, rape was taboo, even in intervillage warfare.[35] Accepted practice in cases of wife battering was for the elders in the community to approach the violator and pressure him to stop the beatings.[36] Customary laws required that a fine be paid to the woman's family.[37] Although in more contemporary times the incidence of rape is attributed to outsiders such as the military or the tourists, there have been cases of rape by men of the Cordillera People's Liberation Army such as the celebrated cases of Delia Mangay-ayam of Tabuk and Julie-An de la Vega of Abra (gang raped by soldiers of the Cordillera Regional Special Action Force).[38]

Cultural constructions of womanhood in the Cordillera were also markedly different from the Christianized majority. Although similarities could be traced in the conflation of "woman" with "motherhood" (for instance, traditionally a Samoki woman's destiny is to give life), the image of the suffering martyr or moral guardian, or the ideology of domesticity, was absent from the official discourses of the feminine in the highlands.[39] Instead, since women were traditionally the primary agriculturalists responsible for swidden farming, the ideal woman was an industrious woman.[40] Kalanguya women were expected to work on their swiddens daily, while their husbands remained at home to look after the children. Women thought to be lazy (*nasadot*) earned the censure of the community because laziness was considered grounds for divorce, even more than allegations of adultery, which took a long time to prove.[41] It was the reputation as an industrious woman that attracted male suitors to a Kalanguya maiden: "industriousness remains their index of social acceptability."[42] Despite the dramatic changes in highland life that has since relegated swidden farming to a lower prestige rank than rice agriculture dominated by men who have since abandoned their large share in child care, women were still identified with the growing of sweet potatoes and "the norm of industriousness persists for Kalanguya women."[43] Since industriousness was inextricably linked to farmwork and more recently food-crisis management, the ideology of domesticity was noticeably absent in the construction of the feminine in highland Philippines.

It is in the political arena where similarities between highland and lowland women concur. Cordillera women were marginalized from political decision making dominated by the male elders of the council of elders (*ator*).[44] Village affairs were considered the domain of men who were the tribal chieftains and the council of elders, making women "almost an invisible sector in village political life."[45]

Specific Issues Raised by Cordillera Women's Activism

The unique features of Cordillera women's activism included campaigns against alcoholism, militarization, the building of dams, and open-pit mining. Innabuyog (whose members were mainly indigenous subsistence peasants) launched a ban on liquor campaign because alcoholism was a serious problem among Igorot men. This was an obvious result of "modernization" that made constructions of masculinity as warriors obsolete, prompting one scholar to name them as "nowhere men" living in limbo.[46] Since alcoholism resulted in domestic violence, women organized themselves to prevent the entry of liquor into their villages by physically stopping vehicles attempting to deliver the product. In addition, they monitored the imposition of a curfew on liquor sales.[47] A liquor ban in Chapyusen, a town in Can-eo Bontoc, was enforced by women. This example was replicated in other parts of the Cordillera, including Besao and Sagada; women in these areas also campaigned for the prohibition of gambling.[48] Whereas temperance was a critical feature of first-wave feminism in the Atlantic world, it was noticeably absent in the suffrage campaigns or early women's movements in the Asian contexts, including the Philippines.[49] In this sense, Cordillera women's activism was exceptional.

Nevertheless, women organized to protect themselves against domestic violence and did not rely solely on the intervention of the council of elders. Some of the women vendors in Baguio, members of the Organization of Women Street Vendors in Baguio (SKNLB; Samahan ng mga Kababaihang Nagtitinda sa Lansangan ng Baguio) who were victims of domestic violence were proactive in using their organization to pressure husbands not to beat their wives:

> Most of our members are battered. During our regular meetings, we discuss what we can do to the husbands who batter their wives. We visit a battered member and drop hints to the husband that we know he batters his wife. Usually this works. The husband loses face and the beating stops. The husband even starts to help take care of the children and do housework. In some cases, we do one-on-one counseling. We choose a person whom we feel the husband would be more comfortable with discussing the problem.[50]

Self-reliance and the support of a sisterhood of women, coupled with a tradition of militancy inspired women to organize to protect themselves from being victimized by men. In the case of the SKNLB discussed above, women used a technique that combined the traditional methods of community pressure (and perhaps the threat of ostracism) with modern psychology. The technique also relied on women's own proactive lobbying as a group rather than reliance on the traditional cabal of male elders.

Cordillera women activists also were proactive in the fight against militarization of the region. In particular, they expressed outrage at the military's use of Cordillera women as mistresses, pretending to be single when they wooed these women only to abandon them (often pregnant with their children) when their deployment to the highlands had ended.[51] This campaign set Cordillera women apart from other Filipinas. Despite the fact that many Filipino men had mistresses and men's extramarital affairs were socially tolerated, the mainstream women's movement still has to raise this issue as a critical priority. Perhaps Cordillera women were comfortable in focusing on this practice as an activist issue because the culprits were clearly outsiders.

The Cordillera Woman as Filipino Woman

Women's organizations consistently represented the Cordillera woman as the most oppressed and exploited of women in the country.[52] But in advocating for the rights of Cordillera women factory workers in EPZs, as peasant women, or as OCWs, Cordillera women were included in the same grand narratives of women's activism. With the exception of the women in mining, as well as the impact of the large military presence in the region, the discussion of the issues facing Cordillera women and the advocacy on their behalf was strikingly similar to the arguments aimed at the rest of Filipino women. A close reading of *Igorota* magazine and the CWERC journals *Chaneg* and *Kali*—revealed astonishing parallels with the experiences reported and discussed in the newsletters of GABRIELA (*Gabriela Update*), DAWN (*Sinag*), and CATW-AP. Part of the explanation could be that Cordillera women's organizations were allies of GABRIELA or that Teresa Dagdag, the editor of *Igorota Magazine* is a Maryknoll feminist nun.

All three magazines used English as the lingua franca and were available for subscription overseas. English was preferred over Tagalog, partly because indigenous peoples interpreted the imposition of Tagalog (Filipino language) as a national language as another attempt by the Christian majority population to impose its hegemony on the highlands.[53] The use of English (a well-known language in the Cordillera region) not only united the various linguistic groups, but also expanded the magazine's audience to include the areas beyond the Philippines. But the use of English probably was also part of the organization's intention to locate Cordillera women's issues in a national and international context.

In my reading, Cordillera women's organizations emphasized Cordillera women's similarities rather than their differences with the rest of the Filipino women, integrating them as active participants in the national women's movements. Although Cordillera women were a designated separate sector, in reality Cordillera women also were peasants, factory workers, vendors, urban poor, and overseas domestic helpers. In documenting the trials of the Cordillera woman, women's magazines quickly identified gender rather than race or ethnicity as the marker for oppression. In doing so, it justified solidarity between Filipino women of the Cordillera and the lowland Christian majority. I am not making a claim that national women's movements made it a deliberate policy to efface the differences between Cordillera women and Christian Filipinas. But cultural and religious differences between Cordillera women and Christian Filipinas were hardly discussed in the magazines' pages. Feminists did not interrogate or problematize the Cordillera woman as an industrious woman tied to cultivating her sweet potato plot. The differences between cultural constructions of the feminine were barely raised. For instance, there was only one themed issue in *Igorota Magazine* on "The Igorots of the Philippines."[54] Instead, the Cordillera woman was represented much like her Christian sister, subjected to the exploitation of international and national capital, militarization, and patriarchal violence. This imagined sisterhood between national and Cordillera women was endorsed during the annual celebrations of IWWD, when Cordillera women's issues were given more "star billing" than they had in Cordillera Day (see discussion below).

Cordillera women's magazines highlighted the experiences of the contractualization of women's labor, particularly in the Baguio EPZ, and denounced globalization, the WTO, and President Fidel Ramos' Medium Development Plan.[55] They discussed the predicaments faced by highland women peasants in the face of rapid changes, and explored the effects of tourism on their women (including prostitution).[56] The displacement of the Cordillera population, a consequence of the infiltration of national and international business and government development projects (for logging, hydroelectric power, mining, and even tourism (e.g., the conversion of Camp John Hay, a former U.S. colonial rest and recreation facility, into a golf and recreation complex), had distinct parallels with the women of the urban poor in Metro-Manila and other cities who faced demolition of their homes.[57] University students were vulnerable to sexual harassment and prostitution, including the exchange of sexual favors for tuition fees.[58] The Cordillera woman as worker experienced capitalist exploitation in the factories and in the fields much like her lowland sisters.[59] And, like her lowland sisters, many Cordillera women have chosen to work far away from home as OCWs.

Although Innabuyog's members were mostly Cordillera peasant women, underscoring the official construction of Cordillera women as peasant women, the tumultuous changes since the 1970s have so altered the region's environment with all the mining and damming; logging and deforestation; and militarization and war, that even Cordillera peasant women had to add on new roles in order to survive or to adjust to these changed circumstances. That Cordillera peasant women were in a constant state of flux is probably evidenced by the fact that only one issue of *Chaneg* was devoted to Cordillera peasant women, whereas globalization and its impact on women became a recurring magazine theme with no fewer than four issues devoted to it between 1994–2006.[60]

The special issue devoted to Cordillera peasant women reported, "Traditional forms of livelihood such as farming and small-scale mining, which the women used to engage in, have drastically declined. This has forced women to look for odd-jobs outside their communities. They work as vendors, laundry women, construction workers, domestic helpers, weaver or take on any other job they can even if these odd jobs are low-paying, unstable and scarce. Others look for employment abroad as overseas contract workers where they often become victims of abuse."[61] In this sense, feminists were aware that classifying Cordillera women as peasants became increasingly problematic as changes attributed to globalization unmoored them more and more from tilling the land.

The "face of globalization in the Cordillera" (to borrow from Jennifer Josef) is manifested in industrialization and tourism, but also in intensified mining activities, the creation of EPZs, and the increase of monoculture agricultural products.[62] The shift to open-pit mining, for example, affected independent scale mining as these small-scale miners become contractual workers. The destruction of the environment made the land infertile, making it impossible for unemployed underground miners to return to farming.[63] The liberalization of agriculture caused a shift from planting staple crops to high-value crops (e.g., asparagus, cut flowers, peas, strawberries) and disadvantaged indigenous communities had to enter into contracts with large corporations.[64] Metro-Baguio developed into a tourist site as well as an urban center for rest, recreation, and housing for investors. This included development projects such as

Camp John Hay (mentioned above), the Cordillera Heritage Village, and the Regional Tourism Manpower Training Center.[65] The designation of Metro-Baguio as an EPZ fostered the contractualization of female labor, and so women in factory work become vulnerable to sexual harassment.[66] Unable to meet their survival needs at home, Cordillera women have been compelled to join their other Filipina sisters as overseas domestic helpers. Cordillerans make up the largest single ethnic bloc of Filipino domestic helpers in Hong Kong.[67] Seven to eight out of every ten domestic helpers in Hong Kong were Cordillera migrant workers who were in high demand overseas because of their command of the English language. An estimated fifty-two thousand migrant workers were from the Cordillera region in 2005.[68] In one village, Sallapadan Barrio, each household had one member who was an OCW (mirroring the national statistics that reported one OCW for every ten Filipinos).[69]

The 1997 financial crisis increased the impetus for outmigration from the farms to Baguio City, and from Baguio City overseas. But even those migrants who became itinerant street vendors in Baguio City were compelled to reinvent themselves from vegetable vendors to *wagwageras* (retailers of secondhand clothing), selling secondhand designer clothing in this rapidly growing retail industry.[70] Ironically, the popularity and trade dynamics of the *ukay-ukay* industry itself are examples of the globalization of clothing, with vendors selling global brand names such as Versace, Prada, Marks & Spencer, Armani, Louis Vuitton, Balenciaga, and other brand names at bargain prices. Globalization's victims responded by participating in the globalization of the fashion industry. In April 2001, there were an estimated five hundred to six hundred *ukay-ukay* establishments in Baguio City.[71] The transformation of the Cordillera peasant woman from agricultural worker to itinerant vegetable vendor to *wagwagera* testified to the resiliency of these indigenous women, underscoring the point that they were not merely survivors or servants of globalization but rather were important actors in the circulation of capital, both economic and symbolic.[72]

Hence, the rapid changes in the life of the Cordillera woman worker were such that in the end their contemporary experiences (since 1985) became more and more like that of Filipinas everywhere. Although there were unique aspects of the Cordillera women's plight, what was more striking was how similar the experiences were between the lower-class Filipina woman as worker and the Cordillera woman as worker. This could be partly explained by the existence of common enemies—globalization, transnational capitalism, and what national democratic organizations including CWERC, Innabuyog, and GABRIELA have labeled feudalism or the dynamics of the Philippine social structure and hierarchy.

But since the rationale for the publications of *Chaneg, Kali,* and *Igorota* magazine was to include the Cordillera perspective to national debates about the Filipina postcolonial condition, many articles were about the struggles of Cordillera women and the women's movements in the Cordillera,[73] as well as the activities of the various women's organizations in Metro-Baguio and beyond,[74] including a lesbian organization.[75] Alliances with lowland women's activists gave Cordillera women the opportunity to include the perspective of a minority group with a long history of resistance to governments, the military, perhaps the church in their evangelizing mission, and multinational corporations. They could call further attention to the region's neglect by successive national governments because the area was in dire need of basic social services in education, health, communication, and transportation.[76] But despite their great jeremiad over the fact that their needs have been overlooked, comparatively speaking, Cordillera feminists were careful to connect their woes to the grand narrative of the women's movements. For instance, while pleading for more improvement of public educational facilities (an area much neglected by the government nationally but even more acutely in the Cordillera), they also clamored for a gender-sensitive education—a demand initiated by the national women's movements.[77]

Topics on rape and VAW, including wife battering, presented the mainstream movements' viewpoints, even though traditional Cordillera cultural norms and practices differed. But Cordillera feminists did not hesitate to critique feminist positions that were at odds with the Cordillera situation. One article was candid about the dilemmas faced by Cordillera feminists who critiqued feminist interpretations of women's marginalization coming from women's domesticity (because Cordillera women had a big role in agricultural production), and dismissed the cynical remarks from the Women's Crisis Center (WCC) that customary fines on perpetuators of VAW were not fair because they went to the woman's family and not to the individual woman.[78] As a whole, though, while topics on women's rights were imbued with a Cordillera flavor many articles integrated the Cordillera position alongside that of the national women's movements.

To plot Cordillera women's struggles along similar lines as the rest of Filipino women required the development of a common epistemology. Hence, Cordillera women took the same basic women's orientation seminars given by GABRIELA (since Innabuyog was an affiliate), which acquainted Cordillera women with the national situation and introduced the national-democratic slant of that branch of the women's movement. The national women's movements consciously included Cordillera women in the national campaigns against, for example, prostitution, against sexual harassment, and against the regime of Presidents Fidel Ramos, Joseph Estrada, and Gloria Macapagal Arroyo. GABRIELA's major advocacy campaigns were reported meticulously and new concepts such as sexual harassment were defined. Even feminist songs, translated into English (from Tagalog originals) sung by women activists all over the country were juxtapositioned with Cordillera feminist songs.

Indigenous peoples have been identified by women's organizations as globalization's victims, more than any other, and yet the experiences of these women mirrored the lower-class women of the Christian lowlands.[79] This is not to imply that the Cordillera case was the same as the situation of the rest of the Filipinas; indeed, the assertion that they have received the worst treatment is valid. Marginalized in both traditional and modern political power structures and constantly exploited by fellow Filipinos because of their rich natural resources and rich cultural heritage, which is also mined as a tourist site, they suffered additional disadvantages from the dominant cultural majority. But as peasants, factory workers, miners, urban poor, vendors, and in particular OCWs or migrants these women were represented as enduring similar experiences to lower-class Filipinas elsewhere.

International Working Women's Day in the Cordillera

If Cordillera Day was a commemoration of indigenous struggles, with Cordillera women participating in auxiliary roles, Cordillera women's activism was celebrated on IWWD commemorating women workers everywhere. The tenor and outlook of both days were vastly different. On the one hand, Cordillera Day marked indigenous as separate from national identity, because the rest of the Filipinos were classified alongside the many oppressors of the indigenous peoples including the colonizers and today's transnational corporations. On the other hand, celebrating IWWD proclaimed Cordillera women's solidarity with women all over the world, not just with fellow Filipinas. One could argue that both days interrogated the geopolitics of nation: whereas Cordillera Day expressed indigenous resistance to national attempts at exploitation and integration, IWWD acknowledged the common experiences of gender oppression that cut across national borders.

One issue of *Chaneg* reported in detail the events of Cordillera Day (on April 24) and IWWD (on March 8) in 1999. Both days received the same space in the magazine, but IWWD was given lead article honors. *Chaneg* reported that celebrations for IWWD spanned more than a month, including workshops and training days, poetry reading sessions from the Lesbians for National Democracy, a regional congress held by Innabuyog, a forum on the effects of globalization on peasant women launched in Ifugao, and an orientation seminar given by CWERC and the women's desk of the Cordillera People's Alliance in Mountain Province.[80] The activities culminated in a rally at the People's Park in Magsaysay Avenue Baguio City and Innabuyog activists distinguished themselves from the women's groups that were perceived to be merely toeing the Philippine government line because they had been formed by government agencies.

Locating itself clearly within the national women's movements, Innabuyog-Metro Baguio identified with activists of national democratic tenor. It was the Cordillera women's groups from government agencies who were clearly viewed as Other. In fact, *Chaneg*'s writer used the word "other" aptly placed under a heading entitled, "The Women and the Other Group of Women."[81] By claiming an identity with the sisterhood of activist women nationally, the Cordillera women's groups underscored that the criteria for Other was not "race," "ethnicity," or "gender," but feminist consciousness. Cordillera women's uniqueness was more likely expressed visually through highland dress and cultural performance: these became the markers for Cordillera identity. Cordillera women wore their traditional dress and accoutrements during IWWD celebrations; for example, *Igorota Magazine* reported that IWWD celebrations included a contest for "Best in Costume" (referring to indigenous dress).[82]

Losing Out as Role Model

Although the Cordillera women were idolized for their militancy by the national women's movement, GABRIELA appropriated the term "militant women's organization" like a badge that they brandished in their self-representation in posters, speeches, statements, and pronouncements. This made it difficult for Cordillera women located within the national movement to claim "militancy" as a specific Cordillera trait, and as a reason for staking an iconic status among fellow women activists. Consequently, Cordillera women were not touted as an alternative role model or idealized as a role model for women activists even though they were touted as an icon of militant activism (remember Mananzan's reference to them as "almost a legend among us").[83] Instead, it was the *babaylan,* the pre-Hispanic priestess, who became the women's movement's ideal because she held religious power denied the Filipina since Spanish conquest in the sixteenth century. Even though indigenous women escaped the cult of virginity, domesticity, and religiosity that accompanied conversion to Christianity, it was not the Cordillera woman that the women's movement turned to in search of traces of the *babaylan.* Instead, they found or imagined the *babaylan* in the foothills of the mystical Mount Banahaw—that liminal area between the town or village and the mountains whose ideal location in between made it the ideal home for many religious sects with a reputation for resistance (see introduction). If the women's movement hoped to fashion women as able to make choices unrestrained by forces such as patriarchal religion and cultural values, the role model of a woman priestess can be more powerful than the militant Cordillera woman represented as constantly besieged by modernity and globalization.

5

"There Is No Need to Endure"

WOMEN'S HEALTH MOVEMENTS

When Anna Leah Sarabia interviewed women of the lower classes for her television show *Womanwatch,* she asked, "Who looks after you when you are sick?" The answer was always, "I just endure it" (*tinitiis nalang*). Women were the last persons in the family to seek health care or to go to hospitals because they were reluctant to leave the family or business unattended without support from husband or kin. Since cultural norms assigned the role of caregiver to women, they did not question the expectation that women place the family first and their own needs last. It was this premise that activists hoped to dismantle. Years later, when Sarabia was asked by the Department of Health to help design a reproductive health campaign, she had the opportunity to alter the belief that women were destined to bear suffering alone.[1] Her slogan, "There is no need to endure," (*hindi kailangan magtiis*) captured both the message and the tenor of the women's health movements. Women activists such as Sarabia wanted women to realize that they were not condemned to a lifetime of pain, sickness, violence, abuse, and ignorance.

Women's health movements, although by no means united, have been consistent in their representation and fashioning of "the Filipina." A majority of women's health activists defined women as agents who needed access to information and services about their bodies. Because women were represented as agents (even though some may have been victimized in the past, see the section below on domestic violence and rape), they must be given the right to make their own choices about their bodies and their health—decisions they should arrive at after being presented with the right information and services. Activists were particularly adamant that women's choices not be constrained by dominant forces such as the Catholic Church, here identified by this branch of the women's movement as their biggest obstacle, even more than the state or cultural attitudes. In contrast with the groups that focused on prostitution, the women's health movements intended to remove the label of "victim" from women, even from those who were victims of rape and domestic violence, preferring to let them process their victimization and then move on to becoming agents. For this reason, the women's health movements did not use oral testimonies in its advocacy because they believed this practice encouraged women to wear the badge of "victim" permanently, blocking women's metamorphosis to survivor and then agent.[2] Even in the edited testimonies of women who experienced domestic violence, published by Women Fighting Against Violence (KALAKASAN; Kababaihan Laban sa Karahasan), the introduction declared, "In this book, the abused women are not victims."[3]

But activists also problematized "agency," "choice," "rights," and "self-determination." They asked, What practical use would it be for women who were given the choice when financial circumstances prevented women from exercising that choice? Women health activists discovered that women's choices had been constrained by poverty; the dogmatic, powerful hold of the Catholic Church and Catholic socialization; and the veil of silence that banned any public discussion of their bodies, including discussion of domestic violence, rape, reproductive health, and sexuality. The taboo on the discussion about "body politics" kept many women ignorant about their bodies and their options (read: the possibility of leaving an abusive spouse), compelling them to endure hardships, often with fatal consequences. Given this context, activists did not just focus on agency, choice, rights, and self-determination, but also on social justice.[4]

In my reading of the discourses, women's health movements made two other significant contributions to fashioning the Filipina: The first was the celebration of the woman as an individual rather than the woman as a relational being as mother, sister, daughter, or wife, and so on, who was connected to the family. Women were encouraged to make decisions as individuals rather than as members of the family. And yet women's primary connection to the family was not totally expunged from their representations. Women were supposed to look after themselves because healthy women were essential to the prosperity and care of the family.

The second contribution was that the women's health activists injected the novel idea that women had the right to be happy, to express pleasure, and to enjoy themselves as individuals, including the right to a happy sex life (not necessarily a heteronormative sex life).[5] The declaration that it is all right to have pleasure was an innovative move in the history of political activism in the Philippines, where activists were told to postpone pleasure or celebration until the movement's aims are achieved.[6] Women's health organizations were not only interested in health and reproductive health—in addition, issues such as domestic violence, rape, and sexuality (including lesbianism) were given high priority.

Domestic Violence and Rape

The sanctity endowed to the Filipino family, particularly the cultural and religious belief that it must be preserved at all costs, caused women's health activists to blame "the family" as the "cherished institution" liable for tacit acceptance of domestic violence.[7] In this scenario, feminists blamed the Catholic Church, particularly with regard to its prohibition against divorce, and the cultural belief that domestic violence was a private matter that should be solved between husband and wife, as the culprit that endorsed society's tolerance for this daily abuse suffered by many women of all classes. Since religious constructions of the feminine anointed women as solely responsible for the success and failure of their marriages, the burden of keeping the family together lay solely on the woman, regardless of her husband's actions. Women who sought advice from religious counselors, as most Filipino women would do due to the lack of counseling facilities, were told to return to their husbands to try and patch up their relationships "for the sake of the children." As Aurora Javate de Dios put it, "Forbearance and patience [pagtitiis at pasensya] are expected of wives who must bear the cross of a philandering and/or a violent husband."[8] In other words, women were told that they had to endure suffering—it was their cross, their earthly test that they had to carry with dignity in order to have the respect of the society and the community. Published testimonies of women victims of domestic violence confirmed social expectations that they accept their situation. In Mariz' story, she was advised by her pastor to "just endure it some more and add to this more prayers to God because he is your husband and you need to understand him."[9] Lorna's religious group also recommended that she leave things as they were because it was just one of God's trials sent to test her.[10] In her own words, Edna equated her abuse as her calvary, which she endured for the sake of her children.[11] The verb "to endure" (*magtiis*) was often invoked in these testimonies (including oral testimonies presented on radio talk shows; see Chapter 6) and in women's narratives of domestic violence given to counselors. One tabloid columnist writing on the topic in 1993 entitled it, "Should I endure it?": "To endure. This is the word that commonly flowed from the mouths of those who want to lecture to wives. Not just in the city but anywhere, when spouses fight, the neighbours do not get involved, even the parents of the woman. What they usually say is 'Endure it because he is already your husband.'"[12]

These examples illustrate the common attitudes about marriage and domestic violence. First, it was assumed that domestic violence was a private issue that concerned only the husband and the wife, and that no one, including the woman's parents, should interfere. In a society dominated by kinship politics, where kinship alliances were essential for survival and protection, the axiom that the kinship group keep out of discussions regarding domestic violence left women isolated or abandoned. Second, the absence of divorce was behind the consistent advice that they were trapped in a marriage that could not be undone. This attitude locked women into the situation, reminding them that the status quo had to be maintained and that they had no choice but to endure it. Finally, cultural and religious factors perpetuated the status of victim: women were supposed to be resigned to their fate as wife of the abuser. The best alternative given to them was to gain status as a dutiful and self-sacrificing wife (the woman as martyr again).

Women victims of domestic violence were blamed for their abuse. The usual response to the confession of a battered woman was, "Maybe the wife did not give him affection."[13] If a woman was beaten or if her husband was a philanderer, the common interpretation was that she must have provoked him. The reason trotted out to explain male violence was women's failure to live up to expectations of the ideal wife or mother. Hence, another reason why women kept their abuse hidden from public view was the belief that they deserved to be abused because they had not lived up to the feminine ideal. The stigma of shame that was attached to both the victim and her family prevented many from exposing their suffering.[14]

Given this cultural template, feminists who addressed the issue of domestic violence focused on sending the following crucial messages:

(1) It was not their fault that the violence was inflicted on them. (2) No one had the right to beat them or abuse them. (3) They no longer had to endure abuse or beatings. The advocacy against domestic violence had several fronts. Women's organizations used the media to advertise services such as women's crisis centers and the availability of counseling, including hotlines. Second, the literature implored feminists to empathize with the women and support their choices, including the decision to stay in the relationship. At least at the discursive level, activists claimed that women should be given the right to choose their destiny even if it meant staying in an abusive relationship.[15]

Third, activists introduced the concept of rights—that no one had the right to hurt another human being, and that women had the right to live a life free from violence. Feminists expanded the definition of domestic violence to include emotional and verbal abuse, infidelity, concubinage (particularly if the husband brings the mistress home), and the withdrawal of financial support. And finally, feminists claimed that domestic violence was not a private issue precisely because no person had the right to be subjected to abuse, including physical abuse.[16] One of the significant victories of the women's movements in the Philippines was the successful campaign to set up women's desks in police stations to deal with cases of domestic violence. First launched in major cities like Quezon City, activists pressured local governments to set up similar women's desks nationwide. Women police, also, were trained to deal with these sensitive situations.[17]

NGOs such as KALAKASAN (founded on May 31, 1991) and the WCC represented the Filipino woman who had endured many years of domestic violence as a survivor and a heroine rather than as a victim. In the introductions to *Tigil Bugbog* (Stop battering), the two-volume series published by KALAKASAN that included an information packet and a collection of testimonies, the organization emphasized that the women were not victims.[18] Because the testimonies published were written by KALAKASAN authors based on interviews with battered women, they could be analyzed as KALAKASAN's representation of the Filipino woman. These women's stories celebrated the end of their suffering: "the end of my stupidity and martyrdom."[19] The climax of almost all stories was the woman's escape from violence and the beginning of a new chapter in her life. The very title of the book of testimonies (also the title of the very first story)—*Sa Akin Pa Rin ang Bukas* (The future is still mine)—projected the viewpoint that it was never too late for women to walk away from abusive husbands because they had the power to direct the future.[20] Feminists did not want to dwell on the past victimization of the women, preferring to imagine a future full of hope and individual empowerment (read: the future is mine!) as women reclaimed their lives and rebuilt their families without husbands. In contrast to the feminists in Chapter 2 who represented prostitutes as victims, the women's health advocates preferred to imagine the battered woman as moving on to a future free of abuse. In these stories, women were represented as heroines for having the courage to leave their abusive husbands to strike out on their own. Representing these women as heroines was not a fantasy on the part of the women's health advocates. In a society where a woman's worth was measured on her ability to attract and keep a man in order to fulfill womanhood (defined as wife and mother), a woman's decision to leave her husband was indeed a revolutionary move, especially bearing in mind that divorce was not allowed and that a woman separated from her husband could not legally remarry.

It was important to communicate to women that there should be no shame attached to their situation because it was not their fault. Hence, the other arm of the advocacy was educational—the introduction of ideas that challenged the cultural construction of the woman as martyr. The methods included the publication of comics, advertisements on television and radio, informance theater (discussed in Chapters 6 and 7), newsletters, pamphlets, and conferences. In addition, the activists focused on providing services. Some of these included the East Avenue Hospital–based crisis center run by the WCC in cooperation with the National Commission on the Role of Filipino Women; the Women and Child Protection Unit of the Philippine General Hospital (run by the University of the Philippines and the Violet Ribbon Campaign of the Department of Health and twenty-five hospitals nationwide); The Haven, a complex of shelters and services established by the Congressional Spouses Foundation Inc. and the Department of Social Work and Development; and KALAKASAN hotline and counseling services. Women were told to go to the women's desks of the police in their local *barangay* if they became victims of domestic violence. Finally, women's organizations formed alliances in order to pressure for legislative changes.

LEGISLATIVE ADVOCACY: THE ANTI-RAPE ACT

Since VAW was a major issue among feminists, alliances of women's groups were formed to lobby for laws that addressed domestic violence, rape, and sexual harassment. But lobbying was a difficult and tedious process that took an average of eight years and required the help of a number of women's NGOs that specialized on legal advocacy (notably the Women's Legal Bureau [WLB] and WomenLead [Women's Legal Education, Advocacy, and Defense Foundation, Inc.]. WLB described itself as "a feminist legal resource NGO servicing women and women's organizations" that "advances women's interests through legal services and development, legal and policy research and advocacy, developmental education and training, and legal information services and development."[21] A pioneer specializing in feminist legal advocacy, WLB also involved itself in community-based work; WLB was founded at the end of November 1990.[22] WomenLead was not only a feminist legal resource institution for the advancement of women's rights by critiquing the legal system, but also was a source of legal services for women that included paralegal training and education, feminist counseling, and legal assistance.[23] (WomenLead was actually formed by members of WLB who left WLB to form their own organization.) It also had a research and publication arm publishing a journal (*Women's Journal on Law & Culture*) and a monograph series. In addition, they published short pamphlets on women and the law, such as *Girls in Law: Laws Affecting Young Women*.[24] In 1991–1992, an alliance of women's organizations formed Women's Joint Initiative for Legal and Social Change (SIBOL; Samasamang Inisyatiba ng Kababaihan sa Pagbabago ng Batas at Lipunan). The nine original members of SIBOL included the Institute for Social Studies and Action (ISSA), GABRIELA, CWR, WomanHealth, PILIPINA, KALAYAAN, WCC, KMK, Philippine Women's Network in Politics and Governance (UKP; Ugnayan ng Kababaihan sa Pulitika), a group committed to support women's candidacy in politics, and two women's institutions that specialized in research and information: the Women's Education, Development, Productivity, and Research Organization (WEDPRO) and the Women's Resource and Research Center, Inc. (WRRC).[25] Two other organizations joined in 1994, the Democratic Socialist Women of the Philippines (DSWP) and Working Women Who Wish to be Free (MAKALAYA; Manggagawang Kababaihang Mithi ay Paglaya). The DSWP was a national federation of grassroots women's organizations promoting socialist feminism through organizing, education, training, networking and advocacy, while MAKALAYA was a forum of women workers from various industries interested in gender issues in the labor sector.[26] Among SIBOL's objectives were "to advance the women's cause in and through the law."[27]

SIBOL's test case was the Anti-Rape Bill.[28] This campaign took six years but the Anti-Rape Act or RA No. 8353 was finally signed into law by President Fidel Ramos on September 30, 1997.[29] The women's movement could take credit for it since most of the language of the bill came from the SIBOL draft legislation. The major victory for the feminists was redefining rape from a "crime against chastity" (that is, virginity raised the penalty, with good reputation as a prerequisite, with force raising the penalty), to "crime against person" (making it a human rights issue).[30] In sum, there were four significant changes heralded by the new law: the expanded definition of rape (to include forms other than penile penetration), the reclassification of rape from crime against chastity to a crime against persons, the recognition of marital rape, and the "rape shield"— that is, the victim's sexual history could not be admitted in court.[31]

The change in the wording of the law was all the more significant when placed in the context of cultural attitudes (exhibited by investigators based on research by the WLB) that rape victims "asked for it" by wearing revealing clothes or by flirting.[32] Feminist psychologist Sylvia Estrada-Claudio's discursive reading of rape stories in the media, from newspapers collected by the WCC in August 1990, concluded that, although rape was pathologized and criminalized, it was condoned. Men were described as being "out of control," whereas women victims were stereotyped as either "generous" or "playing hard to get" (*pakipot*). Women of the former were represented as deserving of the rape because they were sensual women and therefore "without virtue" anyway. The other extreme, *pakipot* implied that because they were only "playing hard to get," they were only "pretending" not to want sex and therefore deserved to be raped, since they really wanted it but were only pretending they did not.[33] Given this cultural mindset, no wonder victims kept quiet. Many were afraid of the great shame they would bring to themselves and the family because the rape was usually blamed on them on both extreme ends of female sexist stereotyping.

Furthermore, the stigmatization of rape victims was enough to deter them from reporting their ordeal.[34] The stigma arose from the designation of rape as "proof enough of the woman's having lost her rightful place among the decent and the respectable."[35] The campaign for the Anti-Rape Act of 1997 was not an easy one, with SIBOL compelled to resubmit their proposals through several congressional sessions.[36] That the act acceded to SIBOL's non-negotiable position that rape be declassified from a crime against chastity to a crime against persons was a major victory for the women's health movements.

Women's organizations also provided practical help for rape victims.

For example, in 2003 GABRIELA founded GABRIELA Circle of Friends, focusing on victims of rape and sexual harassment. Victims of rape would get counseling and legal support from GABRIELA. In addition, this group was intended to act as a support group of families and friends of the victims who were going to appear in court trials to give moral support to the victims. WomenLead also offered legal assistance to rape victims.

ANTI-VIOLENCE ADVOCACY: PROTECTING WOMEN AND CHILDREN

The other major victory for the women's movements was the passing of Republic Act 9262, otherwise known as the "Anti-Violence Against Women and Their Children Act." This act defined VAW and their children, and was signed into law on March 8, 2004, after a nine-year campaign.[37] The history of the bill's passage into law exposed the major ideological, strategic, and personal divisions among women's health activists, with the main lines drawn between those who supported the Anti-Violence Against Women in Intimate Relationships (AWIR) version that did not include the men as potential victims, and those who wanted to include men. Those organizations such as KALAKASAN who wanted the men included only did so under certain circumstances (lower-class men whose partners were more successful than they were, gay men, and men with disabilities).[38] After two years of heated debates, the women's organizations agreed to the version that did not include men but the final law passed at the Senate level included the children of battered women.[39] The definition of VAW and the women's children included threatening to deprive the women access to their families, financial support, or legal rights; preventing the woman from engaging in legitimate professions or business activities; and controlling the victim's money or properties (or solely controlling the conjugal common property). In addition, such violence included "causing or attempting to cause the woman or her child to engage in any sexual activity which does not constitute rape, by force or threat of force, physical harm, or through intimidation," as well as "engaging in purposeful, knowing or reckless conduct" (such as stalking) and "causing mental or emotional anguish, public ridicule or humiliation to the woman or her child."[40] The statute also authorized the issuance of protection orders to prevent further violence on the victims.[41] Feminists from all camps had a huge influence on the actual wording of the final law, although there was the disagreement over whether or not to include men in the law.

Community Organizing: Women
Help Themselves

A more innovative strategy used by activists against domestic violence tapped on cultural notions of shame and community organizing in order to exert everyday forms of resistance against the perpetuators. Communities had to be sympathetic to the plight of the women and willing to use collective action to prevent domestic violence. The strategy involved organizing the community to surround the house of the perpetuator making noise (such as banging pots and pans) calling attention to the man as a wife beater, and appealing to his sense of shame to discontinue his actions. More than shaming the perpetuator, this collective action publicly declared the community's disapproval of the abuse of its women, and confirmed that such actions were not to be tolerated. Lihok-Pilipina, an NGO in Cebu City, named their program Bantay Bana (House watch) and used this noise barrage to prevent violence, with some success.[42] The success of this type of resistance has been documented in a film entitled *No More Sabado Nights* (No more Saturday nights), alluding to the night of the week when male batterers got drunk, came home, and beat up their women.[43] The fifteen-minute short film showed how in one urban slum community (Tawid Sapa) of 550 families in Novaliches Metro Manila, one gender-sensitizing workshop triggered successful collective action against the perpetuators of violence.[44] Other examples of strategies that involved community organizing was the COMBAT-VAW project of Harnessing Self-Reliant Initiatives and Knowledge (HASIK) and the WLB that combined community organizing with legislative advocacy to respond to emergency cases of VAW.[45]

Reproductive Health

The Philippine government since the 1970s has not had a consistent comprehensive national reproductive health policy.[46] Instead, rapid swings between the extreme views of anti-poverty through population control and the official endorsement of Church-approved methods only, characterized the state response to it.[47] Women's advocacy for reproductive health and reproductive rights must therefore be placed in this turbulent context of shifting policies and a conservative backlash. In addition, advocates have had to overcome society's reluctance to talk about the body or even to publicize information about the body, particularly birth control and sex. Women's health advocates themselves were divided on many of the issues. Given the difficult terrain, women's health advocates used several strategies across a spectrum of activities and programs. On the legislative front, they have coalesced under the umbrella of the Reproductive Health Advocacy Network (RHAN). The network has been proactive in the filing in 2001 of the Reproductive Health Bill. On the practical front, organizations such as Likhaan set up local clinics and a mobile clinic to offer health care and counseling, including gender seminars, for women of the lower classes. Information about women's health and reproductive health were disseminated through publications, pamphlets, radio advertisements or plugs (some in conjunction with the Department of Health), posters, radio talk shows, television (see Chapter 6), and informance theater (see Chapter 7). Women's groups also conducted research on the lives and attitudes of women from rural and urban communities, with a focus on the situation of poor women or women from the lower classes. Research methods included sharing life stories, conducting interviews, surveys, sampling, ethnography, focus group discussions, drama forum (narration of life stories in the form of theater), and discourse analysis. The importance of feminist research and methodologies used in research was so crucial that a book on feminist methodologies was published by the University of the Philippines' University Center for Women's Studies, with women's health and sexuality as key topics.[48]

The activist position on reproductive health was summed up in WMC's book *Bodytalk:* Women should have the right to choose "whether to have sex, when and with whom; whether to get pregnant, when, and with whom; whether to have children, how many, and when (including spacing of children); which birth control methods to use—you as a woman have the right to decide all these."[49] But reproductive rights could only be properly exercised if women were given the information they needed to be able to make a decision, and have the appropriate services available to them to exercise such a right. In addition, women would need to be able to have the means to exercise their choices. According to Ana Maria Nemenzo of WomanHealth, Filipina activists were anxious about applying Western concepts of choice in the Philippine situation where poverty and other factors prompted her and her colleagues to ask: "Do we even have the capacity to make a choice?"[50] Given the Philippine situation, activists like Estrada-Claudio suggested that it was not just a question of rights, but also one of social justice.[51] In this sense, women's health activists had their hands full with the important tasks of disseminating information about the body introducing the concept of reproductive *rights,* challenging shifts in government policy, defending themselves against the attacks of the Catholic Church while providing accessible services for free or with minimum charge for lower-class women who needed health care and counseling. Apart from lobbying with the government, and working to alter cultural attitudes, the activists also had to appeal to the health care professionals themselves, particularly doctors and nurses attending to pregnant women and birthing women. Research revealed that many poor women were subject to ridicule, indignities, and insults when they were admitted to public hospitals.[52] Women tolerated this behavior for fear that the professionals would refuse to help them deliver their babies.

"Ignorance was not bliss" claimed the introduction to the WMC's book *Bodytalk, The XYZ Guide to Young Women's Health and Body,* Vol. 2.[53] This aphorism summed up the activists' approach to reproductive health. Women need to be given information about their bodies, and should not be inhibited from talking about their bodies and their reproductive health concerns. The WMC, a longtime women's health advocate, used tri-media (radio, television, and print) to disseminate information about the body and about reproductive health options. The organization identified young women as their target group; their productions and publications were candid about the identification and proper use of contraception. Under the *XYZ* brand, WMC produced *XYZ Young Women's Television,* *XYZone* radio talk show, and an *XYZine* four-page print feature that was a magazine within a magazine, because it was inserted into copies of *Mr. and Ms.* magazine. In addition, WMC published books such as *BodyTalk* Vol. 1 and Vol. 2. The television and radio shows dealt with as many health and reproductive issues as possible (see Chapter 6), dispensing as much information as possible to audiences from very basic answers to questions such as, "What is lesbianism?," to practical advice such as how to use a condom.[54] Since the *XYZ* motto was "Know yourself, trust yourself, respect yourself," these productions and publications hoped to give women information about reproductive health and sexuality in order to enable women to make choices based on their own assessment of their bodies and their situation. Knowledge was the necessary prerequisite towards empowerment, and the motto "Trust yourself" encouraged young women to make decisions based on self-reflection without succumbing to social pressure from society, church, and family, or even from boyfriends or husbands who demanded sex. The *Bodytalk* books, for example, gave women information about all types of contraception available (natural or artificial) without staking a preference for a particular type.

In 1994, Sylvia Estrada-Claudio left GABRIELA to form Likhaan, a women's health organization that offered health services to lower-class women.[55] Likhaan had three "concrete and mortar" clinics and a mobile clinic. The clinics were located in Pasay City, Malabon, and Bulacan province. These clinics provided primary health care and reproductive health services for women, although men and children were not turned away. They conducted Pap smears and fertility management seminars. They had education centers and provided counseling before prescribing contraception. They were all free clinics, and patients were not charged. The organization had a staff of twelve community health workers, two psychologists (to handle cases of domestic violence and rape, for example), and two nurses. They had a cafeteria approach to reproductive health, allowing women to decide which form of contraception to use based on health factors and after consultation with health practitioners.[56]

Since part of Likhaan's aims was the empowerment of grassroots women, community-based health programs organized women to engage in political lobbying in their local constituencies. Likhaan's clients, almost all of them mothers, formed an organization that by 2006 had eight hundred members in Malabon, four hundred in Pasay, three hundred in Bulacan, and three hundred in San Roque, Quezon City. The four organizations formed a federation called United Strength of Women and Children (PiLaKK; Pinagsamang Lakas ng Kababaihan at Kabataan) that included young women and gays; in 2006, PiLaKK boasted three thousand members. It mobilized supporters for demonstrations such as the March 8, 2006, march for reproductive health during which three thousand members participated.[57] The existence of PiLaKK was testimony to Likhaan's success in fashioning women, and in transforming the community through education and training of the urban poor into confident leaders of local women's movements. It could be argued that Likhaan not only fashioned women, but also fashioned men, since women had to negotiate with husbands (who blamed Likhaan for taking their wives outside the home until dinnertime) so that they could participate in women's activism. According to PiLaKK president Lina Bacalando, women in the association had fiery fights with husbands; in the end, though, men appreciated the knowledge women gained from the clinics, information they used to help take care of their families. Included in this information package was women's sexuality (see next section), which PiLaKK members believed contributed to the happiness of couples.[58] The advocacy in Malabon was so successful they convinced the *barangay* captain (local district elected leader) to allocate funds for reproductive services (pills and Pap smears) and a maternity clinic. When I first interviewed her in 2006, Lina Bacalando was head of the health commit-tee of her *barangay*. When I returned in 2008, she was already a *barangay* councilor of Tonsuya Malabon, having won this seat in the local elec-tions of October 29, 2007.[59]

Women Can Have a Libido After All!: Sexuality and the Women's Health Movements

WOMEN'S DESIRE, BEAUTY, AND VIRGINITY

A woman's right to sexuality was not sanctioned by Filipino culture.[60] Sylvia Estrada-Claudio noted that, while sexuality for men was part of becoming male, the suppression of sexuality was an intrinsic part of the cultural construction of being female, with Narzalina Lim, former un-dersecretary of the Department of Tourism, even claiming that females were conditioned to be antisexual.[61] Filipino culture did not imagine women to be agents capable of desire. Instead, women were imagined as beautiful *objects* of desire, while men were perceived to be "naturally" lustful.[62] In contrast, Filipino masculinity, still an underresearched field, and still untheorized, was connected to men's fertility, virility and capac-ity to attract women, his skills as a provider, and his ability to attract fol-lowers or allies.[63] Many Filipino men have mistresses, a practice tolerat-ed by society. In fact, one could argue that a man with a mistress enjoyed considerable status since virility and power were linked. Politicians such as President Ferdinand Marcos, a well-known womanizer, and Joseph Estrada, a movie star with several mistresses, received the popular vote unharmed by the sex scandals in their lives.

But while men's infidelity was tacitly accepted, with the excuse that it was part of their nature to be lustful, women were idealized as pure beings devoid of sexual desire. Yet, although imagined as incapable of lust, women gained status from being objects of desire. They were ex-pected to be beautiful and attractive. A contemporary study conducted in 2001–2002 in two rural communities revealed that, while personal-ity was an important factor in assessing a potential male suitor, "beauty and comeliness underlie one's choice of a wife."[64] Although virility was linked to male power, beauty was linked to female power.[65] The pressure to be beautiful (according to the Filipino cultural measure of beauty) was put on every female, single or married: if a husband had mistresses, the wife was often blamed for not being beautiful enough. Beauty contests were an important preoccupation in local, national, and even international Filipino communities, including the diaspora.

This idealization of women as objects of desire who were unable to perform desire was further affirmed by the intrinsic connection between virginity and women's honor and value. Although it was acceptable for men to be promiscuous, a woman's chastity was critical to her identity. Sex was sinful except in the context of marriage; because women were constructed as being incapable of lust, a wife's submission to her husband's demands for sex was explained in the context of wifely duty.

Given this cultural template on women and sexuality, feminists problematized virginity, beauty, and women's desire. Even feminist nuns contributed to these debates about female sexuality (although they were not too vocal about lesbianism). Mary John Mananzan's (OSB) writings revealed that one of the consequences of linking virginity before marriage with women's identity was that women who were raped or seduced believed that after losing their virginity they had no choice but to become prostitutes or mistresses because they could not regain lost honor.[66]

Beauty as a measure of a woman's worth has yet to be seriously critiqued in the feminist movement. The WMC book *Bodytalk* Vol. 2 began the chapter on "Girls, Boys and Sex" with this:

> The church and older people tell us to "just say no." Virginity, they say, is the best gift you can blah, blah, blah.
>
> On the other hand, media seems to be telling girls to "if you look right, then he'll want to do it with you." Of course, toothpaste and shampoo ads aren't as direct as that. It's just that they play up this "make him notice you" game so much that you'd think making this boy notice you was the only reason you take a bath every morning. They never tell you what do to after he does notice you, and pesters you no end to "prove your love" for him by having sex with him. Neither do they tell you that making him notice you could lead to sexual harassment, rape or unwanted pregnancy.[67]

The contradiction explored in the above passage was that women were expected to be attractive to men but to reject men's sexual advances in order to protect their virginity. Activists were concerned that, while the media and society expected women to be sexually inviting and while a woman's worth was connected to her ability to attract many suitors, no one told these same women what would happen once they captured the attention of these ardent men. In a resolution passed during the first GABRIELA assembly in March 1984, women representatives of the youth sector ended their statement with, "Our self-esteem is built on our ability to attract the opposite sex."[68] The unwritten code was that women were supposed to attract men but delay sex until marriage. Men on the other hand, were expected to pressure women to have sex with them. The predatory nature associated with men's desire was expected to remain with them despite their married state—hence men may have mistresses—while women were expected to attract men, full stop.

The seduction of women per se, though not formally raised or prominently discussed in feminist publications, was nevertheless always present in debates about prostitution and trafficking, which involved the seduction of women, and rape. Feminists such as the WMC attributed women's vulnerability to seduction to ignorance about their bodies, and about sex and sexuality in general. Women's knowledge about sex was confined to the prestige associated with female beauty (read: the ability to be attractive to men), but not about what happens when you become the object of sexual advances, except that, as the quote above said, the answer should be no.

Feminists, however, were aware of this veil of ignorance and hence focused on an information campaign when it came to the topic of body politics, and the right to sexual self-determination. WMC's slogan, "Respect yourself, trust yourself, protect yourself," was the motto behind the publications that gave explicit information about women's health, body, and sexuality. Concepts of sexuality included lesbianism, women's sexual desires, and chastity or celibacy as an individual choice. Activists began to critique the traditional family sanctioned by Catholicism and to offer up alternatives such as single-parent families, and lesbian or homosexual families. Since the practice of keeping mistresses was common, and since Philippine law already recognized children of these liaisons by allowing them to inherit along with legitimate children, illegitimate children (usually hidden from society) were acknowledged by activists as being part of reinventing the Filipino family: after all, the huge number of OCWs separated from families in itself should result in a rethinking of the family.

LESBIANISM

Lesbianism as a feminist issue only entered the public sphere in the early 1990s. Although lesbian sexuality was raised in a conference for the first time in the Sisterhood Is Global dialogues held in the Philippines in

1988 in the panel on sexuality, it barely initiated a discussion. The transcripts of this dialogue, published in 1992 as a book, revealed a lot about what topics activists were willing or unwilling to discuss at that time. The dialogues initiated by WMC's Anna Leah Sarabia were conducted between Filipinos and international feminists in several parts of the Philippines, including Baguio City and Davao. High-profile American feminist Robin Morgan from the Sisterhood Is Global Institute raised the issue of lesbianism in the session on patriarchal culture in the Western historical context; although Aida Santos briefly mentioned that it was practiced as an alternative sexual preference for women by overseas migrant workers, Santos observed, "We don't want to talk about it because it is a taboo issue."[69] The lack of response to these comments reinforced Santos' observation. Sarabia admitted that, for many years, activists were afraid to discuss lesbianism, fearing that critics would dismiss the entire women's movement as composed of lesbians only.[70] Few supported the lesbian arm of the women's movements; as late as 2010, dividing lines were drawn between feminists who were tolerant of lesbians, transgender, and homosexuals "as long as it did not concern them" (or as long as the issue did not have an impact on their personal lives) versus those whose perspective was for recognizing sexual rights or the right to determine one's sexuality.[71]

In November 1990, the issue of lesbianism was raised at the Sixth International Women and Health Meeting (IWHM) in Manila as part of the preparations for the Beijing conference.[72] Prior to this, lesbians were the invisible minority in the country; few lesbians came out, due to lack of support from their families. Anna Leah Sarabia was a pioneer activist on the issue of lesbian sexuality. In 1993, she formed CLIC (Can't Live in the Closet Inc.), a lesbian feminist nongovernment organization (the first lesbian NGO in the Philippines) with its own newsletter (*BreakOut*). Since Sarabia was also founder of the WMC and Circle publications, CLIC published books such as *On Our Terms: A Lesbian Primer* and *Tibok: Heartbeat of the Filipino Lesbian,* a collection of literary works by lesbian Filipinos.[73]

The *Bodytalk* book privileged the issue by placing it prominently in its first chapter; WMC productions also gave it importance (see Chapter 6). Feminists focused on defining lesbianism and describing the difficulties lesbians encountered in the context of Filipino society and the Filipino family. The publications were particularly intent on debunking myths about lesbians (for example, that they were really tomboys who would eventually "straighten out") while advising lesbian readers on how to cope with the enormous challenges of coming out. In addition, they offered support for these women. CLIC described itself as a Filipino lesbian NGO "committed to uphold, protect and promote the human rights of lesbians and other oppressed sectors of society. It envisions a society that does not discriminate against persons on the basis of sex, race, class, ethnicity, and most especially, gender and sexual orientation."[74] CLIC's advocacy focused on education and information through *BreakOut,* its bi-annual lesbian newsletter, and on organizing workshops and forums for lesbians. It was involved in lesbian advocacy using the media or its links with legislative lobbying groups, in communication building, and in support services.[75] Given that sexuality was sublimated in cultural constructions of women who did not desire but who were in themselves objects of male desire, the presence of lesbians—as women who desire other women—was unfathomable. Lesbian activism therefore had to focus on disseminating information on lesbianism and educating society to understand lesbianism and, more important, to stop discrimination against lesbians. The lesbian movement also had transnational links with organizations such as the International Lesbian and Gay Association (ILGA) and the Asian Lesbian Network (ALN).[76] Lesbians have a particularly difficult time in the Philippines: not only was the Catholic Church against them, but also the Filipino family did not tolerate women's expression of sexuality in any form (even heteronormative), even though men's infidelity was tacitly accepted. Hence, many lesbians were isolated from families, friends, and the Church. Given this situation, organizations such as CLIC were crucial for lesbian support. Sarabia has noted that in practice only the financially independent lesbians were able to come out, because they could support themselves if the family disowned them. Tragically, although lesbians supported the family because they had no children, the family was willing to take their money but were not willing to accept their sexuality. At any rate, given the importance of the kinship group in Filipino society it was important to address lesbian advocacy issues with the Filipino family, to appeal for their understanding and support. The Catholic Church's position on lesbians, of course, was an important reason why families shunned lesbian members.

The activist's approach to the issue of sexuality was to send out as much information as possible on the issue and to advertise their advocacies. The information was designed to define issues such as lesbianism, while problematizing concepts of virginity and female beauty (though the beauty contest was denounced only in 1971 by MAKIBAKA, and no other organizations have been known to be publicly against beauty contests in subsequent years). On the other hand, there had been attempts to redefine the Filipino family to include single mothers, lesbian parents, and illegitimate children. For example, when the fourth world meeting for families of the Catholic Church was held in the Philippines on February 9, 2003, the women's groups held their own family day at the University of the Philippines, Diliman with five hundred participants, in response to what was perceived to be the Church's heterosexist view of the family. Likhaan held a special nontraditional family day defining family to include the "the separated," the disgraced, the bastards, and the lesbians (*separada, disgraciada, bastarda, lesbiana*).[77] The event made the front pages of the newspapers, particularly since the special guest was famous celebrity opera singer Armida Ponce-Enrile Siguion-Reyna (the sister of former Defense Minister and Senator John Ponce Enrile), who gave a speech about how miserable it was to grow up as an illegitimate child (*bastarda*). Likhaan also held events that challenged heteronormative rituals, such as a high school prom in 2005 where participants were not required to come as a couple, and where men were allowed to wear formal gowns if they so desired.[78] On the legislative front, lesbians and homosexuals have allied themselves in an attempt to form the first political party for lesbians and homosexuals to run under the party list while advocating for the passage of an antidiscrimination bill.

SEXUALITY

Women activists were keen to discuss the concept of women's desires and women's pleasure in the public arena. The international media's public discussion of sex and women's pleasure (more-explicit and more-regular appearances of sex scenes in movies, talk shows about sex run by psychologists) laid the groundwork for women's advocacy regarding sexuality. One of the popular celebrities in the Philippines is psychologist Dr. Margarita Holmes, who advised women and couples on sex and sexuality. She had a radio show and an advice column, published several books, and had a television segment. In an interview, she revealed that, although she originally wanted to write a column and give advice on the body, most of the letters she received were about sex and sexuality. Thus, her decision to focus on sexuality was based on audience response to her columns.[79] Holmes began writing her columns in 1989, hence it can be assumed that by then it was acceptable for public figures to discuss sexuality openly.

GABRIELA published a chapter in the book *Pagkababae* (Womanhood) in 1991 that had one segment entitled "Sekswalidad" (Sexuality). Although the book was later critiqued by one of its authors for not going far enough and for endorsing the view that celibacy and spinsterhood were against human nature, it was among the first to pioneer the discussion on women's desire.[80] Since then, women's organizations have run regular seminars on sexuality. These workshops had a profound impact on some of the women who attended them, such as PiLaKK president and *barangay* councilor, Lina Bacalando who confided in an interview that it was in those workshops that she realized, "women do have a libido after all!" The discussions opened women's eyes to the possibilities of women's desire. The Tagalog word *libog* (which translates as libido, lust, sexual urge, lasciviousness) was one of those taboo words associated with men but never with women. Feminist activists such as Sylvia Estrada-Claudio wrote on love, desire, and sexuality precisely because exploring the possibilities of women's pleasure was one way to exercise empowerment and experience joy.[81] In addition, Estrada-Claudio introduced a novel perspective into the debate by interpreting celibacy as a subversive option.[82] She critiqued what she believed was society's compulsory genital sexuality and introduced celibacy into the discussion of women's sexuality.[83] This rethinking of celibacy might have a seismic impact on society's dismissal of unmarried women as "undesirable women." According to *Womanhood,* "The term 'old maid' is commonly associated with being undesirable, frigid or even having an abnormal loathing for men by a woman. It seems that being an old maid is viewed by society as a curse that implies celibacy and life-long unhappiness."[84]

Women who have never married have negative capital in the Philippines. They were constructed as grouchy "old maids" because they were unattached to a man or because they failed to live up to definitions of the feminine as "wife and mother." They continued to be women who were pitied, despite the fact that some may be happy fulfilled women. Many of these women assisted relatives by sending children to school, contributing financial support, or fulfilling care duties to children and the aged. And although some of these women were independent, they were still imagined as persons to be pitied in comparison to married women, even though many married women may suffer their husband's infidelities or abandonment. Amaryllis Torres' interviews (2001–2002) with men and women in rural Philippines confirmed this condescending attitude towards single men and women who were not only regarded with pity but were believed to smell like urine.[85] Estrada-Claudio's introduction of celibacy as a form of resistance was a refreshing perspective reinterpreting unmarried women or single women as women who have rejected or resisted traditional constructions of the feminine as wife or mother rather than as women who have failed to fulfill their destiny as wives and mothers.

Who Will Take the Place of the Woman as Martyr?

What new constructions of "the Filipina" did the women's health activists propose to replace the woman who endures suffering? If it is no longer necessary to endure, then what is the alternative? In dismantling the representation of the woman as martyr who acquired status through the fortitude in which she bore her very own calvary, women's health activists attacked the very core of cultural constructions of the Filipina. This ambitious feminist project needed to have a positive goal for women. The alternative was for the Filipina to look after herself (her physical and mental health) so she would be able to look after her family as well.[86] This Filipina would be able to exercise her sexual and reproductive rights free from social criticisms. As an agent, this feminine role model could access information about her body and her health while being aware that no one had the right to access her body without her consent or to commit violence against it. This Filipina also was a woman who was in touch with her own desires. This alternative Filipina imagined as a role model by women's health activists was still an ideal. In the next two chapters, I will discuss the strategies used by activists to fashion the Filipina.

Fashioning Women

6

Women's Studies on the Air

RADIO, TELEVISION, AND WOMEN'S MOVEMENTS

Although the print medium has been used by women's groups since the beginning of the twentieth century, it was not until the 1980s that feminists in the Philippines extended the use of media to include radio and television, which had not been tapped for feminist ends prior to 1985. Anna Leah Sarabia, founder of WMC, pioneered the use of television and radio for the feminist cause when she produced *Womanwatch* (television) and *RadyoWomanwatch* (radio) in 1985.[1] By the 1990s, several women's organizations such as GABRIELA and the Institute of Women's Studies, also began to experiment with the "new" media. Because television was expensive, radio became the preferred option. Radio was portable, making it capable of reaching wider audiences than television. It was a medium that was woman friendly, since women could listen to the radio while multitasking, such as cooking, cleaning, and ironing.[2]

In what sense could these women's programs be viewed as different from the mainstream? First, these programs were unabashedly feminist in orientation and featured the advocacy of women's organizations while highlighting particular women's issues regularly on the air. They showcased the agendas of women as a marginalized group and underscored the reasons for their marginality while advocating equality. The lack of women's programs meant that the topic of women from a feminist perspective was not explored in the media prior to the 1980s. Second (and more important), these programs were conceptualized as educational programs aiming "to reach not to rate."[3] This rationale in itself subverted the mainstream practice that ratings determined the life or death of a particular program. The self-conscious decision by women's groups to place themselves above the ratings game liberated them from being subject to the fickle fate of ratings and responses. Women's organizations did not have to solicit advertising, as a rule; often the advertisements they did carry were for the services of the women's organizations and their allies, including the Department of Health for the women's health programs. The drawback to not being supported by advertising was that they were dependent on the sponsorship of grants from philanthropic foundations or the goodwill of the station. Women's organizations often used their own funds or funds of their allies and sponsors to run the programs; some programs were broadcast from their own radio rooms, in the case of the radio shows such as GABRIELA's *Okay Ka*. Thus, the educational slant and its shift away from ratings and advertising meant that the women's programs were not just peripheral, but also unique as they claimed a space of their own.

This chapter will focus on the use of radio and television for feminist advocacy—exploring, in particular, how women's organizations used radio and television to represent and fashion the Filipino woman. In my view, the radio and television shows were like classrooms, with activists intending to give audiences a basic women's studies course while giving practical advice on how ordinary women could empower themselves. Such advice included information about the kinds of services that these organizations offered to women such as counseling for victims of domestic violence, and health clinics for physical checkups. Two of the producers of the shows discussed here—the WMC and the Institute of Women's Studies—were explicit about their aims: to educate women about feminist issues. The new epistemology of the women's movement was introduced to audiences through a talk show format that allowed resource persons to be brought in as experts to demystify and define complex new feminist vocabularies such as "trafficking," "sexuality," "lesbianism," "sexual harassment," and "reproductive health." As Anna Leah Sarabia disclosed to me in an interview, "We have to define it [feminism] for them, otherwise people will define it for us."[4] Using the Tagalog language (with the exception of *XYZ* television, which was in English) and broadcasting nationally and internationally (through the Internet) women's organizations could be sure that they would be in touch with their target audience—women of all classes in general, and grassroots or lower-class women in particular.

Radio and television programs and their contents (including commercials and plugs) had a unique role to play in normalizing novel feminist concepts. Many of the topics raised such as virginity, sexuality, contraception, lesbianism, incest, rape, abortion, and domestic violence were taboo or considered too sensitive to be raised in the public arena. I do not mean to say that only radio and television gave these issues a public audience: many of these issues were linked to proposed legislation such as the Anti-Trafficking in Persons Act, which passed in 2003, or the Reproductive Health Bill, still being proposed as of this writing, discussed in the political halls. But giving these sensitive topics airtime effectively lifted the cultural ban—making it no longer taboo to talk about sex or no longer shameful to admit one was a victim of partner infidelity or domestic violence.

Sources for this chapter include programs from two television shows (*Womanwatch* and *XYZ Young Women's Television*), and five radio shows (*Okay Ka Mare!* [You are okay, sister!, hereafter *Okay Ka*], *Babae Ka, May Say Ka!* [You are a woman, you have a say! hereafter *Babae Ka*]), *Tinig ng Nursia* [Voice of Nursia, hereafter *Tinig*], *XYZone*, and *Kape at Chika* (Coffee and chat, hereafter *Kape;* see appendix). I listened to a total of forty tapes of radio programs across the five shows (five from *Okay Ka*, three from *Babae Ka*, eighteen from *Tinig*, three from *Kape*, and eleven from *XYZone*) and viewed a select number of television episodes of *Womanwatch* and *XYZ Young Women's Television*.[5] I compiled indexes of all topics, guest speakers, and hosts and anchors of all five radio programs, including all 286 episodes of *Womanwatch*. In addition, I interviewed anchorpersons and producers of several of the shows: Lily Malasa and Rina Jimenez David (*XYZone*); Anna Leah Sarabia, Sinag de Leon, and Congresswoman Risa Hontiveros-Baraquiel (*Womanwatch* and *XYZ*); and Janice Monte and Congresswoman Liza Largoza Maza (*Okay Ka* and *Babae Ka*). Finally, I examined printed materials such as television scripts and records of queries asked by audiences. The episodes I selected were those that tackled the most important or highest-priority issues raised by the women's movement (trafficking, prostitution, women's labor, women's issues in the Philippine context, rape, domestic violence, and sexual harassment) as well as the issues that were controversial or that will set agendas for future priorities (reproductive health, abortion, infidelity). In addition, I selected topics that gave a historical or cultural context to the status of women. One organization produced eight thirty-minute radio dramas, and I was able to listen to one entitled *Huwag Ipabukas ang Ngayon* (Don't postpone the present) about the Pap smear test. Unfortunately, there were no studies of ratings, because this was not a priority for any of the shows' producers. There was one undergraduate thesis that did a survey of audiences of *Womanwatch* television focusing on whether the shows' objectives were realized that affirmed audiences understood and appreciated the educational thrust of the programs.[6]

The five radio programs analyzed here were produced by arguably only two of the major women's organizations: WMC produced *XYZone*, GABRIELA produced *Okay Ka* and *Babae Ka,* and Nursia produced *Tinig* and *Kape.* But since Mary John Mananzan (OSB) was both founder of Nursia and chairperson of GABRIELA it could be argued that GABRIELA and Nursia were similar in outlook and thus Nursia and GABRIELA productions could be classified together as one group. This did not mean, however, that only the organizations that produced the shows were featured in the programs. The alliance between women's organizations and the talk show format that relied on resource persons meant that other women's organizations had opportunities to present their advocacies as guests or resource persons. In this sense, radio showcased the agendas of a plethora of women's organizations.

The Resource Person as Feminist Teacher

The media were primarily used as an educational tool—as "infotainment" to introduce the radical ideas of the feminist movement. The talk show format allowed each radio and *Womanwatch* episode to discuss one topic, giving women's organizations an opportunity to present their own perspective on a particular issue. In this "classroom," the resource person or the episode's guest speaker fulfilled the role of teacher. Resource persons— usually counselors, lawyers, teachers, nuns, doctors, nurses, health care workers, or representatives of particular women's groups—translated the objectives of their organization in simple terms to audiences. Although occasionally survivors of rape, of domestic violence, or of partner infidelity "came out" to retell their stories, and occasionally some women were interviewed to share their particular experiences (as single moms, as overseas workers, or lesbians for example), by and large it was the resource person who had the authorial voice as the recognized expert on the topic. Even when a survivor began the episode by recounting her experiences (which occurred in approximately 2 percent of cases in *XYZone,* although more often in *Tinig* and *Kape*), the resource person had the final say providing the analysis and counsel.[7] Resource persons also were important because they alerted audiences to the various services—women's crisis centers, centers for migrants, legal aid centers, health clinics, or counseling services available to the national audience. In most cases, resource persons represented one particular women's organization or NGO specializing in the topic at hand. This format enabled many of the more prominent women's organizations to advertise their agendas, their advocacy, and their services. Almost all shows advertised a hotline and gave out phone numbers of the various organizations' help desks. Audiences were presented with a smorgasbord of topics on Filipino women, but garnished with the specific advocacy of each organization. Audiences were invited to participate by submitting their queries via e-mail, letter, or telephone.

Introduction to Women's Studies

Tinig's byline "women's studies on the air" captured the trope of the radio and television programs produced by the women's movement. Although *Tinig* was almost an exact replica of a university women's studies subject, complete with a syllabus divided into modules, presented by anchors who were teachers at St. Scholastica's college, the other radio and television programs were more subtle or creative in their approach. For example, one of *Okay Ka*'s regular segments gave household or health tips with a feminist bent.[8] One episode had for its tips the twelve rights of women as outlined by the United Nations, and another episode's tips were on how to get children to help in the housework.[9] The dissemination of practical information and the notion of women's rights or human rights accompanied the introduction of feminist terms and advocacies. Particularly in matters of women's health and sexuality (reproductive health, HIV/AIDS, domestic violence, rape, and so on), the programs focused on giving audiences practical information not easily accessible elsewhere such as how to put on a condom in the form of a quiz, and descriptions of illnesses such as anemia, chronic fatigue, and breast cancer.[10] Since women's rights was a recurring theme, legal information for victims of violence, including rape, sexual harassment, incest, and battering was offered. Although there is no divorce in the Philippines, topics on infidelity and legal separation allowed feminist lawyers to advise women on their rights according to the law. All these pieces of information were not politically neutral, coming as they did from the women's perspective. In addition, the latest research on specific issues such as AIDS or migrant women workers and even the history of women's movements in the Philippines was discussed openly.

Since the programs assumed that audiences were unfamiliar with feminist positions, they made a conscious effort to introduce the new vocabularies of the women's movements. Each show usually began with the definition of terms. Terms such as "prostitution," "trafficking," "lesbianism," "sexuality," "reproductive health," "sexual harassment," "rape," "patriarchy," and "domestic violence"—words already embedded in the epistemologies of women's movements internationally but that are unfamiliar to the general audience—were defined from the perspective of the guest resource person or particular women's organization. I will illustrate precisely how the talk show format was used to achieve this by giving some specific examples on the issues of domestic violence, partner abuse, reproductive health, and sexuality. Chapter 2 has already covered the way prostitution was discussed in radio programs.

Before the 1980s, domestic violence was a taboo subject. Cultural attitudes relegated the issue to the private sphere more appropriately dealt with by the kinship group rather than the police as representatives of the state. The stigma of shame attached to it, the lack of a divorce law, and the cultural expectation that wives had no other option but to endure it with dignity meant that many victims felt trapped and isolated. In testimonies from victims of domestic violence aired on the radio programs, the women talked about having to endure: "take up your cross and endure it."[11] The international campaign against domestic violence made it a public issue for which the community was socially responsible. Media, particularly radio and television, became important vehicles used by Filipina activists to overcome cultural challenges. Resource persons from the WCC defined the forms of abuse, disclosed the relevant statistics, and provided psychological explanations for why men used violence on their partners.[12] Feminists grabbed the opportunity to give new meaning to the term of abuse, extending the concept to include verbal insults, partner infidelity, and the lack of financial support.[13]

Likhaan's Dr. Junice Demetrio-Melgar introduced listeners of *Tinig* to the taboo topic of women's sexuality including virginity and STDs. Because it was a totally new concept, it was important to inform audiences that it encompassed not just women's health and women's bodies, but also sexual preferences and attitudes. For example, Demetrio-Melgar critiqued the cultural preoccupation with virginity defined solely in biological terms (that is, the hymen): "Because they see sexuality based on the hymen so it is something they treasure so when something happens to it their whole self-respect crumbles. Or else they become sex objects."[14] Instead, she offered an alternative definition that stressed personal integrity.[15]

Anna Leah Sarabia also used *XYZone* to debunk myths about lesbians.[16] To demystify the topic, *XYZone* alone ran seven episodes on lesbianism (although this might be partly explained by the fact that the program was produced by Sarabia, who founded CLIC, the feminist NGO that focused on lesbian rights and issues).[17]

In an episode provocatively entitled "Should the Church Interfere in the Reproductive Health Issue?," anchorwoman Rina Jimenez David defined reproductive health for listeners: "the capacity of men and women to fulfill their sexuality, sex, pregnancy and childbirth as well as childrearing."[18] Since the Catholic Church's position on reproductive health was the number one obstacle to the women's health movement, it was a crucial defensive strategy to define reproductive health in a program that advocated that the Catholic Church should not dictate to women on the issue. Given the powerful grip of the Catholic mindset, these programs were very radical indeed.

Some of the new feminist vocabularies were linked to women-centered legislation or legislative advocacy. Programs explained new laws that they hoped would alter cultural attitudes and norms. *Babae Ka* featured the Anti-Rape Law (Republic Act 8353 passed in September 1997) in a program on January 8, 2005, where resource person WomenLead lawyer Claire Lucson explained the shift in the definition of rape from a crime against chastity to a crime against person, illustrating how rape was not an just an infringement or violation of the chastity or virginity of a woman, but a violation of her very essence and human rights. Lucson described the reaction of policemen who claimed that it could not be rape if the man did not have a good time (*hindi siya nasarapan*) as an example of the pervasive machismo of Filipino culture. A major victory for the women's movement was the redefinition of "sexual assault" that was independent of whether or not there was satisfaction of lust on the part of the man.[19] An episode of *Tinig* had attorney Raisa Jajuri of the Alternative Legal Assistance Center (SALIGAN; Sentro ng Alternatibong Lingap Panligal) as a resource person to explain the Family Code's position and grounds for legal separation and annulment.[20] The *XYZone* program on reproductive health was linked to the women's movements proposed House Bill 4110 also known as the Reproductive Health Bill.[21]

Programs were an opportunity to deliver feminist theories in simplified forms. Feminist nun Mary John Mananzan (OSB) explained what she meant by the religious roots of women's oppression in *Tinig* by using references to popular culture (such as computer hardware) to explain how Catholicism was partly responsible for reducing women to companions or "reflected glory" of men that became embedded in the "hard disk of men and women."[22]

The importance of history to the feminist movements was apparent in the number of programs on this topic: there was an entire module on women in Philippine history in *Tinig* (including women in the Spanish, Japanese, and American periods).[23] There were modules on socializing forces, including education (although socialization permeated many topics and was mentioned, in particular, on topics on wife battering).[24] Finally, there were modules about women in Church history.[25] *Babae Ka,* a program that leaned towards the impact of contemporary politics on women of the lower classes, ran a regular segment about either women in history or heroic women. Conscious of the importance of making women visible in history the programs also delivered their own versions of the histories of women's movements in the Philippines.[26] (Dr. Alma Fernandez, a retired professor at the University of the Philippines lamented the absence of women in official histories due to their invisibility in the primary documents written by men in the past.)[27] For reasons discussed in the introduction, the historiography of the pre-Hispanic Golden Age of women's rights that was lost in colonialism was uniformly reproduced in these productions, including the two-part series *Womanwatch* entitled "From Priestess to President" (discussed in the introduction).[28]

WOMEN SECTORS

The simplified versions of Filipino feminist theories translated through media productions also reproduced the representation of women into various sectors—as urban poor, Muslim women, peasants, indigenous women, women factory workers, and so forth. I will give one example here of how radio and television explored the plight of one particular sector of women. The lives of OCWs, particularly domestics, have been given star billing in both the radio and television programs, perhaps because of the feminization of the OCW and her contribution to the Philippine economy in the form of remittances. *Womanwatch,* the show that was among the first to talk about this issue from the feminist viewpoint, aired no fewer than fifteen episodes on this topic, covering domestic helpers in Kuwait, Hong Kong, Spain, Italy, Germany, and Saudi Arabia. The special features included clips of interviews with domestic helpers abroad when the *Womanwatch* crew traveled on location to film the stories.[29] Interestingly, there was only one feature on domestic helpers at home (that is, in the Philippines), a *Womanwatch* program.[30] Radio shows tackled the topic of overseas domestic helpers from different angles: they explored the experiences of women abroad (loneliness, separation, the pain of transnational mothering); they exposed the abuse by agents and employers; and they explored the social costs of migration on the family at home.[31] These included not just psychological effects on the children, but also health impacts including the spread of diseases such as sexually transmitted infections. *XYZone* produced several features on seafarers and WMC aired plugs for the Department of Health reminding overseas workers (particularly men), that if they were unfaithful while overseas, they could be passing on AIDS/HIV or other STIs (sexually transmitted infections) to their unsuspecting partners.[32] Radio programs also critiqued the government for relying on overseas contract labor as a temporary solution to the lack of professional jobs, since many domestic workers were actually nurses and teachers who chose underemployment abroad instead of low salaries at home.[33] Unlike the Kanlungan Migrant Center's blunt stance that migration was risky and best avoided, the radio and television programs were more focused on giving audiences an information package that included the entire gamut of experiences that came with the job of an OCW, including the social costs. In this sense, programs adhered to the women's health activists' philosophy of delivering as much information as possible on a topic or issue to allow women to make choices based on available data. Advocacy was introduced more subtlety in terms of criticisms against government policy or in the discussion of political and legislative lobbying. More important, the content and format of each episode was intended to elicit empathy from audiences for the plight of OCWs represented as lonely, suffering, and hard-working women toiling for the sake of the family (the martyr again), vulnerable to exploitation.

THE SYLLABUS AS ADVOCACY

A women's studies syllabus would not be complete without an in-depth discussion of particular issues raised by the women's movements—critical, sensitive, or controversial topics that received high priority in feminist advocacy. These included but were not confined to, prostitution and trafficking, sexuality including lesbianism, reproductive health, domestic violence, rape (and the "comfort women"), partner infidelity, AIDS/HIV or STDs, virginity, and abortion. The talk show format was a suitable platform for exploring these issues in some depth. In the talk shows, survivors of trafficking, domestic violence, or partner infidelity, for example, shared their stories with the hosts or anchor, the resource persons, and the audiences. Those who shared life stories need not be survivors of some traumatic event, but most were women who had coped with particular challenges. For instance, single mothers and lesbians revealed how they dealt with being outside the normative prescription of the Filipino woman. Women's stories personalized the serious issues being discussed. If no testimonies or sharing was possible, resource persons introduced the topic by referring to contemporary research findings or data from their particular NGO work. Finally, programs were used to advertise the services of women's organizations particularly help lines for victims of trafficking and domestic violence, as well as for OCW victims of exploitation. It also directed women to support groups, feminist lawyers, counseling, and health services or clinics. GABRIELA programs also invited audiences to participate in demonstrations planned by them.

On the issues where the women's movement was relatively united—prostitution, rape, and domestic violence, for example—the women's position was explained directly and with as much detail as possible. Programs would go into some detail about the legislation that needed to be passed while actively lobbying for particular positions. On issues where the movement was extremely divided—such as abortion, reproductive health, divorce, and sexuality (including lesbianism)—the programs showed more restraint, focusing instead on defining what the terms meant and describing the current research findings. It stopped short of advocacy if the topic was considered controversial. In the *XYZone* episode on abortion, for instance, which was carefully titled "Abortion: Illegal but Real," the resource person, Dr. Corazon M. Raymundo from the University of the Philippines Population Institute, trotted out the statistics: although illegal, four hundred thousand women chose to have abortions with one-third losing their lives, and that the decision to abort was largely financial, with poor women who had more than three children likely to consider it. The episode did not advocate abortion as a reproductive right.[34] It is important to note that abortion is a very sensitive issue and that the women's movements remain divided over it. It is taboo to even mention it; journalistic reports on abortion incidents refrain from printing the word, referring to it only as "A."[35] The fact that a radio or television program considered it a topic worthy of public debate signaled a crossing of cultural boundaries.[36]

In the *XYZone* radio program "Women's Rights, Lesbian Rights," the resource person, Anna Leah Sarabia, defined lesbianism and focused her discussion on discrimination against lesbians and the feeling of isolation experienced by lesbians who had no other support but their partners. Although it discussed how cultural constructions of the feminine made it difficult for lesbians, who were deemed outside the "norm" of women, it did not advocate same-sex marriage. Nevertheless, the resource person pointed out that the lesbian groups were advocating for an antidiscrimination act through their allies in the legislature.[37] Although Anna Leah Sarabia questioned the very notion of marriage, she refrained from sharing this view in public.[38]

Kape's episode on partner infidelity included two women sharing their stories of their womanizing husbands while a counselor gave advice and comments. Attorney Raisa Jajuri from SALIGAN was the resource person on the Family Code, and its provisions on separation and annulment. Although she outlined women's options within the limits of the law, the program did not advocate a lobby to pass a divorce law.[39] *Kape* and *XYZone* went on air with two single mothers sharing their stories on parenthood without a partner (in the *XYZone* episode, one of them was a lesbian), but the program did not lobby for divorce as a solution.[40]

"Condoms, Nakatutulong Ba?" (Condoms, do they help?) explored the advantages of wearing a condom but refrained from criticizing the Church's position on contraception (still called family planning).[41] Even the very outspoken episode "Dapat Bang Makialam ang Simbahan sa RH Issue?" (Should the Church interfere in the reproductive health issue?) showed restraint when it refrained from publicly denouncing that the Church was out of line meddling in private affairs or restraining women's choices. Instead, the resource person, attorney Karol Ruiz-Austria from WomenLead, concluded that everyone had the freedom to pronounce their beliefs but that no one had the right to dictate to others what they should or should not do.[42] Radio and television programs were careful not to alienate their listeners but hoped to introduce them gradually to almost all of the issues and topics prioritized by the women's movements and organizations.

Introducing Alternative Role Models

Redefining the heroine became an intrinsic part of the feminist project, and radio and television were perfect media to do this. Programs were able to show real women in color, and audiences could listen to their voices and even talk to them by calling in. Once again, activists saw the potential for redefining heroines. Former survivors were hailed as heroines for having overcome or survived terrible fates. For example, in *Babae Ka,* a segment entitled "Babae Ka, Bayani Ka" (You are a woman, you are a heroine) featured not just activist women in history or women revolutionary heroes (such as Melchora Aquino or Tandang Sora) and Princess Urduja, but also survivors of trafficking, of domestic violence, of rape, of sexual harassment, of partner infidelity and abuse, and of employer abuses (in the case of OCWs).[43] Because it was normative for a woman to endure suffering quietly, the need to destroy this ideal meant that its opposite—a woman who refused to be a victim—was touted as the alternative role model.

Mary John Mananzan (OSB) called attention to the sexist attitude that disparaged assertive women: "When a woman is skilled at making arguments she is labeled as shrewish or feisty but when a man is good at making arguments, they all exclaim 'how great he is!'").[44] Here she showed how social commentary prevented women from excelling or standing up for themselves. Women were meant to be demure (*mahinhin*), not feisty (*mataray*). Labeling a woman as feisty (*mataray*) implied censure, stressing that the woman had strayed from acceptable norms of behavior for her sex. But in the radio programs the qualities of feisty or brave (*matapang*) were encouraged. Senator Loren Legarda advised women to know their rights so as not to be duped by traffickers. If they became victims, though, she advised them to telephone radio anchor Rina Jimenez David (a known feminist journalist) because she is brave (*matapang*), or to approach the senator herself because she is even braver (*mas matapang*) than Rina: "But the important thing is that we know our rights and that we know what we should do and that we should not be afraid. But if you become victims, call Ms. David because she is courageous. Call me because I'm even more courageous! [laughter]" (my translation from Tagalog).[45]

In the episode about the Anti-Rape Law in *Babae Ka,* anchor Janice Monte promised listeners that she would introduce them to courageous women (*matatapang ng kababaihan*); in this particular case, the eleven-year-old rape victim who confronted her congressman rapist and succeeded in having him jailed with the help of women's organizations and a feminist lawyer—attorney Katrina Legarda of the feminist political party Abanse! Pinay.[46] Feminists hoped to fashion assertive women but realized that in order to do so they needed to first remove the negative capital associated with being feisty (*mataray*).

Impacts

What was the impact of feminist radio and television? By commercial standards, a program's success is measured by ratings. Interviews with producers revealed that they had no records of ratings; in some cases, such as *Womanwatch,* no ratings reviews were done because it was aired on a government channel.[47] But since these programs were designed to be educational, women's organizations were more interested in using media as a platform for disseminating their agendas and to gain a mass following. Women's organizations deliberately set themselves above the ratings game and focused on using media as an opportunity to reeducate society into perceiving women's issues as important and to advertise the various women's organizations, showcasing their programs and achievements. Thus, impacts need to be measured in terms of how these programs contributed towards advancing the agendas of women's movements. The fact that all these programs were features appearing regularly for one hour or a half-hour each week meant that women's issues had a spot each week in the audiovisual media, giving women a voice. Sarabia believed that the regular presence of women in media tackling women's issues from a feminist perspective was impact enough.[48] After all, Sarabia claimed that their strategy was to be repetitive (*makulit*), creating an impact through sheer repetition of feminist messages.[49] In calling attention to womanhood and all its pleasures and travails, the programs gave importance to the very experiences of womanhood itself, once trivialized as only domestic.

Impact could also be measured in terms of influence on the many ordinary women who became part of the programs as interviewees or as callers and respondents. *Womanwatch,* which ran for eight years three months, and 286 episodes, and *XYZ* required producers to travel all over the country for segments on themes such as women vendors, women jeepney drivers, women peasants, and so on, talking to ordinary women and not celebrities. Sarabia argued that even a ten-second exposure on television gave these obscure women fame. According to Sarabia, the media exposure not only gave them dignity, but also empowered them.[50] *Kape*'s byline—"Here we are all celebrities. Your story, my story is important"[51]—signaled to all and sundry that every woman's personal story was important enough to be heard and given airtime. *Womanwatch* producer Anna Leah Sarabia regularly featured women jeepney drivers, women farmers, vendors, basket weavers, and indigenous women to show how hard these women worked to survive.[52]

Radio and television were pioneers in breaking cultural taboos. It was a plea from the radio that gave Maria Rosa Henson the courage to be the first Filipina "comfort woman" to come out from the shadows and tell her story.[53] Topics on sex and sexuality were discussed on the air for the first time. Dr. Margarita Holmes, the psychologist who became a celebrity advising the public on issues of sexuality, first appeared on television in *Womanwatch*.[54] In 1991, *Radyo Womanwatch* was still hesitant to discuss lesbianism or "the very sensitive issue of abortion in relation to family planning."[55] But by 1997 *Tinig,* produced by the Benedictine nuns, ran a feature on sexuality with an American nun acting as a resource person.[56] If a religious person, a nun, with symbolic capital and moral legitimacy could talk about sex on the air, then it must not be wrong or sinful to raise sexuality as a feminist issue. Radio and television programs challenged listeners to problematize virginity, to remove their prejudices against gays, lesbians, and single moms.[57] The very sensitive topic of abortion has been opened for discussion, even if the parameters were limited to research findings on abortion. Radio and television programs made it acceptable, or at least less shameful, for women to admit they had been beaten or raped. It gave these victims some dignity, because it transferred the blame from the victim to the perpetuator as women tended to blame themselves for their suffering.

The immediate effect of lifting the cultural ban on certain taboo topics such as the body made it acceptable to demand information on the subjects formerly deemed too private or personal. Many women were ignorant about their bodies—particularly in reference to contraception and health issues. Cultural practices prohibited the discussion of these topics in both the public and the private spheres. But in order to fulfill activist agendas for empowering women, feminists had to traverse forbidden ground in order to deliver the information ordinary women needed to make educated choices about their bodies and their lives. The knowledge gained helped empower them. Although radio and television as I've argued here focused more on informing women than on transforming them into advocates, the information they disseminated was already mediated through a feminist lens. Giving women the information and the options (resource persons always gave them options) was important in instilling feminist consciousness, a necessary step before one could be an advocate. Since these programs were virtually a women's studies course, audiences learned feminist theory and practice. They discovered women's rights, including the right to a happy sex life, and were encouraged to make informed choices and to empower themselves.[58] Actually, the mere fact that an alternative perspective to the conservative Catholic Church was articulated regularly every week to counteract the weekly sermons used by priests to propagate their position on women's issues was significant impact enough. Although women's organizations have stopped short of attacking the church publicly, media at least gave the activists airtime—a regular space to give women an alternative viewpoint from the dominant Church narrative on women. In fact, a member of the Church usually sits on the board of censors, and producers of the above programs have had to contend with censorship from these Church people who constantly label the programs with a PG rating because of the sexual content.[59]

Mimicry is said to be the greatest form of flattery; one measure of the success of the feminist shows has been its metamorphosis and replication in other shows within and outside the Philippines. Marina Mahathir, daughter of then–Malaysian Prime Minister Mahathir Mohammad spoke to Anna Leah Sarabia about doing a Malaysian version of *XYZ Young Women's Television* while another Philippine channel produced a television program entitled "f," which in practice was another version of *XYZ*. Programs also won awards giving them public recognition and encouraging stations to keep them on to give them prestige.[60] *Womanwatch* received the Catholic Mass Media Award in 1987 given by Cardinal Jaime Sin, Archbishop of Manila; that award was in the "Best Women's Program Category." *Womanwatch* received another recognition award from the Cultural Center of the Philippines for making audiences aware of women's rights, for raising controversial issues, and for dispensing practical advice. *XYZone* received the Grand Prize in the AIDS Media Awards in 2001 for "Best News Feature Category for Radio" while the episode on antitrafficking discussed in this chapter was a finalist for the Outstanding Public Affairs Program for the thirteenth Association of Broadcasters of the Philippines (KBP; Kapisanan ng Broadcasters) Golden Dove Awards in 2004.[61] The Department of Health also has used *XYZ on Destiny* (the cable television version of the program) as teaching modules for women's health and sexuality in the public schools.

Women's organizations were acutely aware of the power of the media in constructing female stereotypes, particularly those that represented women as beauty queens or sex objects, or as confined to the domestic sphere. Both television and radio programs ran episodes on precisely the topic of media and women, critiquing mainstream media's stereotypes of the Filipino woman.[62] One classic feminist campaign, taken up by GABRIELA Women's Party in their first election campaign in

2003, was the protest against Tanduay Rum's commercial, "Nakatikim ka ba ng kinse anyos?" (Have you tasted a fifteen-year-old?).[63] GABRIELA succeeded in having the commercials taken off the air. In the late 1980s, *Womanwatch* and the journalists who were part of a media watch group protested against a beer advertisement that used a jingle depicting women as materialistic and dependent on men who were stereotyped as eternal providers. In the lyrics of this infamous jingle, known as the *Bilmoko* jingle, the woman continued to ask the man to buy her things, thus equating love with giving the beloved whatever her heart desired. Protests forced the advertisement agency to revise the advertisement to excise the offending scenes, eventually pulling the commercial off the air.[64] Hence, in dismantling media stereotypes, women's movements intended to use media to present alternative role models for women focusing on women achievers and women who might be outside the contemporary cultural boundaries of the feminine—such as lesbians or single mothers. Obviously, the audience saw even the hosts as role models: two of the television hosts became successful politicians: *Womanwatch*'s Nikki Coseteng became a congresswoman and then a senator, and *XYZ*'s Risa Hontiveros-Baraquiel became a congresswoman. Sarabia admitted that the media exposure as hosts for these television shows were critical to their success as politicians. Both women politicians supported pro-women legislation. Clearly, the television shows had an impact on women voters (and maybe male voters as well). *Womanwatch*'s regular features of women from all walks of life (as vendors, farmers, students, urban poor, peasants, fisherfolk, and businesswomen), and *XYZ*'s regular segments of high-achieving women professionals provided alternative role models for women.

The women's movements in the Philippines have been extremely savvy in their use of the media as a method of introducing counterhegemonic discourses on and about women. They succeeded in marrying advocacy with entertainment even though the programs differed from the mainstream commercial programs. By continuing to air these programs in the vernacular, the women's movements communicated their commitment to becoming a mass movement. But the very premise of "classrooms on the air" had its limitations. The most fundamental problem was that the relationship between the activists and the public (read: mass of women of all classes who composed their audiences) remained fixed in a hierarchy of teacher-student. Even the interactive segments of the programs required audiences to send in their queries or problems to be resolved by the resource person, who retained the privileged voice.

There was a minor exception of some radio shows where audiences were invited to participate in the discussion by calling in. Because of the limitations of radio and television shows in providing a space for audiences to participate more directly in the myriad campaigns of the women's movements, activists resorted to other methods in order to involve members and potential followers. It is these activities—oral testimonies, theater as advocacy, demonstrations, and rituals—that are the subject of the next chapter.

7

Fashioning Women through Activism, Ritual, and Dress

Making Women Activists

How did some women's organizations mobilize followers, and how did some of them intend to fashion women into activists? The formidable task of destroying the "martyr complex" required a complete makeover in cultural constructions of women. The "martyr" had to be reinvented as a militant advocate or activist. Unique strategies had to be put in place in order to transform victims of patriarchy into feminist advocates. If the radio and television programs discussed in the previous chapter introduced audiences to feminist perspectives, the practices analyzed in this chapter (oral testimonies, theater as advocacy, songs, demonstrations, dress, and rituals) could be interpreted as the practicum element of the women's studies courses. These activities were crucial in the formation of feminist identities. Women bonded together by confronting the state, church, and traditional cultural beliefs. By participating in actual protest activities, ordinary women, including former victims, not only became bona fide members of women's organizations, but also became feminist activists.

This chapter focuses on both the content and performance of these practices insofar as they inform us about how women activists represented and fashioned women. Here I concentrate only on those organizations that aimed to transform women into feminist activists through specific practices. It was possible to refashion women through legislative advocacy as well, but this is not the subject of this chapter. Activities run by women's organizations required participation from members. It was through participation in these activities that women followers received their first lessons in political activism and developed identities as feminist advocates. These activities also transformed them in many ways: shy, diffident, exploited workers delivered speeches at demonstrations; survivors of trafficking became amateur actors in theater as advocacy; and victims of sexual violence became full-time activists.

Testimonies

LOLA ASIANG'S STORY

At around 9:30 a.m. on Saturday August 9, 2003, a busload of Japanese tourists, most of them in their early twenties, arrived at Lola's House. Lola's House was the meeting place of Lila-Pilipina, the organization of Filipino "comfort women," victims and survivors of rape and military sexual slavery by Japanese troops during World War II.[1] Vice President/Coordinator Rechilda "Richie" Extremadura introduced the tour group to five *lolas,* all of them in their seventies. ("*Lola*" means "grandmother" in Tagalog, but "comfort women" were affectionately referred to by Lila Pilipina collectively as *lolas.*) Lola Asiang was asked to tell her story. Seated in front of the group and flanked on one side by the Japanese tour guide and on the other by the Filipino translator, Lola Asiang narrated her life story slowly in Tagalog. Every few sentences she paused, to allow her story to be translated into English by the Filipino tour guide, and then into Japanese by the Japanese tour guide.

Lola Asiang began her story in World War II. She was an eighteen-year-old bride, having just been married three months, when the Philippine army from the Central Luzon province of Pampanga recruited her husband. Because he was a leader of the resistance, the Japanese soldiers kidnapped both Lola Asiang and her husband and took them to the jail in *intramuros* (within the walls) of the old city of Manila. It was there that they tortured her husband in her presence. She watched helplessly as they forced him to kneel on salt, had his nails extracted one by one and then had the hair and skin on his forehead scalped with a razor. After her husband was killed, she was imprisoned and raped by an army officer. Then followed six months of daily rape by different Japanese soldiers. At this point of the story, Lola Asiang became tearful. But by the end of her narrative, she had recovered enough to deliver a militant speech in a shrill voice "It has been eleven years and there is still no justice.[2] I thank all of those who have helped us. We are not going to stop; even our president is not listening to us. Thank you to Lila-Pilipina. I only want justice. Tell the government to respect the rights of women who are victims of Japanese soldiers. It is hard to tell my story, I just bear it" (my translation).

I am interested in engaging with Lola Asiang's testimony from two specific angles. First, I focus on what discourses about the Filipino woman emerged from the testimony in particular the replication of the "double narrative"; second, I isolate the testimony as practice—as a ritual used by activists in their attempts to refashion women.

Lola Asiang constructed her life story in terms of a narrative structure emphasizing her transformation from two poles—from "victim" to "activist." It was not a traditional autobiographical text that began with her birth and ended with her current life situation; instead, the first part of the testimony was an account of the circumstances of her rapes in World War II, followed by a pause in the presentation when she broke down in tears, and a fast forward to her present activism. A huge gap in historical time—after the war until her "coming out" in the 1990s—was an interesting case study of memory and forgetting. This problem of remembering did not escape the notice of the Japanese tourists in the audience when they asked Lola Asiang and the four other *lolas* present what happened to them after the war. The response of the *lolas* was unanimous: puzzled by the question, they looked at each other and hesitated before answering that their lives were destroyed since as social outcasts and deprived of an education they were compelled to move to the city and take on jobs as salesgirls or laundrywomen. This part of their life story was absent from the public performance of their oral testimony.

If the *lolas* from Lila-Pilipina came from the urban poor, how did they become militant activists and feminists? Because Lila-Pilipina is affiliated with GABRIELA, the *lolas* were invited to participate in basic women's orientation seminars. In these sessions, their personal stories were linked to Philippine history and gender issues in Philippine culture. Here they learned that the rapes were not just a violation of their human rights, but also of their social rights.

Every oral history or interview is an opportunity for the interviewee to reinvent himself or herself. The performance of oral history transformed these women from survivors to angry, militant feminists demanding justice. Lola Asiang herself admitted that narrating her testimony over and over again was very painful for her. In fact, some Filipina feminists critiqued the practice of oral testimonies because it compelled victims to constantly relive their trauma.[3] Others imputed that the victim's past was being used by feminists for particular advocacies, thus depriving them of their agency once more. The *lolas* in this case were willing to have their pasts used; narrating their stories, though painful, was their contribution to advocacy on behalf of all women raped in war. Lola Asiang in her twilight years was acutely aware of the obstacles facing her. Despite a decade of struggle, none of Lila-Pilipina's objectives had been met. In fact, the *lolas* believed that the Japanese government strategy was to wait for them to die, hoping that the issue would disappear with their demise. As of 2003, thirty-eight of the 173 *lolas* who were members of Lila-Pilipina at the time had died. Among Lila-Pilipina's aims were a demand for an apology and compensation from the Japanese government and a rewriting of official histories. Neither of these two important aims had been achieved. Since both the Japanese and Philippine governments barely responded to the demands, hoping that the protest would "die out" quite literally, the impact of the testimonials has not been in the "big picture" or the rewriting of World War II history in Japan and the Philippines, but in the transformation of the survivor into militant feminist.

ORAL TESTIMONY AS WOMEN'S ACTIVISM

Oral testimonies were used for several purposes: at hearings in the legislature to provide evidence as part of the feminist lobby to alter legal codes, to inform or warn audiences of the experiences of women's exploitation, and to act as a story of inspiration and heroism. Oral testimonies from survivors of rape, trafficking, prostitution, exploitation as domestic helpers or overseas workers, domestic violence, partner infidelity, sexual harassment at work, and discrimination (such as of lesbians) were performed live or published as collective biographies or as fiction.[4] Some other sensitive testimonies were given in closed-door surroundings in court or in legislative hearings for particular legislation such as the Anti-Trafficking in Persons Act of 2003. Because organizations relied on the testimonies of these women as part of the strategy involved in their advocacy work, performing oral histories as public protest was necessary. Oral testimonies were important as evidence of their personal histories of trauma, abuse, and victimization. Without these testimonies, lobbying for compensation or for a change in government laws or social attitudes would be more difficult.

In the campaign to pass the Anti-Trafficking in Persons Act of 2003, survivors of prostitution and trafficking provided their testimonies in public. For example, the survivors who joined TW-MAE-W recounted their stories to women and youth in depressed areas of the Philippines, and were featured on television and on the UNICEF website. These women also accepted speaking engagements as opportunities to present their life histories; they also testified in the United Nations Commission on Human Rights sessions on contemporary forms of human slavery. Some survivors published their stories in a book edited by Rina Jimenez David entitled *Nightmare Journeys;* eight survivors who sought refuge or help from organizations such as BATIS Center for Women, Association of Women in the Streets (BUKAL; Bukluran ng Kababaihan sa Lansangan), Center for Philippine Concerns Australia (CPCA), Kanlungan Center Foundation, Inc., United Women of Angeles City (NKAC; Nagkakaisang Kababaihan ng Angeles City), and Samaritana Transformation Ministries, Inc. (an NGO committed to spreading the gospel among Filipino women in prostitution), published their stories in an anthology entitled *Halfway through the Circle.*[5]

The members of DAWN used testimonies not only to inform the public about what happened to them, but also to dissuade many Filipino women from contemplating a job as an "entertainer" overseas. For example, Mary Joy Barcelona, a former entertainer in Japan, has given her testimony many times to conferences as far away as Africa, and gives her testimony regularly with the Peace Boat.[6] When the United Nations Special Rapporteur for Human Rights of Migrants Gabriela Rodriguez visited the Philippines in 2002, former DAWN members presented their testimonies on their illegal recruitment, detention, and trafficking.[7] Survivors' testimonies were the subject of one of DAWN's published books, and formed the basis for one of the plays performed by DAWN's theater group Teatro Akebono.[8] Testimonies of former prostitutes were also used by CATW Asia Pacific during their conferences, on radio, and in congressional hearings to lobby for the passage of the Anti-Trafficking in Persons Act of 2003.[9]

In *Moving On: Stories of DAWN Women Survivors,* the autobiographies all conformed to the double narrative.[10] All stories began with the woman's desire to escape from a life of poverty and a determination to support her family and ended with the woman's new identity as feminist advocate. In these testimonies, the women represented themselves as innocent victims who were unaware that their work would include something other than singing, dancing, or entertaining at a club. Although some women actually used their singing or dancing skills at the club, most did not. The typical work expectation was to sit and drink with customers, a situation where customers could touch their private parts. A game called jack and poy (rock, paper, scissors) was common: if women won the round, they received tips; if they lost, the men were allowed to touch the women, including their private parts).

Many of the women eventually fell in love with their Japanese boyfriend and ended up pregnant and lonely. Forced to return to the Philippines, pregnant and unmarried, these women were shunned by the very families who had benefited financially from their Japanese sojourn. Desperate, these women ended up joining DAWN. From their self-representation as "victims" the narrative here then shifted to one in which the woman rose above her victimization and transformed herself into a new person, reclaiming her dignity as a weaver, sewer, and a good mother.[11] At the same time, DAWN became their new family, as activities and social excursions brought members closer together. This in itself was something quite radical as the women began the process of rethinking the Filipino "family."

The stories all ended the same—with the women becoming advocates of DAWN, committed to making the public aware of the plight of entertainers and to dissuading other women from considering this occupation. Despite their traumas, they asserted their "new" identities not just as survivors, but also as valiant fighters. Gina in "Picking up the Pieces" ended her story by emphasizing her new militant self: "Though my past was not easy and pleasant, what's important is that I learned to fight and get up from the fall. I'm able to help others become aware of the realities of working in Japan."[12] Angel concluded her narrative with the realization that courage was essential in order to face the challenges of the future: "I know that I have to be strong and brave in facing the odds, for my sake and for the welfare of my children."[13] Women were "dutiful daughters," enduring a life of loneliness and suffering, to support families. But after they joined DAWN, they reinvented themselves as strong and courageous women.

Testimonies helped women reclaim their dignity: in these testimonies, and in the theater protests, they declared that they have been wronged, that their human rights have been violated or taken away from them. By the end of each "presentation," each woman reclaimed a new identity as feminist, human rights activist, or women's advocate, and saw herself as part of the collective identity framed by the organization to which she belonged. By reinventing themselves, these women also altered cultural constructions of the feminine from the woman as martyr to the woman as militant advocate for human rights.

Theater as Advocacy

Women's organizations were fond of using amateur theater because it fulfilled the role of therapy, allowing women to move from "victim" or "survivor" to healing; and political or social theater was an educational tool used to disseminate feminist ideas in a "user-friendly way" through entertainment. WomanHealth Director Ana Maria Nemenzo admitted that a ninety-minute play was more effective than a three-day workshop.[14] Thus, theater also acted as substitutes for women's studies courses or Basic Women's Orientation seminars.

The psychological benefits of theater performances were foremost in the minds of women's organizations. For example, DAWN launched Teatro Akebono, a theater company organized as a "form of empowerment, healing and recovery."[15] Performances were used as vehicles through which former entertainers "process their resentment and feelings of discrimination and move on confident of their ability to have normal lives as well as better interpersonal relationships. With this they can build better lives."[16] Teatro Akebono has gone on tour to Philippine schools in Manila and Philippine provinces, in Japan, and on the Peace Boat. It is through these performances that the women and children realized they had human rights.[17]

The women and children received training in acting and then were encouraged to write scripts for their performances "advocating the issues of women migrant workers and the Japanese Filipino-Children."[18] The plays of the Japanese-Filipino children went on tour to Japan as part of the children's strategic attempts to reunite with their Japanese fathers.[19] Only one play, however was written and performed by the women survivors who were members of DAWN.[20] *The Different Faces of Misty* had each character, all of them named "Misty," share her life story as former entertainer much like the testimonies in *Moving On*. The play was presented in schools in the Philippines and has toured Japan. After each presentation, the audience was invited to address specific questions to the women and Japanese-Filipino children.[21]

TW-MAE-W's counterpart to Teatro Akebono was the theater forum (the group did not appear to have a name). A play about trafficking based on a book by Chris de Stoop entitled *They Are So Sweet, Sir* with input from the life experiences of former prostitutes has been performed in the Philippines and overseas. Twenty-four women, many below eighteen years of age, presented the play in 1995 in Huariou, China, for the United Nations NGO Forum on Women (in collaboration with the San Francisco Mime Troupe) in front of the queen of Belgium and the first lady of Burundi.[22] Similar to Teatro Akebono, the performances included question time when the audience directed questions to the performing artists turned advocates.[23] Like the Misty play, *They Are So Sweet, Sir* was a musical composed of seven scenes depicting women's experiences as trafficked women fooled by agents and club owners and taken overseas. The play, however, ended with women reclaiming agency when they filed a suit against their talent managers and "vowing to continue the fight against international sex trafficking, they sing 'Women Have Their Say,' and invite the audience to sing along."[24] Soledad Perpiñan (RGS) wrote, "The performers evoked tears and laughter from the audience and at the end they received a standing ovation."[25] The play's ending—with the women confronting their oppressors—sent the message that women should fight back. The decision to seek justice was part of the process of reinventing themselves as strong women unwilling to be victimized.

Although DAWN referred to Teatro Akebono as "theatre as advocacy," TW-MAE-W's theater forum was presented as a reverse mission, where survivors as "empowered women" and "valiant survivors," "enlighten scores of people about their situation and the intricacies of the sex industry."[26] The first half of the script depicted them as duped women and the second half focused on their fight for justice; the script ended with a scene in which the women took turns kicking their former manager. This last scene also articulated the position that the managers, syndicates, and agents were the real criminals, not the prostitutes themselves. The grammar of the theater presentations like the oral testimonies reproduced the double narrative but celebrated the process in which the woman rejected her victimization and embraced a new subject position as advocate.

Theater as advocacy has empowered the actors and survivors who have been able to tell their stories and reinvent themselves as feminist advocates. Involvement in the practices of activities run by women's organizations has been crucial in their metamorphosis into new women.

LIBBY MANAOAG: INFORMANCES AND THE MAKING OF A FEMINIST ICON

The late Racquel Edralin-Tiglao, former executive director and cofounder of the WCC, disclosed in an interview, "What we have been doing and can achieve . . . [in] 10 years, PETA [the Philippine Educational Theater

Association] and their theatre can do in two years."²⁷ PETA was founded in 1967 by Cecile Guidote for the specific purpose of performing and educating audiences through the use of Filipino plays that could be performed in schools or in the local communities. It aimed to use theater to generate social change.²⁸ In 1994, PETA established the Women's Theater Program (WTP) to address the issues of gender inequality and women's oppression.²⁹ Because PETA was a professional theater group dedicated to the educational use of theater in the vernacular, with plays usually performed in Tagalog and sometimes in other Philippine languages, and performed in schools and local communities, women's organizations such as the Edralin-Tiglao's WCC could see the advantage in collaborative ventures with them.

Between 1998 and 2002, women's health organizations commissioned PETA to produce two informances. An "informance" is an educational theatrical form with dual goals: to inform and to perform.³⁰ The informances included a built-in post-performance debriefing workshop where audiences participated in a dialogue with the cast and crew. The first play, *Tumawag kay Libby Manaoag* (Call Libby Manaoag, hereafter *Tumawag*), tackled the issue of VAW. Opening night (November 25, 1998) marked the International Day of Protest Against VAW and the start of sixteen days of activism against VAW.³¹ The second play, *The Libby Manaoag Files: Ang Paghahanap sa Puertas Princessas* (The search for the doors to the princess), hereafter *Libby Manaoag Files,* handled the more controversial issue of women's health and reproductive rights. The term *puertas princessas* or "doors to the princess" is a euphemism for the vaginal canal. Both plays went on a nationwide tour, performing to a record number of audiences of around twenty-eight thousand total in forty-one shows for *Tumawag* and twenty-three thousand in twenty-five shows in seventeen towns for *Libby Manaoag Files.*³² Both plays, referred to collectively here as the *Libby Series,* were written by Liza Magtoto and directed by Maribel Legarda. *Libby Manaoag Files* also was produced in VHS video format and was distributed accompanied by a short book described as a "Discussion Guide" as a starting point for a discussion on women's reproductive rights.

The *Libby Series* was more ambitious than the previous amateur productions by survivors because local women's organizations mobilized audiences for collective action after the performance. In addition, women's organizations advertised the services they provided for victims of VAW at the end of the *Tumawag* showings. Moreover, the *Tumawag* informances were accompanied by separate workshops with community-based women's human rights action teams who were supposed to mobilize women to action to address VAW in the family context.[33] Audiences were encouraged and trained to become activists through participation in community-based methods of dealing with the issues of domestic violence. The "action team" could metamorphose into one that agitated for legal advocacy or provide direct services.[34] PETA's allies with the local women's organizations meant that the performances were combined with workshops on how women could mobilize to effect change. This was one important strategy in the women's movements' attempt to gain followers and gain a mass following nationally. In some local areas, there were immediate impacts. After the national tour of *Tumawag*, Councilor Isabelle Climaco passed a resolution in support of family violence prevention. She supported a training seminar for representatives of government agencies where a group succeeded in setting aside a budget of P6 million (approximately US$130,400 at the time) to build a family center.[35] In the Cordillera, PETA WTP facilitated the formation of Teatro Kabbule, a community-based theater group in Ifugao province. Teatro Kabbule produced a thirty-minute play depicting actual cases of abuse against women and children in their community. Similar to the *Libby Series*, workshops were held post-performance. The play was produced as part of the advocacy to raise public awareness and to lobby for the establishments of women's desks and crisis centers in the community.[36] It was important for the highlands to write their own play addressing their unique cultural situation (see Chapter 4).

The main character of both informances, Libby Manaoag, was the medium through which women could tell their stories. In *Tumawag*, Libby was a talk show host who received calls from three women who were victims of violence—Dolor, who is under the control of a strict husband; Bella, a battered wife; and Nina, a victim of sexual abuse by her stepfather. In *Libby Manaoag Files*, Libby had become a television investigative reporter on the trail of missing body parts.[37] Her detective work compelled her to listen to women's stories that tackled six issues all identified in the discussion guide: (1) the right to control one's fertility, maternal morbidity, and mortality; (2) the rights of single mothers and women in same-sex relationships; (3) adolescent sexuality; (4) the right to say no to sex; (5) male responsibility and involvement in reproductive health; and (6) the rights of prostituted women living with AIDS.[38] The play's script "stuck to the main idea—that a woman has the right to decide for her body, herself and her life."[39] In the final scene, the body parts held a press conference where the head declared, "I have a mind of my own and I have a right to choose!" and the vagina celebrated her ability to experience happiness and pleasure.[40]

Because PETA published the journals kept by members while on tour, there exists a documented resource on the debates, experiences, and reactions to the scripts and performances.[41] The *Libby Manaoag Files* went even farther than the public discussions of sex in the media discussed in Chapter 6. The play used words that some Filipinos might consider offensive, openly dramatized women's tactics for avoiding sex with their husbands, mentioned menstruation and sanitary napkins, and showed a PowerPoint presentation of various contraceptive options. Naturally, a common response from the audience was that the play was "shocking."[42] And indeed, this was perhaps the first time that the Tagalog words for private body parts such as "vagina (*puki*)" and "breast (*suso*)" were used in a public performance. Some of the audience complained about the gratuitous mention of these words and some mothers dragged their children out of the theater because they did not want them to be exposed to such "vulgar" language.[43] The mere fact that the title of the play abstained from using the word *puki*, instead using the Spanish euphemism *puerta princessa*, literally "the door to the princess," meant that PETA was aware that they were breaking taboos with regard to language in the play itself, but they refrained from advertising this openly in the play's title. The topic of abortion was completely avoided.

The *Libby Series* succeeded in proposing alternative role models for women. A year after the national tour of *Tumawag* ended, the PETA office continued to receive calls from women looking for "Libby Manaoag." At first, PETA members were puzzled and frustrated by these continuous intrusions in which they had to explain to women callers that Libby was merely a fictional character who did not exist in real life. But the incidents gave Director Maribel Legarda an idea: "Why don't we develop a woman icon?"[44] When women's organizations commissioned another informance, this time about reproductive rights, Legarda thought that it might be good to use the same character but promote her from a radio talk show announcer to a television investigative reporter. There are plans for a third sequel where Libby would be reinvented as a politician—duplicating in fiction the real-life transformation of television celebrities Nikki Coseteng, Loren Legarda, and Risa Hontiveros-Baraquiel into national politicians.

Even members of the audience offered themselves as potential role models. In Leyte, a lower-class woman from the audience approached the microphone and asked the actors why Bella, the battered wife in *Tumawag,* could not leave her husband—contrasting the script with her own response, in which she left her husband. She asked the actors, "Why could she not escape from her situation? I've done better than her. Me, that was my story, but I was able to escape. I am now a community leader here." According to C. B. Garrucho, the audience responded with applause.[45] The audience response could be read as approval of the new role model of the empowered woman and a rejection of the character Bella, who represented the woman as martyr. Through her own efforts, this woman from the poorer classes extricated herself from the position of domestic violence victim to become a community leader.

At the end of the *Libby Manaoag Files,* the fictional character Libby Manaoag confronted the audience with a revelation: "And in this history of women who were strong, principled, and loving, I discovered this woman in them and in myself. I am proud of this woman. But there are also women who have been separated from their being (or self) and cannot make decisions about their own lives, what can we do for these women?" (my translation from Tagalog original).[46]

Libby's farewell address could be read as an open invitation to join the women's movements. Her message articulated the activist strategy of inspiring women with the knowledge that they were capable of empowering themselves on their own. But it also appealed to those empowered women to extend a helping hand to come to the aid of those women less able to help themselves.

Songs

"Sabon" (Soap) a song performed by GABRIELA's performing group *Sining Lila,* based on a poem by Joi Barrios, captured the feminist critique of social constructions of the Filipino woman with wit and humor.[47] It parodied the commercials of the late 1960s and 1970s. Advertisers for the laundry soap Tide guaranteed a whiter wash, even without bleaching in the sun, and a wonderful odor, while Lux bathing soap advertisements displayed a happy man, expressing his delight that his girlfriend's skin was nice to touch after regular use of the product. By equating women's position to a soap inside a box, the lyrics called attention to women's confinement to established roles—here described as either "sublime helpers," such as maids or domestic helpers, or "a decorative object," existing only to please or serve men. At the end of the song, the woman had begun the task of dismantling the box.

"Soap"
Refrain:
    On television the women are in boxes, in boxes like bars of
soap
Laundry soap or beauty soap, women are always heroines.

Stanza 1:
    If it is beauty soap, there is always envy because it enhances
a soft skin; if it is laundry soap, it is fun to pulverize because if
you expose it to the sun it will whiten the clothes.
Refrain

Stanza 2:
    Before our commercial ends, the man gives thanks
The skin of his girlfriend is wonderful to caress
The laundry of the Mrs. smells so good.
Refrain

Stanza 3:
    Here is a question for the heroine who is always in the box.
Doesn't she have dreams or other ambitions? Ultimately only
two positions remain: sublime helper (maid or domestic helper), or decorative object. The soap is melting, the heroine leaves
television in order to face her new ambition: to soap, scrub, and
squeeze dry what had put her in the box! (translation mine)[48]

A lighthearted song with a serious message, "Soap" concluded with
the woman's rebirth (the soap melting) as strong and feisty, optimistic,
confident, and ready to face new challenges. By locating current female
stereotypes in the make-believe world of television, the song called attention to the constructed nature of these women's roles, moored only
in fantasies. Precisely because these images of women were not real, it
was possible to alter them. As the soap melted, the wax could now be
remolded into a different type of woman—one capable of confronting
her oppressors. Songs such as "Soap" made up part of the repertoire
of feminist practices sung during demonstrations, rituals, or even social
gatherings of women's organizations. Much like the genre of songs of
political protest, they became part of the popular culture and practice of
feminist activism. Lyrics of the songs such as "Soap" critiqued cultural
stereotypes of women and offered alternative role models.

Songs, similar to theater as advocacy (many of which were musicals anyway), were an effective way of popularizing feminist ideas. Although radio and television talk shows and theater could explore the entire gamut of issues of women's advocacy, songs were a more limited medium because they were only three to five minutes long. A number of songs grappled with the issues faced by various sectors and roles of women. But a good number of the more popular ones were those preoccupied with "Maria," the generic name for every Filipina. *Sining Lila,* for example, had four songs in their repertoire with "Maria" in the title—all concerned with constructions of the feminine.[49] Songs therefore, also were sites for the women's movements discourses on the Filipino woman. It is this group of songs with which I am most concerned here.

The lyrics of feminist songs regularly appeared in GABRIELA and *Chaneg*'s newsletters, the GABRIELA women's history book, and the transnational feminist theological journal *In God's Image. Kali* (the journal of the Cordillera women), published a special issue that had the lyrics of a group of feminist songs in English, Filipino, and Ilocano.[50] This collection of Filipino feminist songs compiled for women of the Cordillera was probably one strategic move to bring Cordillera activists to the fold of the mainstream national women's movements. Women's organizations that had a cultural arm such as GABRIELA's *Sining Lila* performed feminist songs during demonstrations, rallies, strikes, and rituals, including workshops and special events. At one level, these songs could also be read as women's testimonies. In the musical plays produced by DAWN and TW-MAE-W, each major character sang about her past life. In the *Libby Manaoag Files,* the story of the prostitute with AIDS was told in the form of an aria. The play itself ended with a song about the woman's right to choose her destiny.[51] Some songs such as "Hindi kailangan magtiis" (There is no need to endure; see Chapter 6) that were associated with campaigns by particular women's organizations were played in lieu of commercials at radio programs such as *XYZone.*[52]

A number of songs critiqued the dominant narrative that defined women as tied to the domestic sphere, seen fit only for the kitchen or the bedroom or as toys that could be discarded after use.[53] In keeping with the women's movements' consistent representation of the Filipino woman in a double narrative, the image of the objectified and oppressed domesticated woman was juxtaposed with the alternative role models. In the song "Maria," the role models proposed were Lorena (referring to Lorena Barros), Gabriela (referring to Gabriela Silang), and Tandang Sora (referring to a heroine of the Philippine revolution against Spain).[54] This song was almost an exact replica of the song "Babae Ka" (You are a woman) discussed in the introduction that juxtaposed the enduring nineteenth-century narratives of the Filipino woman exemplified by Maria Clara, Juli, and Sisa, with Gabriela, Teresa Magbanua, Tandang Sora, and the three martial law activists who were killed: Lorena Barros, Lisa Balando, and Liliosa Hilao.[55] In the lyrics, women were told to reject traditional stereotypes. The song "Maria," composed by Kalantog, assured women that they were not pulled from the rib as the pulpit (a metaphor for the Church) claimed, and prefigured the emergence of a "*bagong* Maria" or a "new Maria" who was not tied to the home and who was free to participate in political citizenship.[56]

The songs were obvious feminist propaganda accentuating the serious project of fashioning women into activists. Many of the songs carried the same theme: women should "awake," "rise up," "assert their rights," "break their chains," "move forward," and "fight for your rights."[57] *Inang Laya*'s song "Atsay ng Mundo" (Maid of the world) ended with the question, "When will you fight? When will you be free? When?"[58] The song "March of Women" advised women to arise, unite, and support the women's movement.[59] The song "Hindi Kailangan Magtiis" (There is no need to endure) told women they did not have to resign themselves to a life of suffering.[60]

Songs were therefore an obvious and popular medium used by activists to convey their discourses about the Filipino woman. Lyrics set to catchy tunes or jingles could function simultaneously as entertainment, popular protest, and feminist education. Focusing on the plight of Maria's past, present, and future, they were powerful tools with which to critique stereotypes while proposing an alternative "new Maria"; in fact, one of the songs is entitled "The New Maria." A sense of identity with a sisterhood emerged during the singing, an action that for many might be the first step in their development as an activist.

Demonstrations

When I participated in GABRIELA's demonstration held in August 2003, in support of the Makati Shoemart strike against the contractualization of labor by salespersons on temporary job contracts, the strikers invited me to stand atop a jeepney and denounce President Gloria Macapagal Arroyo as a liar. I noticed various activists took turns doing this, including a group of Belgians who joined GABRIELA as part of their overseas exposure experience. It was a ritual, a rite of passage for one's metamorphosis into an activist. A fairly intimidating experience considering the jeepney faced a group of armed riot police, the act required a militant face. As Mary John Mananzan (OSB) explained to me in an interview, one cannot protest in the streets and assume a "demure" or "sweet" personality asking policemen to "please" give them a space in the streets. One had to be feisty (*mataray*).[61] Some women activists executed daring acts, such as when GABRIELA Deputy Director Emmi de Jesus climbed over the wall into the American Embassy to put up an anti-Gulf War poster inside their grounds.[62]

Demonstrations required women to reinvent themselves using deportment (particularly the clenched fist raised in the air), props (banners and placards for example, dress will be discussed below), and angry chanting or speeches. Because a demonstration was by definition a protest action, participants were required to articulate their demands boldly and loudly. For instance, participants used microphones and loudspeakers. A united front of angry but valiant women was necessary to confront the "oppressors." With clenched fists raised above their heads, they addressed the public space. Participation in demonstrations was an activity that transformed women into strong fighters—the polar opposite of the woman who silently endured her fate.

Demonstrations enabled women's organizations to increase their supporters, extending the membership from the "survivors" to the "sympathizers." During the campaign for the Anti-Trafficking in Persons Act of 2003, for example, CATW-AP invited the women of the elite to join their ranks. Nicknamed "the perfumed ladies" and "bejeweled and beautiful," they were a rare example of elite women's participation in feminist activism since the 1980s.[63]

But out in the streets facing possible violence and riot police, activists bonded together. Although women's movements in the Philippines were divided over almost every issue, participation in particular demonstrations indicated agreement on specific issues across a wide network of organizations. The need to present a mass following—a requirement for the success of a rally—meant that in these particular events women's organizations strived to present a united front. Feminist practices, demonstrations, and rallies communicated, at least at that moment, a feminist identity among participants, while compelling activists to expand their network of followers needed at the barricades. In addition, participation in a demonstration indicated one's commitment to the activist cause. Joining a demonstration was a practice that confirmed that one was a member of the women's movements and affirmed one's identity as an activist.

Precisely because founders of women's organizations were once political activists against Marcos, they were adept at using the power of demonstrations and the picket line as an effective way to claim public space in which to advertise and negotiate their terms. Demonstrations featured highly in the reportage of almost all newsletters published by the organizations discussed in this book. Although demonstrations were used primarily to lobby for political and social change, I want to focus here on the use of demonstrations as feminist practice in fashioning women into militant activists using observations from three demonstrations. All three of these demonstrations were GABRIELA initiatives.

DEMONSTRATION 1: THE "COMFORT WOMEN" PROTEST IN FRONT OF THE JAPANESE EMBASSY

On the morning of Memorial Day, August 14, 2003, Lila-Pilipina held a protest in front of the Japanese Embassy on Roxas Boulevard. A group of fifteen to twenty "comfort women" arrived, accompanied by their children, Lila-Pilipina Director Rechilda Extremedura, and a young GABRIELA representative. They displayed the lilac and red banner advertising their organization, and carried placards with English slogans demanding justice for the "comfort women." Standing on the steps at the entrance with their backs to the embassy, they faced the street where a group of photographers and journalists gathered to report the event. After a marker engraved with the names of members who had passed away was unveiled, speeches were given. After the speeches, women showed their placards, raised their clenched fists in the air, and chanted slogans demanding justice.

The climax of the protest was a short skit written and performed by the *lolas* of Lila-Pilipina. It was composed of only two scenes: one was a dance performance and the other was a mime. In the first scene, six *lolas* dressed in national costume (*baro't saya*) performed a rural folk dance. The second scene showed three *lolas* attacked by Japanese soldiers. It was during this dramatic moment, in which the elderly women were pushed until they fell on the hot, dirty sidewalk, that the skit abruptly ended. Afterwards the women tied black ribbons with the words "Justice Now" around the entrance of the Japanese Embassy and boarded the jeepneys that took them to a picnic at Luneta Park.

DEMONSTRATION NO. 2: GABRIELA AGAINST THE EXPANDED
VALUE ADDED TAX

On January 19, 2005, GABRIELA organized a small protest at the entrance of the legislative building (Batasan) of the house of representatives to protest the rise in the expanded value added tax (EVAT), from 10 percent to 12 percent. The small crowd of around forty to fifty people carried placards and banners communicating their protest in English and Tagalog. Jomes Salvador, the director general of Gabriela-Youth, acted as emcee of the proceedings, leading the crowd as they chanted their protests in anger: (Tutulan! Labanan! Ibasura! "Go ahead! Fight! Junk!"). Salvador introduced the guest speaker, Gabriela Women's Party Congresswoman Liza Largoza Maza, who delivered a short speech discussing the effects of the rise in tax on the food prices and reminded everyone that real minimum wages remained locked at P250.00 (around US$4.50 at the time) per day. Finally, Salvador led the protesters in cries demanding the ouster of President Gloria Macapagal Arroyo. The chants included, "Remove Gloria. It is too much. The hardship is too much!"[64]

DEMONSTRATION NO 3: SHOEMART STRIKE

The demonstration called "Lugawan sa Shoemart" (Congee at Shoemart, referring to the rice porridge with chicken, ginger, and green onions dish served to the participants) was an all-night vigil held on July 22, 2003, to support strikers, who had already been on strike for three months and were against the department store's policy of hiring salesgirls on six-month contracts. The evening program included a performance of a song and dance by GABRIELA's *Sining Lila* (lyrics set to a popular song, "Spaghetti," about the plight of women under the current Macapagal Arroyo administration with appropriate and funny choreography), and speeches by representatives of GABRIELA and other organizations. Finally, the audience was invited to come up to the microphone and declare their individual support. A coterie of armed police officers kept a close watch of the proceedings while a group of young Belgians in their twenties brought sleeping mats, intending to camp out all night with the strikers as a sign of solidarity.

❀ ❀ ❀

All of the demonstrations were typical of GABRIELA-style protests where a chorus of angry women chanted slogans and delivered speeches in combination with some form of entertainment (a skit, or a song and dance). But there was no mistaking the angry tone, the confronting stance, and the militant tenor required of each participant in each demonstration, particularly in Demonstrations 1 and 2. The *lolas* of Lila-Pilipina all carried placards in English, although they did not speak the language, and raised their fists in the air at the appropriate moment. Facing the reporters and photographers, they showed that they were tough. The *lolas* themselves never appeared weak, despite their frail appearance.

The *Lila-Pilipina* skit also reproduced survivors' memories, clearly divided into "good times" and "bad times" typical of oral histories. Before the war, as they remembered it, their lives had been happy and idyllic. The folk dancing, including the costumes of traditional Filipino dress, located them in a rural Philippines undisturbed by modernity.[65] The "bad times" were the memories of rapes, violence, and incarceration during the Japanese occupation. Since demonstrations per se were not the ideal sites for oral testimonies, they used a short five-minute skit. The short scene of the "Japanese soldiers" pushing the frail elderly women onto the hard, hot, dirty sidewalk could not but provoke empathy from the spectators. The "double narrative" was reproduced in the stark contrast between the reenacted victimization of innocent women and the backdrop of *lolas* bearing placards and chanting loudly for justice holding clenched fists above their heads. The Shoemart strike was a classic example of the rites of passage in the making of a militant activist as each "new" supporter was invited to denounce the president over the microphone in front of armed police. Coupled with less intimidating segments such as the dance to the "Spaghetti" song, audiences could choose to participate in different ways. Those who embraced the offer to reinvent themselves as militant personas by accepting the invitation to deliver their message of support publicly and loudly over the microphone marked their initiation as advocates and potential leaders.

The EVAT demonstration was a knee-jerk response to current events with GABRIELA radio show *Babae Ka*'s coanchor Congresswoman Liza Maza explaining the impact of the issue and inviting audiences to organize protests against the increase and to write their politicians registering their complaints against the proposed rise.[66] In this sense, it was the direct opposite of Demonstration 1 by Lila-Pilipina members that aimed to alter official histories and collective memories. But there was no mistaking the similar deportment and tenor of both. In one sense, the physical stance was a reflection of the intrinsic requirement of participants at demonstrations as a whole. While women's studies workshops gave women a feminist perspective, demonstrations allowed them to be practicing activists.

I first met Jomes Salvador in 2003 when I interviewed her as head of GABRIELA-Youth. She was then a student at the University of the Philippines. By the 2005 EVAT strike, she had bloomed into a GABRIELA full-time activist delivering speeches along with Congresswoman Liza Maza. I teased her that the next time we would meet it would be to interview her as a GABRIELA Women's Party congresswoman, and she responded with "not yet." Demonstrations, therefore, groomed activists into becoming future leaders of the organization and perhaps future politicians. After all, not so long ago Liza Maza was doing exactly the same thing Jomes Salvador was doing in the street demonstrations.[67] The presence of GABRIELA Congresswoman Maza at the demonstration site literally a stone's throw outside her office also affirmed the alliances between political activists and the few feminist politicians in office.

Demonstrations also were crucial in developing solidarity or unity in the women's movements. During particular demonstrations, such as in support of the Anti-Trafficking in Persons Act of 2003 or against the Gulf War, the solidarity of the sisterhood was publicly, if temporarily, visible. This was most evident in the annual IWWD marches.

Dress and Feminist Identity

Women activists exploited the semiotic potential of dress. Dress as uniform allowed women activists to present a façade of unity. By dressing in a particular way, individuals identified with the rest of the members of their particular women's organization. It was not merely a coincidence that one women's organization called itself Kilos Kabaro (translated as "Act Sister"; it literally means those of us who wear the same dress will act) and that activists referred to other women as *kabaro* (we who wear the same dress). Two types of dress as costume were favorites—national dress in the form of the *baro't saya* of the nineteenth century or the *terno* and *pañuelo* of the 1920s, and the Western T-shirt emblazoned with the insignia or slogan of a particular women's organization. Although these types of dress were visually opposite, since Western dress was normally the Other of national dress, in practice, both types of clothing were used interchangeably.[68] Cordillera women preferred to wear indigenous dress during protests in a visual display of difference from their Christian sisters, while activists located overseas were keen to wear national dress to underscore their identities as Filipinas. The feminist nuns were not above the strategic use of dress. Becoming political activists right about the time of Vatican II encouraged them to discard the habit and wimple, but they were reluctant to dispense with an emblem that held symbolic capital.

Instead of the modern *terno* (which was without *pañuelo*) popularized by former First Lady Imelda Marcos during the martial law regime of 1972–1986, activists were partial to an earlier version of it—the *terno* and *pañuelo* style of the 1920s and 1930s or the *baro't saya* fashion of the nineteenth century. WMC's Anna Leah Sarabia chose to revive what she called the *baro't saya* as homage to the suffragists who were rarely seen without this form of dress (technically, they wore the *terno* and *pañuelo*).[69] In the end, Sarabia succeeded in popularizing not one but two types of dress: the *terno* and *pañuelo* of the 1920s style worn by the suffragists and the *baro't saya* style of the late nineteenth century albeit with smaller sleeves. The main difference between the two types of clothing was that in the *baro't saya* the blouse was separate from the skirt and usually made of a diaphanous material worn above a shirt, while in the *terno* they were joined and often of the same material. Although the modern *terno* from the 1950s and 1960s onwards was without a *pañuelo,* contemporary women activists restored the *pañuelo* back to the *terno* almost fifty years after it had been discarded.

As producer of *Womanwatch,* Sarabia had the opportunity to fashion activist dress. The *baro't saya* became the signature attire of *Womanwatch* host Nikki Coseteng. The two-part documentary "From Priestess to President: The Story of Women's Struggle in the Philippines" had the two hosts C. B. Garrucho and Lily Lim wearing 1920s-style *terno* and *pañuelo.* This revived versions of both types of dress had slightly smaller tubular sleeves than the original nineteenth century and 1920s versions. By circa 2000, this type of national dress had become fashionable, even among upper-class women who were not feminists or activists. From this angle, the wearing of the 1920s-style dress was an attempt by feminists to connect the women's movement to the struggle for suffrage in the early twentieth century. Dress linked Filipina feminists from the first wave to the present, showing, at least visibly, an imagined unity of the sisterhood across time. It also reinforced the activists' sense of history.

The *baro't saya* also became the uniform for "comfort women" activists. In my description of the Lila-Pilipina demonstration above, I noted that the *lolas* in Scene 1 of the skit wore *baro't saya* (those who played male roles wore pants and male rural peasant clothing). According to Extremedura, the *baro't saya* reminded the *lolas* of the prewar days, when this attire was the fashion in the rural areas, that remained idyllic in their memories as a time of innocence. Extremadura also noted that this costume was the preferred dress chosen by the *lolas* for public events, including the presentation of oral testimonies to Japanese lawyers in their advocacy to seek an apology and compensation from the Japanese government.[70] When I visited the office of Lolas Kampanyeras, another organization of former Filipino "comfort women," I noticed that the photographs that adorned the walls of the sitting room were of members of the organization attired in *baro't saya*. The organization's leader Nelia Sancho confirmed in an interview that *baro't saya* was their preferred mode of dress.[71] Thus, one could argue that the *baro't saya* was intrinsic to the self-representation of the former "comfort women" who wore this attire whenever possible as their "uniform."

The Western T-shirt with its ability to send written messages and reproductions of paintings and photographs, and the ease in which it could be mass-produced, not to mention that it was more comfortable to wear in the Philippine climate especially during demonstrations, made it a popular choice of attire for women activists. Some women's organizations such as GABRIELA and its affiliates had a special T-shirt designed as a uniform that could be worn during demonstrations so participants could express their identity with that organization. When I arrived early at the setting of the Shoemart strike, the strikers welcomed me to the picket line because I wore the GABRIELA T-shirt and jeans. A T-shirt bearing the name of an organization or just an ordinary T-shirt with blue jeans became the regular uniform for women activists, who were seldom seen in any other attire. This quotidian garb linked them to the lower classes they claimed to represent, as well as to women activists all over the world.

Dress was also used as a strategy for intimidation to pressure legislators into discussing the Anti-Trafficking in Persons Act of 2003 before it was passed into law. CATW members and their allies dressed in white and occupied the visitor's gallery of the senate session scheduled to discuss the proposed legislation, becoming a sea of white confronting the legislators.[72] Survivors of trafficking joined demonstrations in support of the Anti-Trafficking in Persons Act of 2003 attired in black with their faces painted in white such as Kabuki artists in order to allow for anonymity.[73] GABRIELA's Circle of Friends, the organization founded to support former victims of sexual abuse and sexual harassment, designed a special T-shirt that members wore during the trials against the perpetuators. The intended effect was an intimidating presence directed at the defendant and visual evidence of moral support for the victim.

IN AND OUT OF THE HABIT

The reforms of the post-Vatican era included radical alterations to religious dress in the 1960s and 1970s. The majority of women in the noncloistered orders were asked to exchange religious habits for secular fashions. The habit was meant to obliterate individual identities because it prioritized the collective identity and commitment to the Roman Catholic Church.[74] Filipino nuns were asked to discard their habits so they would blend more easily with the community and be exempted from special privileges such as seats on full buses, for example.[75] In the Philippines, because religious persons were highly respected, nuns interviewed claimed that the habit gave them "symbolic capital."[76]

The initiative to dispense with the habit and wimple raised interesting dilemmas for Filipino nuns at a time when they were political activists against a repressive regime. Determined to continue their political activism and aware that they had some advantages over Marcos—their "moral power" and credibility as defenders of social justice—the nuns chose to wear their habits as a "costume" during demonstrations and rallies. Gertrude Borres of the Religious of the Assumption reflected on how the habits made their protests more effective:

> So that was the thing, in the 70s members of the church we
> also went through a stage . . . the church renewal after Vatican
> II and so one of the things was "Go Lay," meaning that the
> church was such a strong power so you should already try to
> be less visible in your thing, but mix with the people. Just dress
> the way they do so that when you take a bus, people will not
> offer you a chair, you know that kind of thing. But the thing
> was, at the same time that this was happening, on the other
> hand, when there were mass demonstrations everyone was
> there in their full gear, seminarians in their *sutanas* (laughter),
> sisters in their habits [laughter], because then you had to be
> visible, you had to dress as religious.[77]

The nuns' habit and wimple advertised the moral power and the legitimacy of the wearer. The habit proved to be useful attire for political activism. According to Mariani Dimaranan (SFIC), a priest told her when she was president of TFD, "If you were not a nun with a veil, the TFD would no longer be around."[78] Nuns confessed to smuggling documentation on the plight of political prisoners under their habits when visiting prisoners.[79]

Nuns were acutely aware of the power of religious dress in the Philippines; some religious orders and individual nuns have been flexible about the use of the habit and wimple. Soledad Perpiñan (RGS) worked with prostitutes so wearing the habit to the various bars where prostitutes worked would only elicit hostility from bar owners who feared that the presence of a nun at a bar would scare customers. Perpiñan did not wear the habit when she visited the bars, but when she represented the TW-MAE-W she wore the habit, sometimes with the veil, sometimes without.[80] Mary John Mananzan (OSB) wore the habit in the Philippines but not on her overseas sojourns. She confessed in an interview that it was more practical to travel in lay clothes because it was not possible to lie down in the departure lounge of an airport wearing the habit and wimple. On the other hand, she was forthcoming in admitting that the habit was "symbolic capital" in the Philippines where religious persons were respected.[81] If she appeared on television criticizing the government, she wore her habit and wimple. In the People Power 1 "revolution" that toppled the Marcos regime, the nuns were conspicuous in their habits and wimple, linking arms in the front lines protecting the lay people from the armed soldiers and armored personnel carriers sent to attack the defenseless public. In this case, the nuns faced the macho military; armed only with rosaries and their moral power, they were critical in the effort to persuade the soldiers not to fire a single shot. Even after the restoration of democratic institutions in 1986, Filipino nuns remained strategic about the habit, using it when they needed to present the collective identity of the Catholic Church and discarding it when it became more effective to assume personal identities as leaders in women's movements.

Dress was not merely an accessory in the struggle for social transformation. Activists were strategic in their choice of clothing. But since dress was a visible expression of particular identities, the adoption of uniform dress by organizations had the effect of displaying, at least visually, an identity and unity in feminist movements, or at least within their organization.

Rituals

On August 23, 2003, GABRIELA Circle of Friends, an organization devoted to women survivors of rape and domestic violence, was officially launched. I had the great fortune to be invited to join the half-day schedule of activities that marked the birth of the group. The event was hosted by GABRIELA and held in their headquarters in Quezon City.

The workshop began with the performance by *Sining Lila* (GABRIELA's cultural group) in which the entire group, about thirty to thirty-five people, rose and joined in the singing and dancing. After the show, a GABRIELA representative delivered a short speech of welcome. Then everyone was divided into small groups with the aim of drafting an agenda for the new organization. After about thirty minutes, psychologist Obeth Manthres chaired a general discussion that collated the proposals of each small group. During the discussion time, two women delivered oral testimonies. They told the audience that they were once domestic violence victims who saw themselves as "quiet" and "shy," but who were transformed into confident members of GABRIELA. One of them obtained a permanent full-time job working for GABRIELA. The other one gratefully acknowledged GABRIELA's role in her transformation from shy victim to confident activist. Although these women could not hold back their tears during the presentation of their oral testimonies, they were role models for the rest of the group. After these moving speeches, everyone supported Manthres' proposal that members appear at the court trials to support the victims. A roster was tacked to the wall with the dates of court hearings and everyone was encouraged to commit to attending at least one of them by signing on the sheet. The formal section of the day ended once everyone agreed to a regular monthly meeting on the twenty-seventh of each month.

The day ended with a touching ritual. Every participant was required to write a message to GABRIELA Circle of Friends on a small piece of paper. Some instrumental music was played in a small cassette player and a candle was placed at the center of the room. One by one, participants read their personal messages aloud and attached the pieces of paper to a long string. The entire group began to form a big circle, each holding part of the "string of messages." When the big circle was formed, the ritual ended.

The circle of women connected by one piece of string symbolized the elusive dream of a united sisterhood bonded by the desire to fulfill feminist agendas. It was a fitting culmination of the day's proceedings. Former victims gathered together to form an organization that would support their agenda for punishing the men who had hurt them. They heard oral testimonies of survivors who have become GABRIELA activists and who were held up as new role models for members of the audience. By the end of the afternoon, they had agreed on a platform of action where each participant committed to a particular task. The string of messages held together by members was not just a literal representation of their organization's name (GABRIELA Circle of Friends), but also gave them a clear identity and unity as an activist group.

This chapter focused on practices of the women's movement—oral testimonies, theater as advocacy, demonstrations, and rituals—as important rites of passage in the process of becoming an activist. The practices discussed here initiated ordinary women into the membership of a women's organization; these initiations brought them into the fold of the women's movements. Practices also trained women to become militant activists, a metaphorical army of feminist revolutionaries. They participated in the various demonstrations and rallies organized by specific women's organizations. Here, they learned how to give speeches, carry placards, raise clenched fists in the air, and shout slogans. From an intellectual awakening received from the Basic Women's Orientation Seminars, they received a new deportment, new dress, and new personas. Whether they were once victims or survivors, or merely ordinary women who have been affected by the women's studies courses "on the air," on the stage, in the streets, or in special rituals, these new followers become the mass followers of the burgeoning women's movements.

Locating Women

8

Women's Movements in Transnational Spaces

Locating Women's Movements

Philippine women's movements must be located in the international arena and international networking of feminists everywhere. Filipino organizations since the 1980s argued that activism must be global.[1] They participated in the international women's movements (through international conferences or in meetings with the United Nations) and were proactive in hosting international conferences in the Philippines. Two important priority feminist issues—trafficking and migration—required networking or lobbying across national boundaries. Activists lobbied several governments—Greece, Hong Kong, Italy, Singapore, Spain, and the United States, and countries in the Middle East, to name a few— and international organizations such as the United Nations. Women's organizations relied on a huge international network in their advocacy work and engaged with the world as transnational subjects.

This chapter will focus on the transnational nature of the women's movements. The term "transnational" is understood to mean the movement of people, ideas, technologies, and institutions across national boundaries.[2] The recently published *Palgrave Dictionary of Transnational History* declares that authors on a long list are interested in "links and flows, and want to track people, ideas, products, processes and patterns that operate over, across, through, beyond, above, under, or in-between polities and societies."[3] Ellen Carol DuBois, contributing to that peculiar dictionary in an entry on women's movements, points out, "the intellectual content of women's studies is decidedly transnational," and indeed, because Asian feminist theories developed partly as a rethinking of the applicability of Western feminism in local contexts, it might be possible to argue that Asian feminisms were transnationally produced (Ian Tyrrell, for example, has argued that the American nation-state was transnationally produced).[4] In this book, I use the term "transnational" to refer to this movement of ideas about women's status and rights across national borders, as well as the across-the-border organizing between women activists from different countries.

I argue that some activists' decisions to locate themselves in the interstices has proved to be an effective strategy. Straddling national borders allows them to have a continuing dialogue with feminists of all color, injecting Philippine perspectives into international women's movements, and in so doing affecting international feminist debates and international activism on behalf of all women. Transnational activism also has an impact on the perspectives of Filipina activists who developed an international outlook. Although Philippine-based organizations are outward looking—analyzing the global context that affected the Filipina worker at home (for example, the EPZs), and abroad (as OCWs), those organizations based overseas look towards home, since helping the Filipina migrant abroad required understanding the roots of her socialization. Maitet Ledesma, director of *Pinay sa Holland* (a GABRIELA affiliate based in the Netherlands) explained to me in an interview that in order to become effective activists on behalf of Filipina migrants for marriage in the Netherlands, members had to first attend Basic Women's Orientation seminars that deconstructed the history and status of women in the Philippines.[5] Thus, women activists on opposite ends of the world looked towards each other, and discussed "the woman question" in a special transnational space.

This transnational orientation inspired them to think globally. CATW-AP and TW-MAE-W both aimed for "a world without prostitution" or "an end to prostitution and trafficking," while Lila-Pilipina hoped to help bring about "a world without war."[6] TW-MAE-W staked the entire developing world as their territory, while CATW-AP claimed the Asia-Pacific as their space, with the former having United Nations consultative status and the latter being active in the United Nations conferences in the area of trafficking in women. GABRIELA conceived of hosting a biannual Women's International Solidarity Affair (WISAP) because "the issues that beset people have a global dimension, and the specific concerns of women are worldwide phenomena. Invariably, women are patriotic and feminists must also be internationalists."[7] One could argue that these nuns and laywomen activists refused to be confined by the geographical borders of the nation-state. As feminist nun Amelia Vasquez (RSCJ) told me in an interview, "the world should set our agenda."[8] When women's organizations marched on IWWD, they expressed in symbolic terms their wish, no matter how elusive, for a global sisterhood.

The Filipino Catholic Nun as Transnational Feminist

The nuns' unique location in the interstices—as transnational feminists who moved constantly from the local to the international—was what made them effective activists in the women's movement. This extraordinary group lived in and out of the convent, part-time with the poor and part-time with their congregation. As members of international religious congregations, these nuns were plugged into the global networks of the "mother house," able to access the latest developments in Western feminist theology, and theology from the developing world. Informed by the local knowledge of their mission work in the Philippines, they became spokespersons for Filipina activism abroad as representative of transnational women's organizations, some of which they founded themselves, speaking for Filipina women around the world. Their extraordinary position straddling several spaces made them perfect conduits translating Western feminism for the Philippine context while injecting a Filipino perspective to feminist debates overseas. Their status as religious persons further legitimized their radical agendas, including their critique of patriarchy in the Catholic Church. The Church is still regarded as the most powerful obstacle to women's movements. Since Filipino feminist theorizing inevitably confronted cultural constructions of the feminine imposed by the Catholic Church since the sixteenth century, audiences were more likely to accept a challenge to this dominant narrative if the activist was a Catholic nun.

Nuns were able to be proactive in the multiple tasks of dismantling grand narratives precisely because of their ambiguous position unmoored in space and place. From their regular sojourns overseas, they imbibed the theories of Western feminist theology, but these theories were tempered by their analysis of poor women's experiences based on their work and life with the lower classes in the city and the provinces. Constantly moving here, there, and everywhere—from their mission work with the urban poor or in the provinces, to the convent in Metro-Manila and the "mother houses" abroad—these nuns connected with the *barangay,* the village, the city, and the metropole.

The nuns' continuous movements affected their subjectivities as feminist women: a peripatetic lifestyle gave them multiple perspectives and the credentials to speak for and about the many aspects of the Filipina postcolonial condition. They had local knowledge, Western knowledge, and global links—assets they mined to create a unique eclectic perspective to their activism. For example, they had the vocabulary of Western feminist theology from which to articulate the many experiences of the women of the lower classes. Distinct from the other middle-class laywomen leaders of the women's movements who may have been empathetic to the plight of the poor but did not live with them, the nuns' choice to live with the poor part of the time earned them the credentials to speak for Filipinas, while the overseas networks gave them opportunities to have their voices heard internationally. In sum, their shifting subject positions were what made them effective political activists.

Filipino feminist nuns traveled between nation-states as advocates of the international project of women's activism in the late twentieth century. Members of EATWOT, they participated in the project of putting a Southern perspective to Eurocentric theological discussions. They were founding members of the journal *In God's Image,* EATWOT's feminist mouthpiece, where they published articles on practicing feminist theology in a developing world context. In fact, nuns staked the entire developing world or Asia-Pacific as their home territory. For example, the Institute of Women's Studies and the Institute of Formation and Religious Studies looked at the developing world as their student body; Soledad Perpiñan's (RGS) women's organization was called the Third World Movement Against the Exploitation of Women, or TW-MAE-W. St. Scholastica's Institute of Women's Studies published an *Asia Pacific* journal, ran a dormitory for international visiting scholars, and hosted international conferences.

But the lifestyle that included living part-time with the poor also involved continuing overseas travel, travel that often was linked to the organizations the nuns founded in the 1970s and 1980s. It was difficult for me to arrange interviews with the nuns because they were great world travelers and have been since the 1970s. Vasquez told me (facetiously) that Fabella's ambition was to set up a travel agency when she retired because she loved the traveling associated with her mission work.[9] When

Mananzan was elected prioress of her congregation in 2004, the Institute of Women's Studies staff joked that for the first time the nun would experience being "grounded" from traveling abroad (she has been to forty-five countries). In my first interview with Perpiñan she relished giving me an account of her many travels on behalf of her organization.[10]

Perhaps precisely because the nuns quite literally lived in international or transnational "homes," the women's organizations they chose to lead had transnational bases. In 1998, Mananzan was elected national chairperson of GABRIELA, a position she still holds as of the present writing in 2010. Perpiñan received some funding from Europe and private individuals.[11] Due to its prominence, TW-MAE-W was given consultative status in the United Nations Economic and Social Council in 1985.[12] This nun has drafted statements for the Commission on the Status of Women for the United Nations.[13] Here was one clear example where Filipino women had an impact on United Nations' policies governing women, particularly with regard to prostitution and trafficking.

This location in the interstices enabled them to have an impact on the women's movements—not just in the Philippines, but also in the very transnational spaces they inhabited. Nuns founded feminist organizations with transnational moorings and a transnational perspective, seeking to foster feminist identities cross-culturally and across nation-states. In particular, they saw their role as articulating the Filipino "woman question" in a dialogue with the North and the South. But their positions in transnational organizations, for instance in the United Nations, meant that they also had a global impact. Nuns exploited their substantial connections: Perpiñan, for example, was able to get a letter to the pope during his visit to Manila to appeal on behalf of prostituted and trafficked women during the authoritarian regime of Marcos, and Mananzan was able to get funding from overseas (Spain) for feminist organization WMC for its feminist radio program *Radyo Womanwatch*.[14]

Women's Organizations in Transnational Spaces

The international orientation of Filipino women's organizations was obvious from its beginnings in 1986. The WMC invited a small group of prominent international feminists from Iran, New Zealand, and the United States to a series of national conferences on various women's issues in 1986–1988.[15] In 1986, too, GABRIELA held its first WISAP conference as part of the IWWD celebrations. Sixty women from thirteen countries around the world attended the event.[16] GABRIELA made it a point to hold WISAP conferences every two years, often publishing the papers and minutes, with each conference tackling a particular theme. By 1989, they boasted an increase to seventy-two women activists from thirty-two countries.[17] That the activists addressed themselves to the entire world was reflected in the types of resolutions passed by the conferences. In the WISAP 1991 conference, whose theme was "The Culture of Foreign Domination: Women's Issues, Alternatives and Initiatives," delegates from twenty-four countries passed resolutions condemning the killings in Sri Lanka and Palestine.[18] Speaking at the 1998 WISAP whose theme was "Advancing the Women's Movement in the Era of Globalization," Secretary General Liza Largoza Maza revealed the ambitious nature of the women's agenda: "For our aim is not just to rock the boat but to shake the world and with other oppressed and exploited peoples bring down imperialism."[19] Her statement identified her national-democratic color, but, more important, it reinforced the international perspective of the GABRIELA coalition. The women's health movement was also proactive in the activities of the global health movement offering to host the sixth IWHM in November 1990.[20]

Because of sheer logistics alone, activism on behalf of overseas contract or overseas migrant workers needed organizational structures across national borders. For example, DAWN's advocacy on behalf of entertainers in Japan who had children by Japanese fathers required a branch in Japan (DAWN-Japan) to help locate the fathers and to pressure them for financial assistance. Kanlungan Center Foundation, Inc. networks with Philippine embassies abroad and has satellite offices in the host countries of Filipino workers. GABRIELA has chapters all over the world, notably GABRIELA-USA and *Pinay sa Holland* in the Netherlands. Emily Cahilog, director of GABRIELA's international relations department, traveled to five cities in the Netherlands linking the situation of Filipino women in the Philippines with the issues of Filipino marriage migrants in that country. Her visits were instrumental to the formation of *Pinay sa Holland*, the GABRIELA chapter there.[21]

Successful international campaigns such as Violence Against Women mobilized women from all parts of the world, including participants from Bangladesh (working on dowry-burning), Chile (Mujeres por la Vida), and India; the Philippines was represented by GABRIELA.[22] GABRIELA later launched its own worldwide campaign against trafficking of women. In 1999, the campaign was launched all over the world through the GABRIELA international chapters, with activities held in the Resistance Theater in Park Slope, Brooklyn, New York, "Purple Rising" on April 10 that included videos, storytelling and a concert), and in Holland where *Pinay sa Holland* sold the special Purple Rose pin.[23] Initiated to raise awareness about sexual violence and human rights abuses against women, it targeted men as well as women, and demanded a commitment to oppose the trafficking of women and a promise not to patronize the sex trade.[24] The pin came with a pledge that needed to be signed and returned to the GABRIELA network.[25]

Women organizations also internationalized "local spaces" by inviting overseas advocates to participate in Filipino activism. For example, GABRIELA's international relations department arranged "exposure trips," where young people from overseas (particularly from Korea and Belgium) joined GABRIELA's activities, such as standing in picket lines and visiting urban poor communities.[26] When I did fieldwork in Metro-Manila in 2003, a group of Belgians arrived to show support for the Shoemart strike and a Belgian woman was completing a year of volunteer work with GABRIELA. In July 2008, Fiona Seiger from Vienna started a six-month internship with DAWN.[27] When I interviewed Soledad Perpiñan (RGS) of TW-MAE-W, a Filipina-American was also assigned as an intern there. Likhaan's Filipina-American intern became the model for the cover of one of the pocketbooks published by the organization (see Chapter 9). Philippines-based activism had international actors, and international activism included Philippines-based actors.

Carmelita Nuqui, executive director of DAWN, organized "home stay" visits as part of organized Japanese study tours. Included in the travel itinerary were visits to recruiting agencies, NGOs, and Sikhay.[28] Young Japanese activists volunteered to work with DAWN on various internship programs arranged by DAWN-Japan and coordinated by Chiho Ogaya, an academic from Japan who could speak Tagalog. But the exchange was a two-way process: former entertainers revisited Japan to encourage the healing process, and Filipino-Japanese children visited Japanese primary schools to perform their plays as Japanese children welcomed them with a serenade of Tagalog songs.[29] DAWN-Japan also organized study tours in Japan where participants were taken to the clubs where entertainers worked, to the Catholic Church where Filipino entertainers congregated on their days off, and to a Filipino restaurant for a meal.[30] A unique activity was the Peace Boat, an NGO that organizes cruises during which NGOs deliver lectures. Nuqui often joined the cruise in its Southeast Asian leg to deliver lectures about DAWN's advocacy and to sell Sikhay products.

Former entertainers also toured Japan performing the musical *The Different Faces of Misty*. The performances were accompanied by a symposium. During the post-performance discussion, Nuqui told audiences that DAWN's advocacy not only focused on helping former Filipina entertainers and their children, but also aimed to help Japanese families affected by the cultural practice where married men visit bars and have relationships with Filipinas. In response, Japanese men defended their practice of visiting the bars after work while their wives chastised them. This was one instance where Filipino activism has initiated public debates in Japan about the cultural practices of both countries.[31] DAWN had hoped to deliver its message across Philippine geographical borders and had hoped to transform not just Filipino society, but also Japanese social relations in a truly transnational approach to advocacy.

The 1990s saw an increased level of funding for NGOs working on human rights; because the feminist catch cry became "women's rights are human rights," women's organizations benefited greatly from this international financial support.[32] Funding bodies not only brought dollars, but also created allies. At the same time, links with overseas organizations had an impact on the rhetoric, epistemology, and vocabulary of the Filipina activists. For example, the women's health movements showed an evolutionary language from "reproductive health" to "reproductive rights" to "reproductive self-determination," reflecting shifts in the perspectives of the international women's health movements. But, as I will argue in this chapter, it was never a one-way transfer of knowledge or even of ideological feminist positions. Filipinas also had the opportunity to influence international feminists.

Local disagreements, conflicts, and differences between activists also were played out in transnational spaces. Activists from the myriad organizations competed fiercely for access to the finite number of "reserved seats" allocated to country representatives at overseas conferences, venues, talks, or meetings. Foreign aid, though welcomed, opened a Pandora's box of potential conflict. Foreign aid was not perceived to be politically neutral; some women's organizations such as GABRIELA were not comfortable with receiving foreign aid for ideological reasons (GABRIELA was national-democratic). The question of whether to accept foreign aid was fundamental enough to cause the splintering of some major organizations. One of the founding members of Likhaan, Sylvia Estrada-Claudio, was formerly a member of GABRIELA. One of the reasons she left that organization was disagreement with the GABRIELA leadership on whether or not to accept funding from international bodies (Likhaan was in favor, GABRIELA was not).[33] In my interviews with them, activists raised the personal and ideological conflicts between them but only "off the record" since these were interpreted to be very sensitive and highly personal. Activists also were perhaps reluctant to reveal to "outsiders" any evidence that might show a fracturing of the sisterhood.

International activists sometimes found themselves caught in the middle of national disputes. The Sisterhood Is Global dialogues in Manila, 1988, had originally planned a culminating activity—Filipino Women's Day of Protest. But one month before the event, one organization (GABRIELA) decided to pull out to stage its own march with the Sisterhood Is Global Institute as guest participants. The fallout from this was an extra session of "evaluation and sharing" where participants, local and international, did some self-reflection on the frustrations that were part of the dynamics of activist movements everywhere and the unique characteristics of conflict in the Philippine cultural context.[34] Both Filipina feminists and international guests raised the negative consequences of various splits in the sisterhood at this "evaluation" and "sharing" session. Anna Leah Sarabia looked for a way to get PILIPINA and GABRIELA to work together, while invited international feminists Marilyn Waring and Robin Morgan empathized with the women's movements' challenge of forging unity in diversity when "this country is drowning in groups."[35] The internal disputes were obvious to the international guests, who were clearly affected emotionally by the fraught nature of the division among activist groups. As Marilyn Waring expressed it, "[T]he precise meeting at which the split in GABRIELA occurred is extremely disconcerting."[36] In the end, Robin Morgan communicated her personal wish that, "The diversity of the Philippine women's movement is, I hope, a strength, not a pain."[37]

From Filipina Feminist Activist to
International Feminist Activist

Similar to the feminist nuns, leaders of women's transnational organizations lived a peripatetic life. Choosing 2004 as a random year to describe her travels, Carmelita Nuqui counted six visits to Japan plus two visits with the Peace Boat.[38] Aurora Javate de Dios was required to do the traveling necessary as a member of the CEDAW group of experts in 1994–1998 (twice a year for one month each time to review ten country and government reports). But she also traveled regularly to the United

States, and to international conferences. Overseas travel was complemented by local travel within the Philippines—for example, to Davao to
attend meetings with Muslim women.[39] Emily Cahilog traveled regularly
within the Philippines (she has worked in the Cordillera) and internationally (to link up with GABRIELA's international chapters).[40] Anna
Leah Sarabia's travels have put her in touch with the International Lesbian and Gay association (ILGA) and introduced her to feminists all over
the world, some of whom she invited to the 1986 Sisterhood Is Global
dialogues in the Philippines.[41]

This peripatetic lifestyle also enabled them to be proactive in the
international feminist movements. The need to give the global wom-
en's movements an international face required the voices of Southern
women, and Filipinas were uniquely qualified to fulfill this requirement.
They spoke English, were well organized locally and well networked
overseas, knew the particular debates, had good diplomatic and technical skills, and had the patience for NGO work.[42] Hence, Filipinas were
often invited to assume roles such as chair or rapporteur. For example,
Jean Enriquez of CATW-AP was rapporteur in the world conference
in 2002, while Jeanne Frances Illo acted as chair in the various international meetings she attended.[43] Four Filipinas had served as chairs for
the Committee on the Status of Women in the United Nations, including
during 1994, prior to the Beijing Conference, and two Filipinas served as
experts in the CEDAW committees, two of them in preparation for the
significant Beijing and Nairobi conferences.[44] The dominant presence of
Filipina activists in international meetings has been observed by other
countries prompting former CSW chair Patricia Licuanan to rise to their
defense, saying, "We can't help it!" "because we are so good"—underscoring the point that Filipinas "initiate," "to just start the ball rolling,"
and were proactive in the international women's movements.[45]

And yet activists participated in a conversation with international
women from the perspective of the national—most of them were invited
to attend international conferences and meetings as Philippine specialists. In time, some of these transnational actors began to speak for wom-
en of one region or for women all over the world. Nuns such as Soledad
Perpiñan of TW-MAE-W had a larger impact because of the consultative status with the United Nations, affecting policy that concerns trafficked women who may or may not be Filipinas. Aurora Javate de Dios
spoke on behalf of trafficked women everywhere, whereas Patricia Licuanan was identified as the expert on migration and trafficking.[46] Letitia
Shahani, also a former CSW chair, was one of the authors of CEDAW.

Chapter 1 discussed the role of Filipina feminist nuns in international feminist theologizing, including their leadership roles in the Women's Commission of EATWOT. The fact that Filipinas enjoyed leadership positions in the international feminist world attests to their credibility not just as Filipino feminists, but also as transnational feminists, speaking for the interests of women around the world.

The decision to become a transnational activist had a seismic impact on the perspectives and strategies of the women's movements in the Philippines and on the subjectivities of the transnational actors themselves. Filipinas aspired to take leadership roles in these international organizations along with First World feminists. In doing so, they moved from interrogating "the Filipina woman" to engaging with "the international woman."

9

Women's Movements in Liminal Spaces

ABORTION AS A REPRODUCTIVE RIGHT

Although abortion is illegal and punishable by law in the Philippines, democratic institutions do not prohibit citizens from public advocacy for the pro-choice cause. But because of the political hold of the Catholic Church and the global neo-conservative swing, anyone brave enough to openly endorse the legalization of abortion as recently as 2010 risked severe public censure. Any individual or organization that so much as hinted at legalizing abortion even if in whatever limited form (for instance, for rape victims) was immediately demonized. Given this environment, there has been no overt proactive lobby or networking for absolute reproductive rights in the legislature, although there have been attempts to legalize abortion under special circumstances. Women activists knew it was futile to campaign publicly for the legalization of abortion in a social climate where they had no chance of success. In order to avoid censure, contempt, and ostracism, women activists who grappled with this sensitive and complex matter had to tread carefully. They had to explore alternative methods of subtle propaganda, attempting to elide the condemnation of the Catholic Church and its conservative political allies. In this sense, feminists operated in a metaphorical liminal space—sometimes above ground, sometimes below ground. They could not openly advertise their cause, and so adopted innovative methods with which to disseminate ideas considered too radical or revolutionary for their time.

Operating in an amorphous liminal space required creativity, at least in the sphere of advocacy. Instead of public testimonies by women who have had abortions, women's stories were published in fictionalized form and were published as pocketbooks or novels that could be read *privately* by women readers. Likhaan commissioned one musical play *Buhay Namin* (Our lives), but even though it was produced through a consultancy with PETA, it did not go on nationwide tour such as the *Libby Manaoag* series had done. It was performed at the University of the Philippines; in addition, Likhaan sold or distributed film versions of the play in DVD format. The University of the Philippines offered a secular space for women advocates eliding the extensive hold of the Catholic Church. In 2006, for example, Estrada-Claudio's Women in Development class held an open forum on abortion as a reproductive right, with guest speakers from the women's movement including GABRIELA, Likhaan, Woman-Health, and the WCC.[1] But, by and large, anonymity was a rule; since some activists worked for Catholic institutions, they could not afford to have their names associated with anything that might be interpreted as pro-abortion.

This chapter will focus on this radical aspect of the women's movements. Because of the delicate nature of this issue, I focus here on the one organization that has given me permission to mention their name and their stance on the issue: Likhaan, the NGO discussed in Chapter 5. After internal debate, Likhaan put forth an official position via their chair, Sylvia Estrada-Claudio's speech to Amnesty International in London, in June 2005: "In the end, we took a position for legalization for economic reasons, in cases of threat of life to the mother, in cases of severe fetal deformity, in cases of rape. We also set the cut-off point for access to below the age of viability."[2] Material from WomenLead, a Likhaan ally (some Likhaan people were members of the first WomenLead board), also was used, particularly on the legal side of abortion advocacy. I have mentioned names where I have been given permission, while in all other instances I protect their anonymity. Sources here include interviews with women activists, published materials from Likhaan and other women's organizations, posters, and one play in the genre of theater as advocacy. In addition, I analyze six pocketbooks published and sold by Likhaan as part of their strategy for opening up the discussion on abortion. This last source is unique, although at this stage it is still too early to predict its impact on women readers. Since Likhaan chose the genre of the romantic fiction, it has the potential to reach a significant number of women readers.

My reading of the evidence suggests that activists (at least until 2008) have been preoccupied with the task of making the society culturally prepared for the public discussion of abortion as a feminist issue. Activists worked from the premise that this cultural preparation would take a long time. Advocacy was generally limited to an appeal for empathy for women who made these decisions at great risk to their lives, and for nondiscriminatory postabortion care in hospitals. A request for the legalization of abortion was only ever hinted at, in the dialogues of the pocketbooks; the critique of the Church was restrained, through the use of the dialogues delivered by the characters of the fictionalized stories. But a major part of the cultural preparation was a message that abortion was a reality for many women in the local community. Thus, the emphasis was on the number of abortions that occurred, and the number of deaths or hospitalizations that occurred because of clandestine botched abortions. These statistics also were disseminated to illustrate the unnecessary cost of the illegal nature of abortion.

One might be tempted to ask, What was this cultural preparation for? An article by WomenLead lawyers provides part of the answer. Entitled "From Mortal Sin to Human Rights: Redefining the Philippine Policy on Abortion," it articulated the activist goals of shifting the discourse on abortion from a religious one (sin, guilt, shame, punishment), to a discourse on human rights (entitlements).[3] This is an ambitious scheme in the Philippine context due to the powerful political influence of the Catholic Church, and ambitious in a Catholic culture where it was still impossible to divorce discussions of abortion from its religious moorings. Thus, it makes absolute sense for women activists to focus on preparing the public minds (and in particular women's minds) for this new paradigm shift that must accompany any discussion on the decriminalization of abortion in the Philippines.

Andrea Whittaker's seminal work on abortion in Thailand focused on the public discourses of women who abort and self-representations of women who have had abortions.[4] My discussion shifts the analytical lens to an examination of how activists introduced a counter-hegemonic discourse. In the process, feminists hoped to be fashioning a new hegemony where the future Filipina will enjoy reproductive and sexual rights.

Research on Abortion in the Philippines

One important aim of women's movements was to make public the fact that abortion was a reality of life for many women from all classes.

Though abortion was prohibited under Philippine law unless it was to save a woman's life, and although it was not easily accessible even for this reason, statistics show that between 155,000–750,000 abortions were performed each year (with the research conducted by the Guttmacher Institute claiming that 473,000 occurred in the year 2000).[5] The women who had abortions came from all classes with a majority of them poor Catholic married women, who already had several children. The reasons for the abortion could be classified in three categories: 72 percent of women cited economic costs of raising a child, 54 percent stated they already had the number of children they desired, and 57 percent reported that they had become pregnant too soon after the last pregnancy.[6] In addition, an estimated seventy-nine thousand women were hospitalized due to complications incurred from the abortions, with an estimated eight hundred women dying per year from complications of an unsafe abortion.[7]

Article II, Section 12 of the Declaration of Principles and State Policies of the 1987 Constitution states, "The State recognizes the sanctity of family life and shall protect and strengthen the family as a basic autonomous social institution. It shall equally protect the life of the mother and the life of the unborn from conception."[8] But the constitution failed to define when conception occurred and nowhere in the Revised Penal Code could one also find a legal definition of abortion.[9] In September 2006, when I was invited by Likhaan to accompany them in the hearings with the Committee on Revision of Laws regarding House Bill 4643 (banning the use of certain drugs classified as "abortifacients") and House Bill 5458 (which increased the penalty for those medical practitioners who have been involved in abortion), the legislators not only failed to come up with a definition of an "abortifacient," but also had to ask resource persons for help. It was Dr. Sylvia Estrada-Claudio, a doctor of medicine as well as a psychologist, who reminded the lawmakers that the definition of "abortifacient" was incumbent on the definition of "conception."[10] Women who had an abortion and those who came to their aid were penalized under the Revised Penal Code with criminal liability. The relevant section of the Code read as follows:

> AR 256. Intentional Abortion.—Any person who shall intentionally cause an abortion shall suffer:
> The penalty of reclusion temporal, if he shall use any violence upon the person of the pregnant woman.
> The penalty of prison mayor if, without using

> violence, he shall act without the consent of the woman.
>
> The penalty of prison correccional [*sic*] in its medium and maximum periods, if the woman shall have consented.
>
> AR 258. Abortion practiced by the woman herself or by her parents—The penalty of prison correccional [*sic*] in its medium and maximum periods shall be imposed upon a woman who shall practice abortion upon herself or shall consent that any other person should do so.
>
> AR 259. Abortion practiced by a physician or midwife and dispensing of abortives.—The penalties provided in Article 256 shall be imposed in its maximum period, respectively, upon any physician or midwife who, taking advantage of their scientific knowledge or skill, shall cause an abortion or assist in causing the same.[11]

Since the law punished abortion without defining either conception or abortion itself, feminist lawyers argued that the criminalization of abortion was a consequence of religious beliefs that regarded it as a mortal sin, a heinous crime, and an "evil" that "offends established norms."[12] Because attitudes towards abortion could not be separated from religious belief, activists had the formidable task of introducing a new paradigm shift in which abortion would be seen in terms of a rights discourse instead of a religious discourse. Women who have had abortions also spoke of it in moral and religious terms, carrying the burden of guilt and shame, compelled to keep their experience a secret. The concept of rights or entitlements was still relatively novel even at the end of the twentieth century. To most ordinary Filipino women resigned to "fate," or the dictates of cultural constraints, the very notion that abortion could be a human right was inconceivable.

Narratives of Abortion in the Trope of Romantic Fiction

In 1991, Likhaan conducted in-depth interviews with thirty women who had abortions. The material from these interviews was used not only as empirical evidence for their research papers, but also mined for advocacy work. Because these women were viewed as criminals and murderers, they could not "go public" or "come out" to speak for themselves in their own voices. Instead, the interview material was used by feminist literary writers as the basis for writing fiction. Likhaan's ingenious approach was to commission feminist creative writers to use the data from the interviews to write "fiction" or "faction" and then publish them in the form of pocketbooks.

Between 2004 and 2006, Likhaan published six pocketbooks. They were written by two authors; one of the authors, Lualhati Bautista, was an award-winning writer and novelist. The pocketbooks written by Carmen Cabiling were distinguishable from Bautista's because they were grouped under a series called *The Scarlett Diaries* where the main characters of each book were close friends of one local nonmetropolitan community named Gian. These pocketbooks were packaged in the genre of romance novels much like the Mills and Boon or Barbara Cartland books. But it was the issue of "abortion" rather than "romance" that received "star billing" in these novels. Although romance novels followed the quintessential formula that commenced with " boy meets girl" and ended with "boy gets girl," the pocketbooks by Bautista began with "girl gets pregnant" and was preoccupied with "girl and abortion." In addition, although the visual appearance of the publications were in the trope of the cheap romantic paperback novel, the content of these particular books captured poignantly the women's struggle with the decision to have an abortion—there represented as a decision that involved not just the woman herself, but also her kinship group, the father of the child, and her friends—and the difficulties in finding an abortionist, including complications that might have arisen due to the clandestine nature of it. Although Carmen Cabiling's *The Scarlett Diaries* series privileged the "romance plot" over the "abortion plot" (*Erika, Serena,* and *Angelika*), Lualhati Bautista's books stand out as serious feminist fiction where debates on abortion took center stage and any small vestige of "romance" was a side issue (*Hugot sa Sinapupunan* [Taken from the womb, hereafter *Hugot*], *Desisyon* [Decision], and *Ang Kabilang Panig ng Bakod* [The other side of the fence, hereafter *Ang Kabilang Panig*]).[13]

Likhaan commissioned the writing of the pocketbooks based on the stories of thirty women interviewed by the organization for its research advocacy arm. The decision to use this genre was the extreme popularity of romance pocketbooks in the 1990s; they replaced the comics of previous years.[14] The books were written in conversational, colloquial Tagalog, with an emphasis on dialogue rather than on literary description. All were short novels, of around 125 pages long, and were published in newsprint. A print-run of six thousand copies or one thousand per pocketbook was published. Many of the pocketbooks were handed out free of charge to audiences or participants in Likhaan's forums, training sessions, community educational activities, and mobilization events and to patients benefiting from their medical outreach services. The audience or recipients of the books included community women, medical providers (doctors, nurses, midwives, *barangay* health workers, community health workers, NGOs, and people's organizations (POs) were the usual participants of the above activities run by Likhaan. In addition, the books were sold at a minimum of 5 pesos each (a few cents), a huge price drop when one compares it with the P40.00 (or US$1.00) price tag on commercial pocketbooks. In addition, Likhaan has sold five hundred copies through consignment with a University of the Philippines writer-artist who sold it to college students and personal friends. By October 2007, only three hundred copies remained.[15] All books brandished the Likhaan name and logo and were sold by Likhaan. The conspicuous absence of any explicit descriptions of sex in the novels themselves was probably intentional, because Likhaan was not shy about discussing sexuality. Because the purpose of the books was to inform, sex scenes that had the effect of titillating readers would only blunt the powerful message introduced by the narratives. Despite the cheap packaging and risqué series title (*The Scarlett Diaries*), these books handled the issue of abortion in a sophisticated and poignant way, delivering their attacks on the Catholic Church and the state through the intense dialogue of the characters. In this sense, the proverbial "do not judge a book by its cover" was appropriate. These pocketbooks subverted not just the sociocultural and legal mores of their time, but also the romance trope in which they were packaged. Perhaps that is why these books were seen as a potential subversive tool. But the aim was to introduce the delicate issue of abortion to mainstream society, epitomized by the target readers. One could also detect a certain irony in the use of the romance novel as a way of refashioning readers, since readers of romance fiction were not usually perceived to be susceptible to feminist ideas.

The stories that were told through the medium of these pocketbooks blurred the lines between fiction, romance, and autobiography. All books carried the following acknowledgment: "Although all the people and events in this story comes from the imagination, we wish to thank all the women who opened their doors and hearts to us who in minor or major ways have been the inspiration of this literary work or book." But even if the readers bothered to read the acknowledgment, unless they were aware that Likhaan conducted pioneering qualitative research on women who have had abortions in the last decade, they would remain blissfully unaware that the pocketbook they were reading so avidly had an empirical basis. Hence, this method of advocacy had a huge potential for the women's movement.

The six pocketbooks introduced in various ways the life experiences of women who have had abortions. They point out that abortion is not uncommon, that it is an issue that cuts across class, that women who abort try all sorts of drugs to induce abortion, that it is difficult and dangerous to find a person who is willing to perform the abortion, that those experiencing complications from botched abortions were reprimanded at hospitals, and that women who abort were perceived to be criminals and judged as sinners. The novels also explored the variety of reasons why women seek abortions: they are poor and cannot afford to support another child, they got pregnant too soon after the last birth, they already have many children and cannot cope with another pregnancy, they are too young and are not ready to be a mother, or they are abandoned by their lovers who are either married men or unavailable (e.g., a priest). The novels also show how poor women were dehumanized by doctors, nurses, and midwives. This inhuman treatment robbed these women of the joys of motherhood. The plot of *Ang Kabilang Panig* was the search for a safe, reliable, abortion clinic. This clinic, of course, is never found, compelling the characters to send Sandra (the teenager who wants an abortion) to Hong Kong to obtain her abortion.

Although the narratives of the novels gave details about the experiences and reasons for abortion, the dialogues were used to articulate some of the feminist responses to the issues of abortion, sexuality (including virginity), womanhood, motherhood, and reproductive health and rights. Some of the issues such as the lack of access to contraception and the women's right to choose when and if to get pregnant, treaded familiar ground, while others such as the appeal to legalize abortion (only hinted at through dialogue) were more radical.

Bautista's *Ang Kabilang Panig* was the most candid in advocating the legislation of abortion as a reproductive right. The book was about the search for a safe abortion clinic that does not exist: the characters attack the government for failing to address this issue, particularly difficult for poor women who could not afford to go overseas for the procedure.[16] The title of the book itself refers to other countries such as Hong Kong where abortion is legal and where women can be assured of a relatively safe environment in which to access a procedure that might endanger their lives. In *Hugot,* the character Ging delivered the activist position, "It should not be prohibited. If the government and the church were really humane they would think about saving women's lives (or think about preventing dangers to women's lives)."[17] In Estrada-Claudio's 2005 speech to Amnesty International, the official position of Likhaan was the legalization of abortion under specific circumstances only. But in the novels, not all the characters could be said to fit into these specific circumstances defined by the organization. By advocating abortion as a reproductive right, these pocketbooks articulated a position even more radical than Likhaan's own official position on abortion.

One of Bautista's themes was the formation of a sisterhood of feminist women referred to in *Desisyon* as "bonding." Three women friends from different classes—Luisa an obstetrician, Juliet a nightclub singer, and Sam a beauty parlor entrepreneur—bonded together as women at the end of the novel *Desisyon.* An unusual female bonding also occurred between Juliet and Marjorie, where the mistress and the wife share the similar experience of being women betrayed (fooled) by the same man. In *Hugot,* estranged sisters Angeli and Ging bonded after Angeli's abortion. Bautista introduced the concept of a feminist sisterhood, where two biological sisters who were not originally close bonded together through the experience of abortion and through the discussion of women's rights. In both books, the trauma of abortion was cushioned by the sisterhood.

In order to shift the discourse on abortion from "morals" to "rights," the books needed to address feminist positions on reproductive health rights. Both authors were clearly aware that, in the Philippine context, not only was the issue of the woman's right to choose or determine the fate of her body including reproductive health a new idea, but also women's choices were constrained by cultural mores that controlled women's actions through social censure and public disapproval, including gossip. In *Ang Kabilang Panig,* Karla advised her pregnant sister Sandra that it was her choice whether or not to have the baby, and in Carmen Cabiling's *Serena,* Leya defended Serena's decision to have an abortion with the statement that women had the right to decide what to do regarding their bodies: "A woman has the rights over her own body. She is the one who knows whether or not she wants to have children."[18]

In contrast to the stories of former prostitutes that labeled them as "victims" (Chapter 2), or the victims of rape and domestic violence who were cast as heroines (Chapter 5), the novels did not stereotype women who had abortions. Instead, the characters critiqued existing ideal stereotypes of the Filipina woman. Characters such as Louisa in *Desisyon* questioned why marriage and motherhood should be the "be all and end all" of women's roles.[19] They challenged the valorization of motherhood and rejected the negative capital attached to single women.[20]

Representations of the men also mirrored the women's movement's position that men should not be viewed as enemies. Instead, they suggested that a collaboration between the sexes was necessary and desirable for a future of gender equality. The male lead characters in the novels were not demonized. With the exception of Ismael, the married man who gets Juliet pregnant in Bautista's *Desisyon,* and Alex, Luisa's philandering husband in the same novel, the male characters, though flawed, were redeemable, with some of them eventually coming around to the women's point of view. The men in the novels, with the exception of Doc Ago in *Angelika,* were against abortion at the start of the novel but by the end of the books become more understanding of why women chose it. Ernesto in *Hugot* reconciled with Angeli in the end after his new role as househusband gave him a glimpse of what it was like to be in Angeli's shoes. Even Rosendo, the priest who impregnated Luisa in *Desisyon,* empathized with her choice. In *Angelika,* Father Romano (Angelika's biological father) had always been motivated by love and concern for his biological child, and the estranged father in *Ang Kabilang Panig* came to the rescue by paying for a plane ticket for Sandra's abortion in Hong Kong. Needless to say, the male romantic heroes in the novels were generally good men at heart who were all supportive of their lady loves.

In her introduction to the play *Our Lives,* scriptwriter Lualhati Bautista addressed the audience with the statement that women reclaimed their honor only when they exercised the right to make decisions over their bodies, but that women could work towards this goal with the help of their partners, the men.[21] In Bautista's template, women should not be hostile to men who could help them in the activist cause. These characters sent separate messages to men and women. Men were meant to realize that they did not have to be macho to be masculine, while women confronted with these male characters could begin to question why the men in their lives did not behave like them. The books' male characterizations, however, remain much idealized—more revealing about how women wished the men would behave than a projection of how Filipino men behaved in practice. It is these characterizations that unmasked the authors as women writing about men. But it also revealed the women's movements' optimistic view that men too could become feminist advocates and embrace the women's point of view while the state and the Church remain closed.

Fashioning the Filipina of the Future?

Since it was necessary to protect the identities of women who had abortions, women's activists spoke through the voices of fictional characters. But these imaginary characters could be read as alternative role models. In all the novels discussed above, the female lead characters were strong, intelligent, and independent women. They also were able to question social mores and religious morals. In this sense, they were admirable heroines. In the prologue to the DVD version of the Likhaan musical play about abortion entitled *Our Lives,* based on the interviews with the thirty women who had abortions, Sylvia Estrada-Claudio informed audiences that these women were *dakila,* or noble women.[22] Although they may not realize it, Estrada-Claudio claimed, they were noble because they risked their lives each time they gave birth, and were prepared to stake their lives to protect their loved ones.[23] An important distinction should be made here. It was not the abortion itself that made them noble, but their self-sacrificing nature, and their willingness to risk their lives to bear children, since most women who had abortions were those who already had several children.

Carmen Cabiling's character of Angelika that dominated the novel of the same name was one example of an alternative role model. Angelika was introduced in the novel as an unusual woman, a controversial figure in the high schools in which she has taught. The daughter of a priest and reared in the seminary, Angelika's unusual upbringing located her as a marginal person, but these unique credentials made her attractive. This alternative woman believed that women were not destined merely to become wives and mothers; at the end of the novel, when she finally accepted Ago's marriage proposal, she decided not to take his name—not accepted practice in the Philippines.[24] But Angelika was not represented as being an extreme radical, either: she was described as a beautiful woman, so much so that even her female student Gian developed a crush on her; by the end of the story she had agreed to marry Doc Ago and therefore would become a wife and mother. She was not just a typical Filipino woman subscribing to the traditional parameters of the social ideal because she believed in a woman's right to make choices about her life and her body and was open-minded about reproductive health issues, including abortion. Her discussion on abortion included knowledge of the numbers of women who abort, abortion due to date rape, and the discrimination against women who have had abortions.[25] In this sense, the character of Angelika (who does *not* have an abortion in the novel) could be read as the women's movements' future Filipina—still a Catholic but unconstrained by Catholic dogma. (For example, she did not meekly submit to her father's will, even if all along she knew in her heart that Father Romano was her biological father—a possible metaphor for the Filipina's Catholic socialization.) The woman whose face graced the cover of this particular pocketbook was a Filipino-American mestiza (only 25 percent Filipino) who had worked as an intern with Likhaan. Perhaps the choice of a mestiza as Angelika conformed to the ideal yardstick for beauty that still dominated popular culture.

Likhaan's musical play, *Our Lives,* represented women who had abortions as militant women. The play was set at the site of the funeral of Mary Ann who died from complications of a botched abortion. Women from the community who attended the funeral shared their experiences of abortion and advocated women's reproductive rights.

The play focused on a conflict between parents—between the pro-choice and pro-life stance over their pregnant teenager's (Lyn) decision to have an abortion. Lyn's father was against the abortion, demanding instead a marriage between the lovers. The mother accused her husband of placing more importance on his honor than on the well-being of his daughter. The words of Lyn's father's endorsed social expectations: "You got pregnant, you endure it."[26] On the other hand, Lyn's mother provided the alternative option: that women should have the freedom to decide.

The climax of the play was a scene, entitled The Church's Proclamation on Abortion, that takes place at the funeral of Mary Ann, inside the church. The priest saying mass announced that some abortions could be forgiven, and that the bishops were coming to a decision about the maximum number of abortions women could have before they were condemned to eternal damnation. Women reacted to this sermon by striking the priest with their red scarves, seizing the coffin, and taking it out of the church. The penultimate scene, entitled "Prayer of the New Women," featured the women reciting a litany of prayers without the priest as the lights faded out.[27] The "new women" were imagined to be brave enough to challenge the Catholic Church. This was a much more radical act than demands for political space or political and social reform, given the powerful hegemonic hold this institution has on society and politics.

Once again, similar to the pocketbooks, the sisterhood of feminist women supported each other. It must be emphasized that the imagined new Filipina was still seen as spiritual, but was no longer bound by the strict rules of the Catholic Church. This Filipina engaged in a major act of resistance and subversion, including assuming the role of priest, a role denied them in the Catholic Church.

This alternative role model—whether it is beautiful sweet Angelika or the women in *Our Lives*—was quite radical and revolutionary. Filipino women had been marginalized from religious power and leadership since Spanish colonization. Filipina nationalist heroines and activists had previously been depicted as staking their lives for an imagined Filipino nation, but rarely as women who defied the Catholic Church.

Abortion is likely to continue to be a divisive issue. Pro-Life Philippines Foundation Inc., founded by Good Shepherd nun Pilar Verzosa in 1975, represents the other end of the spectrum from Likhaan. It sees itself as "the lead organization in the Philippines dedicated to promoting respect and care for human life from conception to natural death; by promoting a culture of life and love in accordance with the Catholic Church's teachings."[28] Pilar Verzosa (RGS) also has acquired celebrity status as the leader of the pro-life movement and is visible in the public sphere and in the legislative halls whenever the issue of abortion comes up. Her position is clear. Most other organizations are less clear or more ambivalent. Amihan, the peasant women's organization, includes the issue of abortion within the discussion of reproductive rights in their women's orientation workshops.[29] Lines are drawn between those who are in favor of protective abortion or qualified abortion versus those who advocate abortion as a full right.[30] WomanHealth has not come up with an official position about abortion despite their unequivocal stance that women's right to choose should be respected.[31] During the development of the PETA-produced informance *Libby Manaoag Files*, the issue of abortion was uncomfortable and highly emotional. It divided the cast to the point that some members threatened not to take part in the production if abortion were mentioned.[32] In the end, after much reflection, they decided to remove the scene on abortion because "it was too complex an issue that it merited a more nuanced dramaturgy."[33] The internal conflict within PETA mirrored the fraught nature of the debate in the public sphere. The solution—to remove it from public debate—also reflected the general consensus among feminists that the time is not yet ripe for the public discussion of abortion as a reproductive right.

I've discussed Likhaan's innovative use of pocketbooks to create a counter-hegemonic discourse by subverting the romance genre. Even these radical ideas were packaged in the narrative of romance. Perhaps cultural preparation required hints rather than blunt demands. Linking abortion to the larger issue of reproductive rights connected it with the overall women's health movements' advocacy. Those who were empathetic to women's health movements might be persuaded to see the rationale behind the abortion advocacy. In the meantime, women readers of romantic fiction have been introduced to the serious topic of abortion, although it was accompanied by a happy ending.

Conclusion

After a little more than two decades of vigorous activism, Filipino women's organizations have become well-entrenched in civil society. In the ambitious aim of targeting the country as a site for a feminist re-education camp and every individual as a potential women's studies student, they aimed for much more than the creation of a mass following. To fulfill the aims of improving women's status they confronted the state, the Catholic Church, and international bodies and governments. In all these maneuvers they had to grapple with their own internal disagreements and divisions. Lessons learned from past experiences taught them to focus on winning strategies, such as lobbying politicians (since feminist activists had less success in gaining political office) and tapping the media for feminist ends. And, in the process of negotiating for power, they deployed the double narrative, making it a successful discursive strategy despite the inherent contradiction between woman as victim and woman as agent.

The many discourses on the Filipino woman—from victim of violence, agents, society's coping mechanism or payment of debt, suffering martyr, oppressed daughter or worker, modern slaves, survivor, militant activist, to *babaylan*—displayed the many possibilities of theorizing the feminine in the Philippines. This book has explored how activists imagined, represented, and fashioned the Filipina woman in advocacy in order to alter social norms internalized since the Spanish colonial era.

Although the women's movements have not really dismantled the grand narrative of woman as wife and mother, they have nonetheless shaken the fundamental beliefs about womanhood. New discourses that urged women to refuse to bear suffering alone, that redefined virginity, and that expanded the concept of women's rights to include reproductive self-determination and a happy sex life, had a seismic impact on perceptions of womanhood that cut across class. The breakdown of taboos such as public discussion of domestic violence, sex and sexuality, contraception, reproductive health, and even abortion had the effect of a succession of tidal waves tearing down rigid structures and opening up ways of rethinking women's roles in the family and indeed the very notion of family itself.

An enduring legacy of the women's movements is the offering of alternatives to the grand narrative of the woman as wife and mother and the ideal woman as "mater Dolorosa." These new images of the Filipina woman acted as counterhegemonic discourses to sexist media stereotypes and the Catholic Church's projection of the ideal woman. Feminists have begun the project of extending normative "woman" to include other roles that once held negative capital such as feisty women, militant activists, soldiers, revolutionaries, single women, and breadwinners away from the home. In addition, the adjective "heroic" has been redefined to include survivors of rape, incest, domestic violence, and partner infidelity. The value of motherhood was increased as mothers were in turn pronounced to be noble (*dakila*), an adjective usually attributed to male national heroes. Hence, activists made headway in the ambitious project of redefining the feminine on their terms. The obstacles to change are massive, given the neoconservative backlash and the strong hold of traditional beliefs. After twenty years, the main impact of the women's movements was to remove the one-dimensional image of womanhood and offer the possibilities of multiple or other definitions of "woman." Instead of one grand narrative of the woman as "wife and mother," beauty queen, or moral guardian (including the suffering martyr), activists have introduced a counterhegemonic discourse and proposed alternative role models. These cultural rebels have begun the process of altering centuries-old feminine stereotypes.

Tinkering with constructions of the feminine must inevitably impact on masculinities—the Other of woman. At the time of this writing in 2010, activists have not yet launched a full-on critique of Filipino cultural constructions of masculinity, nor have they attempted to rethink or resocialize males into taking on domestic tasks such as child minding, cooking, or cleaning to ease the women's "double burden" (except see Chapter 3). Although feminists have begun the process of challenging the culturally inscribed belief that men are naturally lustful, there are still no big campaigns encouraging men to do domestic chores or to inscribe domestic chores as part of masculinity or responsible parenthood. Perhaps this might be because middle-class activists have domestic helpers, making the need to pressure men to perform domestic chores or alter definitions of masculinity to include domestic tasks less urgent, although the women's movements self-consciously claimed to have embraced the perspective of the lower class. Although feminists have begun the process of radically altering feminine stereotypes, there is still the need to embark on the process of transforming masculinities. In Alicia Pingol's case study, it was women's roles are breadwinners rather than explicit feminist activism that resulted in the remaking of masculinities in Ilocos when men inadvertently become househusbands.[1]

A challenge to existing definitions of masculinity might take feminists to the highly sensitive and divisive issue of absolute divorce, an area that will perhaps mark the next stage of feminist activism. It is interesting that, unlike their sisters in Indonesia, Filipina feminists have not seriously raised polygamy as an issue.[2] Feminist lawyers, in interviews, responded that because the law only allows one wife it was difficult to launch a legal campaign: the problem was not law but cultural practice.[3] The social acceptance of the *querida* system (men's taking of mistresses) meant that in actual practice men were polygamous and that wives were abandoned for mistresses. An attack on the *querida* system would also strike the very heart of constructions of Filipino masculinity because of its link with virility and the belief that men were naturally lustful. A move to the project of remaking masculinity as well as femininity would also benefit the feminist project, since women blamed themselves for not being beautiful or not living up to feminine ideals when their husbands take on a mistress.

Activists displayed much creativity and commitment in the cultural project of interrogating "the Filipina woman," an enterprise that had great revolutionary potential. The variety of activities and strategies used by activists to disseminate their ideas about the Filipina woman has been phenomenal. These activities and strategies tapped the wide gamut of cultural production: from the use of radio, television, informance theater, comics, romance novels, dress, rituals, demonstrations, oral testimonies, radio dramas, workshops, seminars, lectures, publication of educational materials, and women's studies courses. Tapping popular culture such as

Right page (201):

comics, talk shows, the use of the vernacular, and the new media, including the Internet and the cell phone, activists exploited all sorts of ways to get their message across.

It is difficult to measure the composition of the women's movements in quantitative terms. Membership of women's organizations has fluctuated over the years. KMK had forty thousand at its peak in 1998, GABRIELA had fifty thousand in 2006, according to Mary John Mananzan (OSB), while KABAPA was known to have a mass base of twenty-eight thousand in 1990. Amihan's membership fluctuated but could boast of twenty thousand in 2003.[4] But there is also the practical problem of who counts as a feminist following. PETA informances had nationwide audiences of twenty-eight thousand for *Tumawag* and twenty-three thousand for *The Libby Manaoag Files*. Should we include them in the tally? How about the graduates of the basic women's orientation or those who tuned in to the radio and television programs and joined cultural events such as the nontraditional family day, or those who participated in local community organizing against domestic violence? It could be argued, after all, that these people had taken the first step towards developing a feminist consciousness because their actions in small ways could be seen to be advancing the agendas of women activists. In time, they may wish to become active members of women's organizations. One could posit that the women's movements have already begun to have a mass following uniquely straddled across national borders, as Filipina activists at home and in the diaspora looked towards each other, locked in a conversation about womanhood.

Looking Back, Looking Forward

Filipino women are imagined in terms of sectors (women workers, peasants, youth, migrants, etc.) and class (with an emphasis on the lower classes or grassroots women), with the national women's movements including indigenous women and Muslim women (both also classified as sectors). Increasingly, the Filipino woman is envisioned as a transnational subject as more and more women become migrants due to the feminization of the global labor force and through marriage migration. Although it is indeed true that the diversity of the women's movements means that many more women sectors will be included in the feminist project and more voices are generally welcomed, one cannot dismiss the terrible consequences resulting from the fraught divisions between activists. Foremost among these is the need to sustain a viable women's

Left page (206):

APPENDIX 1

CWNGO	Cordillera Women's Non-Governmental Organization
CWR	Center for Women's Resources
DAWN	Development Action for Women Network
DSWP	Democratic Socialist Women of the Philippines
GABRIELA	General Assembly Binding Women for Reforms, Integrity, Equality, Leadership, and Action
GABRIELA circle of friends	General Assembly Binding Women for Reforms, Integrity, Equality, Leadership and Action. An organization devoted to women survivors of rape, sexual harassment, and domestic violence
GABRIELA-USA	GABRIELA in the United States
GABRIELA-Youth	GABRIELA for youth
GLOW	Gloria's League of Women
HASIK	Harnessing Self-Reliant Initiatives and Knowledge, Inc.
IFRS	Institute of Formation and Religious Studies
Igorota	Organization of women in the Cordillera, founded by a feminist Maryknoll nun
ILGA	International Lesbian and Gay Association
Innabuyog	Organization of women in the Cordillera
Institute of Formation and Religious Studies	Provides academic training for religious women, men, and lay workers
Institute of Women's Studies	An affiliate unit of St. Scholastica's College in Manila; sometimes called "Nursia," the name given to the three-story home of the Institute that houses the staff and has facilities for women's organizations
ISSA	Institute for Social Studies and Action
KABAPA	Katipunan ng Bagong Pilipina (Collective of New Filipinas)
Kabataan Makabayan	Nationalist Youth, formed in 1960s as an ally of the National Democratic front
KAIBA	Women for the Mother Country (Kababaihan Para sa Inang Bayan
KALAKASAN	Women Fighting Against Violence (Kababaihan Laban sa Karahasan)
KALAYAAN	Organization of Women for Freedom (Katipunan ng Kababaihan Para sa Kalayaan)
Kanlungan Center Foundation Inc.	The feminist NGO for migrant workers. "Kanlungan" means "sanctuary" or "to care" or "to shelter."
KMK	Women Worker's Movement (Kilusan ng Manggagawang Kababaihan)
Likhaan	This organization does not use an English translation, but Likhaan suggests a space for women's creativity. Likhaan is a word that means a place of honing or developing women (Linangan ng Kababaihan).

Appendix 1

ALN	Asian Lesbian Network
Amihan	Harvest Wind; National Federation of Peasant Women
AWIR	Anti-Violence Against Women in Intimate Relationships
BATIS Center for Women	A service institution focusing on the needs of distressed overseas Filipina workers
BBWERC	Baguio Benguet Women's Education and Resource Centre
BEGNAS	Name coined from the indigenous Kankany-ey custom "begnas," meaning a cultural rest day observation after harvest.
BUKAL	Association of Street Women (Bukluran ng Kababaihan sa Lansangan)
CATW-AP	Coalition Against Trafficking in Women, Asia-Pacific
CATW-International	Coalition Against Trafficking in Women, International
CEDAW	Commission on the Elimination of Discrimination Against Women
CLIC	Can't Live in the Closet
CMC	Center for Migrant Advocacy
CPCA	Center for Philippine Concerns, Australia
CRJA	Centre for Restorative Justice in Asia
CSW	United Nations Commission on the Status of Women
CWERC	Center for Women's Resources, Cordillera

comics, talk shows, the use of the vernacular, and the new media, including the Internet and the cell phone, activists exploited all sorts of ways to get their message across.

It is difficult to measure the composition of the women's movements in quantitative terms. Membership of women's organizations has fluctuated over the years. KMK had forty thousand at its peak in 1998, GABRIELA had fifty thousand in 2006, according to Mary John Mananzan (OSB), while KABAPA was known to have a mass base of twenty-eight thousand in 1990. Amihan's membership fluctuated but could boast of twenty thousand in 2003.[4] But there is also the practical problem of who counts as a feminist following. PETA informances had nationwide audiences of twenty-eight thousand for *Tumawag* and twenty-three thousand for *The Libby Manaoag Files*. Should we include them in the tally? How about the graduates of the basic women's orientation or those who tuned in to the radio and television programs and joined cultural events such as the nontraditional family day, or those who participated in local community organizing against domestic violence? It could be argued, after all, that these people had taken the first step towards developing a feminist consciousness because their actions in small ways could be seen to be advancing the agendas of women activists. In time, they may wish to become active members of women's organizations. One could posit that the women's movements have already begun to have a mass following uniquely straddled across national borders, as Filipina activists at home and in the diaspora looked towards each other, locked in a conversation about womanhood.

Looking Back, Looking Forward

Filipino women are imagined in terms of sectors (women workers, peasants, youth, migrants, etc.) and class (with an emphasis on the lower classes or grassroots women), with the national women's movements including indigenous women and Muslim women (both also classified as sectors). Increasingly, the Filipino woman is envisioned as a transnational subject as more and more women become migrants due to the feminization of the global labor force and through marriage migration. Although it is indeed true that the diversity of the women's movements means that many more women sectors will be included in the feminist project and more voices are generally welcomed, one cannot dismiss the terrible consequences resulting from the fraught divisions between activists. Foremost among these is the need to sustain a viable women's political party in the long term. The challenges that lie ahead include the potential to use politics and political campaigns, including elections for feminist ends, and to elect more politicians with a feminist consciousness (whether male or female) to the legislature and local politics.

It is interesting that, although Filipina feminists have been particularly attracted to the *babaylan* and despite the importance of Catholic nuns among leading activists, there is no obvious demand for women's religious power; this is different from Thailand, for example, where the feminist movement is linked to women's demands for ordination to the Buddhist monkhood.[5] Perhaps it is because Filipino feminist nuns do not wish to be ordained subject to the current Catholic Church hierarchy (see Chapter 2), and the knowledge that it is practically futile to confront the international institution of the Catholic Church, that prevents them from embarking on such a quixotic quest. But the fascination with the *babaylan* as feminist muse suggests that the Filipina woman with religious power remains an elusive dream for today's feminist activists.

The transnational spatial context of advocacy means that Filipino women's movements have traversed national borders; the discourses about the Filipino woman already take place in an international context. With Filipinas in the United Nations or in internationally placed NGOs, or acting as chairs or rapporteurs during international meetings, they have the opportunity to influence international feminist debates and the international feminist movements. As this happens more and more (and assuming that other Southern countries also contribute), feminism will lose its association with "Western" culture.

The feminist project has been very much a women's history project. But activists did not want to rewrite history merely to make women visible. Filipina feminist theory was embedded in a particular historical narrative that theorized womanhood from the precolonial times to the present. This interpretation of women's history became politically charged from the campaign for suffrage in the 1920s to the post-1980s activism. Although at the present writing this nonlinear chronology of women's history is still unnuanced and unchallenged, the argument that women wanted to reclaim rights previously lost to colonialism defended them from any claims that their activism was Western or that their feminist agendas were alien or incompatible with Filipino culture. This feminist grand narrative also functioned as counteroffensive strategy when they were attacked for adopting feminist theories from the West that were seen as alien or imperial.

The journey to the past also suggested alternative role models from the *babaylan* who had religious power, to the women who fought colonial and authoritarian regimes, and to the survivors of male abuse. The process of rethinking the Filipino woman is ongoing; despite the neoconservative backlash, some activists continue to be committed to ensuring that the future of this woman is defined by women themselves rather than by political, social, and cultural institutions such as government policies or the Catholic Church. Invoking discourses such as human rights, and nationalist discourses such as the *babaylan* and the precolonial past glory, activists continue to remind audiences that the Filipino woman is still at the center of debate in the women's movements.

Appendix 1

ALN	Asian Lesbian Network
Amihan	Harvest Wind; National Federation of Peasant Women
AWIR	Anti-Violence Against Women in Intimate Relationships
BATIS Center for Women	A service institution focusing on the needs of distressed overseas Filipina workers
BBWERC	Baguio Benguet Women's Education and Resource Centre
BEGNAS	Name coined from the indigenous Kankany-ey custom "begnas," meaning a cultural rest day observation after harvest.
BUKAL	Association of Street Women (Bukluran ng Kababaihan sa Lansangan)
CATW-AP	Coalition Against Trafficking in Women, Asia-Pacific
CATW-International	Coalition Against Trafficking in Women, International
CEDAW	Commission on the Elimination of Discrimination Against Women
CLIC	Can't Live in the Closet
CMC	Center for Migrant Advocacy
CPCA	Center for Philippine Concerns, Australia
CRJA	Centre for Restorative Justice in Asia
CSW	United Nations Commission on the Status of Women
CWERC	Center for Women's Resources, Cordillera

CWNGO	Cordillera Women's Non-Governmental Organization
CWR	Center for Women's Resources
DAWN	Development Action for Women Network
DSWP	Democratic Socialist Women of the Philippines
GABRIELA	General Assembly Binding Women for Reforms, Integrity, Equality, Leadership, and Action
GABRIELA circle of friends	General Assembly Binding Women for Reforms, Integrity, Equality, Leadership and Action. An organization devoted to women survivors of rape, sexual harassment, and domestic violence
GABRIELA-USA	GABRIELA in the United States
GABRIELA-Youth	GABRIELA for youth
GLOW	Gloria's League of Women
HASIK	Harnessing Self-Reliant Initiatives and Knowledge, Inc.
IFRS	Institute of Formation and Religious Studies
Igorota	Organization of women in the Cordillera, founded by a feminist Maryknoll nun
ILGA	International Lesbian and Gay Association
Innabuyog	Organization of women in the Cordillera
Institute of Formation and Religious Studies	Provides academic training for religious women, men, and lay workers
Institute of Women's Studies	An affiliate unit of St. Scholastica's College in Manila; sometimes called "Nursia," the name given to the three-story home of the Institute that houses the staff and has facilities for women's organizations
ISSA	Institute for Social Studies and Action
KABAPA	Katipunan ng Bagong Pilipina (Collective of New Filipinas)
Kabataan Makabayan	Nationalist Youth, formed in 1960s as an ally of the National Democratic front
KAIBA	Women for the Mother Country (Kababaihan Para sa Inang Bayan
KALAKASAN	Women Fighting Against Violence (Kababaihan Laban sa Karahasan)
KALAYAAN	Organization of Women for Freedom (Katipunan ng Kababaihan Para sa Kalayaan)
Kanlungan Center Foundation Inc.	The feminist NGO for migrant workers. "Kanlungan" means "sanctuary" or "to care" or "to shelter."
KMK	Women Worker's Movement (Kilusan ng Manggagawang Kababaihan)
Likhaan	This organization does not use an English translation, but Likhaan suggests a space for women's creativity. Likhaan is a word that means a place of honing or developing women (Linangan ng Kababaihan).

Lila Pilipina	An organization of former "comfort women"
Lolas Kampanyeras	An organization of former "comfort women"
MAKALAYA	Working Women Who Wish to Be Free (Mangga-gawang Kababaihang Mithi ay Paglaya)
MAKIBAKA	Free Movement of New Women (Malayang Kilu-sang ng Bagong Kababaihan)
Malaya Lolas	An organization of former "comfort women," it literally means "Free grandmothers"
NCRFW	National Commission on the Role of Filipino Women; renamed the Philippine Commission on Women
NKAC	United Women of Angeles City (Nagkakaisang Kababaihan ng Angeles City)
Nursia	Institute of Women's Studies, St. Scholastica's College
PETA	Philippine Educational Theater Association
PiLaKK	United Strength of Women and Children (Pinagsa-mang Lakas ng Kababaihan at Kabataan)
PILIPINA	One of the two top feminist organizations
Pinay sa Holland	A Gabriela affiliate based in the Netherlands
RHAN	Reproductive Health Advocacy Network
SALIGAN	Center of Alternative Law Groups (Sentro ng Alternatibong Lingap Panligal)
SAMAKANA	Association of United and Free Women; Samahan ng Malayang Kababaihang Nagkakaisa
Samaritana Transformation Ministries	A religious, nonprofit organization that offers services to help women move out of the prostitution industry
SIBOL	Women's Joint Initiative for Legal and Social Change (Samasamang Inisyatiba ng Kababaihan sa Pagbabago ng Batas at Lipunan)
SKNLB	Organization of Women Street Vendors in Baguio (Samahan ng mga Kababaihang Nagtitinda sa Lansangan ng Baguio)
TW-MAE-W	Third World Movement Against the Exploitation of Women
UKP	Philippine Women's Network in Politics and Gov-ernance (Ugnayan ng Kababaihan sa Pulitika)
WAGI	Women and Gender Institute, Miriam College
WCC	Women's Crisis Center
WEDPRO	Women's Education, Development, Productivity, and Research Organization
WIWA	Women's Industrial Workers Alliance
WLB	Women's Legal Bureau
WMC	Women's Media Circle Foundation Inc.
WomanHealth	Organization that focuses on women's health and reproductive rights

Women and Child Protection Unit of the Philippine General Hospital	Founded in 1997 to care for abused children
WomenLead	Women's Legal Education, Advocacy, and Defense Foundation, Inc.
WRRC	Women's Resource and Research Center, Inc.
WTP	Women's Theater Program of PETA

Appendix 2

*Time Span: Shows begin in 1986 (*Womanwatch Radyo *and TV); most are from 1995 or 1998; some are from 2002 to the present.*

Radio

Babae Ka, May Say Ka! (You are woman, you have a say!); Saturdays 3:00–4:00 p.m., DZXL RMN. Began in 2003—still on the air in 2006. This program was available on the Internet via the GABRIELA website in 2006. Anchors: Rep. Liza Maza, Janice Monte

Kape at Chika (Coffee and chat); Sundays 8:00–9:00 a.m., DZRJ AM 810. Began in August 2002 and ran until December 2003. Anchors: Becky Padilla Marque, Kristina Gaerlan

Okay Ka, Mare! (You're all right, sister!); Wednesdays 11:30 a.m.–12:00 p.m. and Sundays, 11:00 a.m.–12:00 p.m., DAWN 1206 khz. Was on the air from 1990 until 2002. Hosts: Janice Monte, Brenda Lumeda

Tinig ng Nursia (Voice of Nursia) "Women's Studies on the Air"; Mondays at 2:30 p.m., half-hour K-Love Radio. Began in October 9, 1995, and aired until December 1997. Anchors: Mary John Mananzan (OSB), Arche Ligo, Kristina Gaerlan

XYZone; Saturdays 10:00 a.m.–12:00 p.m., Boss Radio RJ (DZRJ 100.3 FM), then Saturdays 12:30 p.m.–1:30 p.m., DZAR 1026 AM. Began in October 1995. Hosted by Ida Vargas, with Anna Leah Sarabia as cohost. Moved to Angel Radyo (DZAR 1026 AM) in June 2001 and aired until January 31, 2005. Its anchors were Rina Jimenez David with Risa Hontiveros-Baraquiel, Karen Kunawicz, and Apol Lejano; eventually it was hosted by Rina Jimenez David and occasionally by Lily Malasa.

Television

Womanwatch, Saturdays 7:30 a.m. and then 8:30 a.m., People's Television
(PTV-4). Began on September 24, 1986, every other Wednesday 10:30 p.m
and became a weekly program after two months; also appeared Wednesdays at 9:30 p.m. Ended January 25, 1995. (The final episode was supposed to air February 1, 1995, but was not permitted to air because host
Nikki Coseteng was running for office again. She filed her certificate of
candidacy one day before airing date.) Host: Nikki Coseteng

XYZ Young Women's TV. One-hour magazine format show (with "Bodytalk" as
its banner segment), began May 24, 1996, Fridays 10:00 a.m. over People's
Television 4 (PTV-4), then Saturdays 6:00 p.m., then Sundays 11:30
a.m.–12:30 p.m. Aired on PTV-4 until March 28, 1999. Transferred to
ABS-CBN News Channel (ANC 21) and began airing December 12, 1999,
Sundays 12:00 p.m., then Saturdays at 7:00 p.m., airing until October 13,
2001. Hosts: Risa Hontiveros-Baraquiel, Karen Kunawicz, Apol Lejano

XYZ Young Women's TV also aired over Destiny Cable from 1998 to 1999 with
a show titled "XYZ on Destiny." It was a thirty-minute show featuring
selected, edited segments of *XYZ Young Women's TV;* each episode was
anchored by an *XYZ* host who gave an opening and closing talk.

Notes

Introduction

1. The role models touted were Lorena Barros, who founded MAKIBAKA, the feminist arm of the Communist Party of the Philippines, and was killed by the military in the early 1970s; Gabriela Silang, who led the revolt against the Spaniards in the eighteenth century; and Tandang Sora, who helped soldiers in the Philippine revolution against Spain in 1896. "Maria," Sining Lila, CD, 2002. Words are reproduced in Tagalog in GABRIELA, Convention Proceedings, March 2–3, 1985, 51.
2. "Sabon," Sining Lila, CD, 2002.
3. "Babae," in Sining Lila, CD, 2002, and quoted in Santiago, *In the Name of the Mother,* 43–44. This song was composed by a man, Mon Acyo, but was sung by women activists, particularly during demonstrations.
4. "Bangon Maria," Sining Lila, CD 2002. Song's lyrics also are reproduced in *Chaneg,* 9, no. 1 (January–June 2000): 35.
5. Aguilar, *Toward a Nationalist Feminism,* 70.
6. Over the years, anthropologists and feminist scholars, in particular, have grappled with the concept of agency, with some arguing there must be multiple theories of agency and power. See Comaroff and Comaroff, "Introduction," in *Of Revelation and Revolution, Anthropology in Theory: Issues in Epistemology,* ed. H. Moore and T. Sanders (Malden, MA: Oxford and Melbourne, VIC: Blackwell Publishing, 2006), 382–396; and F. Wolf, "Introduction," in *Europe and the People Without History, Anthropology in Theory: Issues in Epistemology,* ed. H. Moore and T. Sanders (Malden, MA: Oxford and Melbourne VIC; Blackwell Publishing, 2006). A recent article specifically tackling Asian women's agency has offered an excellent reframing of the concept (see Hilsdon, "Introduction: Reconsidering

Agency," 134). Aware that modern agency ("understood as individuated and reasoned consent" has been tapped by Asian women in their struggles against forms of authority, the authors of the special issue on reconsidering agency opted to interpret Asian women's agency as "hybrid forms" "where freedoms are regulated—arising as they do from within dominant discourses which women have never been able to completely escape," as Ram is quoted in Hilsdon, "Introduction: Reconsidering Agency," 134–135. Writing on the global discourse on prostitution in Cambodia (incidentally reproducing only the victim narrative because it read Cambodian prostitutes as sex slaves), Sandy discussed agency as "constrained choice." See Larissa Sandy, "Just Choices: Representations of Choice and Coercion in Sex Work in Cambodia," in *The Australian Journal of Anthropology* 18, no. 2 (2007): 194–206.

7. Hilsdon, "Introduction: Reconsidering Agency," 134–135.
8. These types of organizations were created mostly for charity or civic work. See Roces, *Women, Power and Kinship Politics,* Chap. 2.
9. Interview with Emily Cahilog, Quezon City, August 18, 2003; interview with Nanette Miranda, Quezon City, August 26, 2003; interview with Cathy Estavillo, Quezon City, August 23, 2003; interview with Ana Maria "Princess" Nemenzo, Quezon City, October 10, 2006, and interview with Jeanne Francis Illo, Quezon City, August 7, 2003.
10. Interview with Aida Santos, Makati City, October 11, 2006; interviews with Sylvia Estrada-Claudio, Quezon City, September 18, 2006 and October 6, 2006.
11. Interview with Josefa Francisco, Quezon City, July 28, 2010.
12. Ibid.
13. Ibid. and interview with Sylvia Estrada-Claudio, Quezon City, July 6, 2010.
14. See Roces, "Is the Suffragist an American Colonial Construct?," 24–58.
15. Santos Maranan, "Towards a Theory of Feminism," preface.
16. Garcellano, Lolarga, and Sarabia, eds., *Sisterhood Is Global,* 180, 186–187. See also Santos Maranan, "Towards a Theory of Feminism," 77–78; interview with Nemenzo; and interview with Fe Mangahas, Manila, February 1, 2005.
17. Angeles, "Feminism and Nationalism," 183–185.
18. Sobritchea, "Women's Movement in the Philippines," 103.
19. Tancangco, "Voters, Candidates, and Organizers," 70.
20. "Feminist Forum," column in *Laya* 1, no. 1 (2nd quarter 1992): 32.
21. Sobritchea, "Women's Movement in the Philippines," 105; interview with Josefa Francisco, July 27, 2010; interview with Anna Leah Sarabia, Makati City, July 24, 2010; and interview with Estrada-Claudio, July 6, 2010.
22. The term "comfort women" has had a controversial history in the politics of naming. I've used the term in quotation marks because I am reproducing how it was used by the women's organizations in the Philippines, including Lila-Pilipina and Lolas Kampanyeras.
23. Sobritchea, "Women's Movement in the Philippines," 105–107.
24. Ibid. and Aguilar, *Toward a Nationalist Feminism,* 70.

25. Aguilar, *Toward a Nationalist Feminism,* 70.
26. Sobritchea, "Women's Movement in the Philippines," 104.
27. Ibid., 115. The word "contractualization" is the term used by women's activists and refers to the fact that employment is by short-term contract only and therefore women do not have employment benefits and are vulnerable to exploitation. In the chapter on women workers (Chapter 3) I discuss the increasing trend towards employing women as contract laborers only, as opposed to continuing appointments. This has been a major issue for the women's movements.
28. Veneracion-Rallonza, "Women and the Democracy Project," 223–230.
29. Quimpo, "The Left, Elections, and the Political Party System," 11.
30. Angeles, "Feminism and Nationalism," 201.
31. Quimpo, "The Left, Elections, and the Political Party System," 14.
32. Veneracion-Rallonza, "Women and the Democracy Project," 239; and Josefa Francisco, *Women's Participation and Advocacy in the Party List Election* (Quezon City: The Center for Legislative Development, Occasional Paper no. 3 1998), 2.
33. Veneracion-Rallonza, "Women and the Democracy Project," 240.
34. Interview with Congresswoman Patricia Sarenas, Makati City, January 18, 2008.
35. One important issue was whether the party should include those who were not formally members of PILIPINA. Interview with Sarenas.
36. Interview with one of Abanse! Pinay's founders, Attorney Katrina Legarda, Makati City, January 20, 2005; and interview with Sarenas.
37. Francisco, *Women's Participation and Advocacy,* 11–13.
38. Josefa Francisco, "Introduction," in *Gaining Ground? Southeast Asian Women in Politics and Decision-Making, Ten Years After Beijing, A Compilation of Five Country Reports* (Pasig City: Friedrich Ebert Stiftung, 2004), 9; and Sobritchea, "Women's Movement in the Philippines," 107.
39. NCRFW Pearl Anniversary Brochure 1975–2005, *Empowered Women Stronger Nation.*
40. Sobritchea, "Women's Movement in the Philippines," 108–116.
41. Interview with Aurora Javate de Dios, Quezon City, August 8, 2003; interview with Mangahas; interview with Josefa Francisco, July 23, 2003; and interview with Illo.
42. Rebecca Sullivan, *Nuns, Feminism, and American Postwar Popular Culture* (Toronto: University of Toronto Press, 2005).
43. Filipino concepts of power see power held not just by the individual in political office, but also by the kinship group. Hence, women also exercise unofficial power through kinship and marriage ties with male politicians. See Roces, *Women, Power and Kinship Politics.*
44. The term "servants of globalization" was coined by Parreñas, *Servants of Globalization.*
45. See Olivia H. Tripon, ed., *Shaping the Women's Global Agenda: Filipino Women in the United Nations Commission on the Status of Women/CEDAW Committee* (Manila: National Commission on the Role of Filipino Women, 2006).

46. Sobritchea, "Women's Movement in the Philippines," 107.
47. Although Filipino feminist theory is taught as part of the syllabus in women's studies in places such as St. Scholastica's College, there is yet no scholarly book study on the topic. There is, however, an anthology on Filipino-American feminisms that initiates the process of deconstructing what is distinct about Filipino feminisms abroad, see Melinda L. de Jesús, ed., *Pinay Power: Peminist Critical Theory Theorizing the Filipina/American Experience* (London: Routledge, 2005). A short summary of Filipina Feminist theory is in Mina Roces, "Rethinking 'the Filipino Woman': A Century of Women's Activism in the Philippines, 1905–2006," in *Women's Movements in Asia: Feminisms and Transnational Activism,* ed. Mina Roces and Louise Edwards (London: Routledge, 2010), 34–52.
48. I refrain from using the term "Sister" before each nun's name to avoid repetition. I am a little uncomfortable with the possibility that it might appear less than polite, since it is the custom to address these women as "Sister." As a compromise, I have added the nun's religious affiliation (OSB, MM, RGS, ICM, RSCJ, and so on) after their names to indicate their status as religious persons.
49. "Women's Studies in the Philippines," in Mary John Manzanan, *Challenges to the Inner Room: Selected Essays and Speeches on Women by Sr. Mary John Manzanan OSB* (Manila: The Institute of Women's Studies, 1998), 190–192.
50. http://www.cwrweb.com/packages.htm, accessed 2009.
51. "Women's Studies in the Philippines," in Mary John Manzanan, *Challenges to the Inner Room: Selected Essays and Speeches on Women by Sr. Mary John Manzanan OSB* (Manila: The Institute of Women's Studies, 1998), 194.
52. Purcell, *Coming of Age,* 134–135.
53. Ibid. and Sylvia H. Guerrero, "Broadening the Concept of Reproductive Health and Thinking Feminist," in *Gender-Sensitive and Feminist Methodologies: A Handbook for Health and Social Researchers,* ed., Sylvia H. Guerrero (Quezon City: University of the Philippines Press, 2002), 13.
54. Judy Taguiwalo revealed in an interview that activists have "an acute sense of history." Interview with Judy Taguiwalo, Quezon City, January 7, 2008.
55. Arriola, *Si Maria, Nena, Gabriela Atbp* [Maria, Nena, Gabriela and others], 15.
56. Manzanan, ed., *Essays on Women.*
57. See Arriola, *Si Maria, Nena, Gabriela Atbp.*
58. There are several histories by academics that I have not considered here, in particular the literature on women in the Philippine revolution and the histories of the women's movements in the American period up to the early 1980s.
59. See Arriola, *Si Maria, Nena, Gabriela Atbp,* 55–56; "From Priestess to President: The Story of Women's Struggle in the Philippines," *Womanwatch,* Women's Media Circle, 1986; and Judy M. Taguiwalo, "Ina, Obrera, Unyonista, Ang Pagkakaisa at Tunggalian sa Pananaw sa Kababaihang Manggagawa Sa Panahon ng Kolonyal na Paghahari ng Amerikano sa Pilipinas Isang Panimulang Pag-aaral" [Mother, worker, unionist, unity

and conflict from the perspective of women workers in the American colonial period in in the Philippines: A preliminary study] unpublished paper, 1997–1998.

60. "Tatlong Dantaong Hinubog ng Prayle" [Three centuries of being fashioned by friars] (1521–1896), in Arriola, *Si Maria, Nena, Gabriela Atbp,* 16.

61. Carol M Añonuevo, "Ideology and Cultural Practice," unpublished manuscript, 1990, quoted in Estrada-Claudio, "The Psychology of the Filipino Woman," 188.

62. Santiago, *In the Name of the Mother,* 14, 23–47.

63. John Schumacher, *The Propaganda Movement: 1880–1895* (Manila: Solidaridad Publishing House, 1973), 196–220. Rizal's last poem ("Mi Ultimo Adios" [My last good-bye]), refers to the Philippines as "Nuestra Perdida Eden" [Our lost Eden].

64. Mary John Mananzan (OSB), "The Filipino Women: Before and After the Spanish Conquest of the Philippines," in *Essays on Women,* ed. Mananzan, 34.

65. Ibid., 13.

66. Ibid., 34.

67. "From Priestess to President: The Story of Women's Struggle in the Philippines," *Womanwatch,* Women's Media Circle, 1986.

68. "Trailblazers: Mga Babaeng Nanguna" [Trailblazers: Pioneering women] *XYZone,* Broadcast 120, September 7, 2002.

69. Guerrero, "The Babaylan in Colonial Times," 178.

70. See Roces, "Is the Suffragist an American Colonial Construct?," 24–58.

71. Mary John Mananzan (OSB), "The Filipino Women: Before and After the Spanish Conquest of the Philippines," in *Essays on Women,* ed. Mananzan, 34.

72. Arriola, *Si Maria, Nena, Gabriela Atbp,* 23.

73. Carol M Añonuevo, "Ideology and Cultural Practice," unpublished manuscript, 1990, quoted in Estrada-Claudio, "The Psychology of the Filipino Woman," 188.

74. Ibid.

75. Ibid.

76. Mananzan, *The Woman Question in the Philippines,* 4; Fabella, "Mission of Women in the Church in Asia," 166–167; Arriola, *Si Maria, Nena, Gabriela Atbp,* 25; de Dios, "Hidden No More," 157.

77. Santos Maranan, "Towards a Theory of Feminism," 38.

78. Rizal, *Noli Me Tangere [The Social Cancer].* This construction of woman as martyr may be traced farther back than the nineteenth century, although not farther than the period of Spanish colonization (sixteenth century), because the pre-Hispanic Filipino woman was a priestess and had religious power.

79. Santiago, *In the Name of the Mother,* 29; Santos Maranan, "Towards a Theory of Feminism," 37. See also Judy Taguiwalo, "Women as Society's Coping Mechanism," *Laya Feminist Quarterly* 1, no. 4 (1992): 15–21.

80. See Ma. Teresa H. Wright, *Rulebook Women* (Manila: De La Salle University Press, 2004).

81. Santiago, *To Love and to Suffer.*
82. Rizal, *Noli Me Tangere.*
83. Encanto, *Constructing the Filipina*, 24.
84. Santiago, *In the Name of the Mother*, 40.
85. See the more detailed discussion of this in Roces, "Is the Suffragist an American Colonial Construct?," 24–58.
86. Nakpil, *Woman Enough and Other Essays*, 30.
87. Santos Maranan, "Towards a Theory of Feminism," 38.
88. Arriola, *Si Maria, Nena, Gabriela Atbp.*
89. Ibid., 31, 39, 63, 71.
90. Ibid., 31.
91. Ibid., 26, 51.
92. Ibid., 83, 86; interview with Taguiwalo; and footnote explanations to "Babae Ka," *Chaneg* 6, no. 2 (May–August 1997): 43.
93. Santiago, *In the Name of the Mother*, 151.
94. Interview with Mangahas.
95. Quoted in Santiago, *In the Name of the Mother*, 43–44.
96. One feminist writer has critiqued this tendency of the historiography on the Philippine revolution to measure women's contribution to it in terms of the male yardstick for valor. See Santiago, "Ang Salaysay ng Babae" [The discussion on woman], 32.
97. "Trailblazers," *XYZone*, Broadcast 120, September 7, 2002; Louise Edwards and Mina Roces, "Orienting the Global Suffrage Movement," in *Women's Suffrage in Asia: Gender, Nationalism and Democracy*, eds. Edwards and Roces, 5–8; "From Priestess to President: The Story of Women's Struggle in the Philippines," *Womanwatch*, Women's Media Circle, 1986.
98. Leticia Ramos Shahani, "Foreword," in *Centennial Crossings*, ed. Mangahas and Llaguno, 13.
99. Leny Mendoza Strobel, "The Filipina Babaylan in the Diaspora: Encounters in Filipino American Literature," in *Centennial Crossings*, ed. Mangahas and Llaguno, 156.
100. Santiago, *In the Name of the Mother,* 4, 45; Mananzan, *The Woman Question in the Philippines*, preface, 5. Both Fe Mangahas and Mary John Mananzan (OSB) use the words "dangerous collective memory." See Fe B. Mangahas, "The Babaylan Historico-Cultural Context," in *Centennial Crossings*, ed. Mangahas and Llaguno, 42; Mary John Mananzan (OSB), "Welcome Address" National Chairperson GABRIELA in *Gaining Ground, Building Strength: Advancing Grassroots Women's Struggles for Liberation, WISAP '94* (Quezon City: GABRIELA, 1994), viii.
101. Mila D. Aguilar, "Babaylan, Tumanda Ka Na," in *Centennial Crossings*, ed. Mangahas and Llaguno, 173–174.
102. Mangahas, "The Babaylan Historico-Cultural Context," in *Centennial Crossings*, ed. Mangahas and Llaguno, 37–40; Brewer, *Shamanism, Catholicism and Gender Relations*; Guerrero, "The Babaylan in Colonial Times," 170.
103. Guerrero, "The Babaylan in Colonial Times." 167–179,
104. Mangahas, "The Babaylan Historico-Cultural Context," in *Centennial Crossings*, ed. Mangahas and Llaguno, 40; Brewer, *Shamanism, Catholicism and Gender*

Relations; Salazar, *Ang Babaylan sa Kasaysayan ng Pilipinas* [The babaylan in
the history of the Philippines], 52–72; Guerrero, "The Babaylan in Colonial
Times," 167–179; Mangahas, "The Babaylan Historico-Cultural Context,"
in *Centennial Crossings*, ed. Mangahas and Llagunoa, 21–46; Fe B. Mangahas,
"Are Babaylans Extinct? How the Spanish Colonialists Banished the Native
Priestesses in the Philippines," *In God's Image* 12, no. 3 (1993): 27–32.
105. Salazar, *Ang Babaylan sa Kasaysayan ng Pilipinas* [The priestess or *babaylan* in
Philippine history], 25, quoted in Mangahas, "The Babaylan Historico-Cultural Context," in *Centennial Crossings*, ed. Mangahas and Llaguno, 22–23.
106. Brewer, *Shamanism, Catholicism and Gender Relations*, 127–140, esp. 136.
107. Guerrero, "The Babaylan in Colonial Times," 167.
108. Ibid., 168. See also Brewer, *Shamanism, Catholicism and Gender Relations*.
109. Arche L. Ligo, "Searching for the Babaylan in Ciudad Mistica de Dios,"
in *Centennial Crossings*, ed. Mangahas and Llaguno, 75–91; Consolacion
R. Alaras, "Body Narratives, Metaphors, and Concepts in Philippine
Indigenous Religion," in *Gender/Bodies/Religions* ed. Sylvia Marcos
(Mexico: ALER Publication, 2000), 181–191; Mananzan, "Suprema
Isabel Suarez," 129–135.
110. Arche L. Ligo, "Searching for the Babaylan in Ciudad Mistica de Dios,"
in *Centennial Crossings*, ed. Mangahas and Llaguno, 83.
111. Ninotchka Rosca, "Race and Sex Discrimination: Aspects of the Culture
of Foreign Domination," in *The Culture of Foreign Domination: Women's
Issues, Alternatives and Initiatives, Women's International Solidarity Affair in the
Philippines '91* (Manila: GABRIELA, 1991), 18.
112. "Day 1–August 30, 1991," in *The Culture of Foreign Domination: Women's
Issues, Alternatives and Initiatives, Women's International Solidarity Affair in the
Philippines '91* (Manila: GABRIELA, 1991), 45.
113. The prologue began, "This compilation on the *babaylan*, the Filipina's
foremother, culminates a year-long celebration of the feminist centennial
in the Philippines (1905–2005). . . . [T]he babaylan, although ancient
and unknown to most feminists in the country, is alive, and lingers as the
"political consciousness" of women in this part of the world." Mangahas and Llaguno, "Prologue," in *Centennial Crossings*, ed. Mangahas and
Llaguno, 15.
114. Mary John Mananzan, (OSB), "The Babaylan in Me," in *Centennial Crossings*, ed. Mangahas and Llaguno, 145–146. See chapters by singer Grace
Nono and dancer Myra C. Beltran.
115. "Prologue," in *Centennial Crossings*, ed. Mangahas and Llaguno, 17.
116. Ibid., 15.

Chapter 1 The Religious Roots of Women's Oppression:
Feminist Nuns and the Filipino Woman
1. Exceptions to this are Anne O'Brien, *God's Willing Workers: Women and
Religion in Australia* (Sydney: The University of New South Wales, 2005);
and Rebecca Sullivan, *Visual Habits: Nuns, Feminism, and American Postwar
Popular Culture* (Toronto: University of Toronto Press, 2005).

2. Rebecca Sullivan, *Nuns, Feminism, and American Postwar Popular Culture* (Toronto: University of Toronto Press, 2005).

3. Ibid., and Marta Danylewycz, *Taking the Veil: An Alternative to Marriage, Motherhood, and Spinsterhood in Quebec, 1840–1920* (Toronto: McClelland & Stewart, 1987).

4. Marta Danylewycz, *Taking the Veil: An Alternative to Marriage, Motherhood, and Spinsterhood in Quebec, 1840–1920* (Toronto: McClelland & Stewart, 1987); Anne O'Brien, *God's Willing Workers: Women and Religion in Australia* (Sydney: The University of New South Wales, 2005); and Rebecca Sullivan, *Visual Habits: Nuns, Feminism, and American Postwar Popular Culture* (Toronto: University of Toronto Press, 2005).

5. Coeli Maria Barry, "Transformations of Politics and Religious Culture Inside the Philippine Catholic Church (1965–1990)," PhD diss., Cornell University, Ithaca, NY, 1996; and Claussen, *Unconventional Sisterhood.*

6. Anne Harris, *Dare to Struggle Be Not Afraid: The "Theology of Struggle" in the Philippines* (Quezon City: Claretian Publications, 2003).

7. Mary John Mananzan, "Redefining Religious Commitment Today: Being Woman Religious in a Third World Country," in *Challenges to the Inner Room,* ed. Mananzan, 4.

8. Interview with Amelia Vasquez (RSCJ), Quezon City, August 19, 2003.

9. Interview with Virginia Fabella (MM), Pasig City, Metro-Manila, January 18, 2005; interview with Vasquez; interview with Leonila Bermisa (MM), Quezon City, July 20, 2003.

10. Interview with Fabella.

11. Mananzan, *Woman, Religion and Spirituality in Asia,* back cover.

12. Amelia Vasquez (RSCJ), "Fidelity in Vowed Life: Matrimony and Religious Life," *Religious Life Asia* 5, no. 1 (March, 2003): 55.

13. Interview with Vasquez.

14. Floy Quintos, "The Gentle Activism of Sister Sol," *Metro-The City Life* (March 1993): 34.

15. Short bio of Soledad Perpiñan in Mary Soledad Perpiñan (RGS), "Muffled Voices," Paper/lecture, nd, in the personal papers of Mary Soledad Perpiñan (RGS), TW-MAE-W Office, Quezon City.

16. Interview with Emelina Villegas (ICM), Quezon City, January 10, 2005; Margaret Lacson (MM), "Questing Woman-Spirit," *In God's Image* 12, no. 3 (1993): 14.

17. Interview with Rosario Battung (RGS), Quezon City, January 23, 2005.

18. Fabella, *Beyond Bonding,* 36.

19. See Kwok Pui-Lam, *Introducing Asian Feminist Theology* (Cleveland: The Pilgrim Press, 2000), Chap. 6, where Mananzan's and Fabella's contribution to theological debates are summarized. See also Virginia Fabella, "Contextualization and Asian Women's Christology," lecture presented at Ewha Women's University, Korea, September 7, 1994, in personal papers of Virginia Fabella.

20. See also, for example, Mananzan, "Theological Perspectives of a Religious Woman Today," 340–349; Fabella, *Beyond Bonding,* based on Fabella's thesis on the history of the Women's Commission of EATWOT;

Fabella and Park, *We Dare to Dream;* Fabella and Torres, eds., *Irruption of the Third World;* Battung (RGS), Bautista, Lizares-Bodegon, and Alice G. Guillermo, eds., *Religion and Society;* Apuan, Battung, Bautista, eds., *Witness and Hope.*
21. Fabella, Lee, and Suh, eds., *Asian Christian Spirituality;* Fabella and Torres, eds., *Doing Theology in a Divided World;* Fabella and Park, *We Dare to Dream;* Fabella, ed., *Asia's Struggle for Full Humanity;* Fabella and Sugirtharajah, eds., *Dictionary of Third World Theologies;* Fabella and Torres, eds., *Irruption of the Third World.*
22. The special issues were *In God's Image* 12, no. 3 (1993) (a special issue on "Reclaiming Women's Partnership with the Earth"); *In God's Image* 21, no. 2 (June 2002) (a special issue on Women and Just Relationships); and *In God's Image* (March 1989) (a special issue on the meaning of Easter).
23. Virginia Fabella, Carmela Carpio, Emelina Villegas, Marianne Katoppo, Elizabeth Tapia, Maria Riley, and Sr. Filo Hirot, "Woman and the Churches: It's the Men's Problem," *In God's Image* (April 1983): 11–12; Fabella, "Mission of Women in The Church in Asia"; *In God's Image* (December /February 1985/86): 4–9; Sr. Lydia L. Lascano, "The Role of Women in the Church and in Society," *In God's Image* (December /February, 1985/86): 9–14; Fabella, "Asian Women and Christology," *In God's Image* (September 1987): 14–20; *In God's Image* (September 1987): 14–20; Virginia Fabella and Margaret Lacson, Editorial, *In God's Image* (March 1989): 3–4; Lydia Lascano, "Signs of New Life," *In God's Image* (March 1989): 5–8; Emelina Villagas (ICM), "Lita: Worker, Wife and Mother, An Interview," *In God's Image* (March 1989): 9–10; Teresa Dagdag (MM), "Why a Women's Movement?," *In God's Image* (March 1989): 14–16; Mary Rosario Battung (RGS) "From Zen to God the Mother," *In God's Image* (March 1989): 20–27; Virginia Fabella (MM), "Symbols in John's Resurrection Scene Reflections on the Garden and Mary Magdalene," *In God's Image* (March 1989): 37–40; Mary John Mananzan (OSB), "Coup Reflection," *In God's Image* (December 1989): 46–47; Amelia Vasquez (RSCJ), "Meditation on War," *In God's Image* (December 1989): 47–48; Margaret Lacson (MM), "Questing Woman-Spirit," *In God's Image* 12, no. 3 (1993): 11–14; Mary John Mananzan (OSB), "Who Is Jesus Christ? Responses from the Philippines," *In God's Image* 12, no. 3 (1993): 39–41; Rosario Battung (RGS), "Woman of Compassion: A Filipino Image of Mary," *In God's Image* 12, no. 3 (1993): 42–47; Virginia Fabella (MM), "Report on the EATWOT Women's Philippine Consultation: Spirituality for Life: Women Struggling Against Violence," *In God's Image* 12, no. 3 (1993): 63–68; Mary John Mananzan (OSB), "Feminist Theology in Asia: A Ten Year's Overview," *In God's Image* 14, no. 3 (1995): 38–48; Mary John Mananzan (OSB), "Jubilee in the Wake of Globalisation: From an Asian Woman's Perspective," *In God's Image* 19, no. 1 (2000): 2–14; Felice Imaya Calingayan (OSB), "Indigenous Sense of Justice," *In God's Image* 21, no. 2 (2002): 3–6; Leonila V. Bermisa (MM), "Justice: The Way to Reconciliation and Healing," *In God's Image* 21, no. 2 (2002): 7–16; Emelina Villegas (ICM), "Out of the Struggles Come Hope," *In God's Image*

21, no. 2 (2002): 17–21; Mary John Mananzan (OSB), "Globalization and the Perennial Question of Justice," *In God's Image* 21, no. 2 (2002): 22–27; and Leonila V. Bermisa (MM), "Word, Sacrament and Liturgy: Philippine Experience," *In God's Image* 23, no.1 (2004): 50–56.
24. Gaerlan, ed., *Women Religious Now,* 56, 71–72, 75–79.
25. Interview with Vasquez; interview with Fabella; and interview with Villegas.
26. Interview with Villegas; interview with Fabella.
27. Interview with Battung.
28. Interview with Vasquez.
29. Interview with Soledad Perpiñan (RGS), Quezon City, August 28, 2003.
30. Interview with Christine Tan (RGS), Leverisa, Malate, Manila, February 7, 1995.
31. *Sister Stella L.,* 1984. See also Emmanuel Reyes, *Notes on Philippine Cinema* (Manila: De La Salle University Press, 1989), 10–15.
32. When I suggested to Mariani Dimaranan, president of the TFD, that nuns had no political power, she replied, "But we have moral power." Interview with Mariani Dimaranan (SFIC), Quezon City, February 3, 1995.
33. Interview with Tan.
34. Interview with Helen Graham (MM), Quezon City, August 1, 2003.
35. Ibid., and interview with Bermisa.
36. Interview with Tan.
37. *International Viewpoint,* no. 145 (July 11, 1988): 14 and 16.
38. Mary John Mananzan (OSB), "Benedictine Values and the Woman Question," in *Challenges to the Inner Room,* ed. Mananzan, 59–60.
39. Mary John Mananzan (OSB), "Feminist Theology in Asia: A Ten-Year Overview in *Challenges to the Inner Room,* ed. Mananzan, 117.
40. Ibid.
41. Jurgette Honclada, "Notes on Women and Christianity in the Philippines," *In God's Image* I (1985): 13–20.
42. Ibid., 16.
43. Fabella, "Inculturating the Gospel," 123.
44. Fabella, "Christology from an Asian Perspective," 7.
45. Ibid., 10.
46. Mary John Mananzan (OSB), "Paschal Mystery from a Philippine Perspective," in *Concilium 1993/2: Any Room for Christ in Asia?,* ed. Leonardo Boff and Virgil Elizondo (Maryknoll, NY: Orbis Books, 1993), 86–94, summarized in Kwok Pui-Lam, *Introducing Asian Feminist Theology* (Cleveland: The Pilgrim Press, 2000), 83.
47. Fabella, "Mission of Women in the Church in Asia," 166–167.
48. Interview with Villegas.
49. Mary John Mananzan (OSB), "Emerging Spirituality of Women: The Asian Experience," in *Essays on Women,* ed. Mananzan, 176.
50. Mananzan, "Redefining Religious Commitment in the Philippine Context," 111.
51. Kwok Pui-Lam, *Introducing Asian Feminist Theology* (Cleveland, OH: The Pilgrim Press, 2000), 82–86; Fabella, "Christology from an Asian

Woman's Perspective," 10–11; Fabella, "Mission of Women in the Church in Asia," 7, 159–170; and Mananzan, *Challenges to the Inner Room*, 16–19.

52. Mananzan, "Redefining Religious Commitment in the Philippine Context," 110.

53. Mananzan, *The Woman Question in the Philippines*, preface; and Mary John Mananzan (OSB), *Ang Pagkababaihang Isyu sa Pilipinas* [The woman question in the Philippines], (Manila: Institute of Women's Studies, 2001), 20–25.

54. Mananzan, *Challenges to the Inner Room*, 81, 185, 181.

55. See for example, "Liturhiya 2" [Liturgy 2], in *On the Wings of a Dove*, 68, 72.

56. See Angelina Almanzor, "Mary John Mananzan Filipina Christian Activist," in *Exploring Feminist Visions*, ed. Frances Maria Yasas and Vera Mehta (Bombay: Streevani/Ishvani Kendra, 1990), 330–359.

57. Teresa Dagdag, "Why a Women's Movement?," *In God's Image* (March 1989): 16.

58. "DAWN Expands to Japan," *Sinag* (April–June 1998): 1.

59. Interview with Soledad Perpiñan (RGS), Quezon City, July 28, 2003.

60. Interview with Mary John Manazan (OSB), Manila, July 17, 2003; interview with Estrada-Claudio, September 18, 2006.

61. Interview with Villegas; and interview with Fabella.

62. Interview with Perpiñan, July 28, 2003.

63. Mananzan, "Redefining Religious Commitment Today," 14.

64. Interview with Bermisa.

65. Interview with Perpiñan, July 28, 2003; interview with Villegas; interview with Vasquez; interview with Bermisa; interview with Fabella; and interview with Graham.

66. Some nuns such as Tan, Fabella, and Borres were from the upper-class elite families, and Mananzan was from an upper-middle-class family.

67. Interview with Bermisa.

68. Interview with Tan.

Chapter 2. Prostitution, Women's Movements, and the Victim Narrative

1. This recent polarization of the debate has been given an excellent in-depth discussion by Elaine Jeffreys. Elaine Jeffreys, *China, Sex and Prostitution* (London: Routledge, 2004), 70–95.

2. Mananzan, ed., *Essays on Women*, 196–208; "Prostitution Profits from Women's Bodies," *Piglas-Diwa*, 9, no. 1 (1999); Cynthia Enloe, *Bananas, Beaches and Bases: Making Feminist Sense of International Politics* (London: Pandora, 1989); interview with Aurora Javate de Dios, CATW-AP, Quezon City, January 26, 2008.

3. DAWN Brochure, 2005, Manila.

4. These women sometimes are referred to as "Japayuki," but this term is pejorative so I prefer to use the term "entertainers." Japayuki-san is a pun on Karayuki-san, which refers to the nineteenth-century Japanese women who traveled to Southeast Asia as prostitutes.

5. Montañez with Sicam and Nuqui, eds., *Pains and Gains;* and Nuqui and Montañez, eds., *Moving On.*
6. Primer on TW-MAE-W, Quezon City, 2003.
7. CATW-AP, Second Board of Trustees Meeting, 1996, from the Papers of CATW-AP, Quezon City.
8. www.catwinternational.org/campaigns.php, accessed April 2008.
9. Syndicates in this context are underground coalitions of groups involved in prostitution as a business.
10. Entertainers composed part of the overseas contract workforce whose remittances totaled 110 billion pesos or US$12.8 billion. See "2007 Survey on Overseas Filipinos" in http://www.census.gov.ph/data/sectordata/sr08353tx.html, accessed August 8, 2008; "Philippine 2006 Overseas Remittances Hit Record 12.8 Billion Dollars," Yahoo! News Asia, http://asia.news-yahoo.com/070215/afp/070215073037eco.html, accessed August 8, 2008; and "Philippines' Reliance on Foreign Remittances Carries Significant Costs," *The Nation,* http://www.nationmultimedia.com/2007/05/01/opinion/opinion_300330988.php, accessed August 8, 2008. The Philippines by the year 2002 was sending forty thousand entertainers to Japan every six months. This prompted journalists to refer to this regular 'export' of overseas performing artists as the "vaginal economy."
11. Chant and McIlwaine, *Women of a Lesser Cost,* 1–81, 211–212.
12. Eviota, *The Political Economy of Gender,* 137–139.
13. Chant and McIlwaine, *Women of a Lesser Cost,* 63 and 65.
14. Cynthia Enloe, *Bananas, Beaches and Bases: Making Feminist Sense of International Politics* (London: Pandora, 1989); "Prostitution Profits from Women's Bodies"; "Exploitation of Women in Olongapo and Angeles," *Coalition Asia-Pacific Report* (March 2002): 8–9; and Chant and McIlwaine, *Women of a Lesser Cost,* 1–81, 211–212.
15. Tadiar, *Things Fall Away.*
16. Montañez with Sicam and Nuqui, eds., *Pains and Gains,* 2.
17. Nelia Sancho, who heads an organization of "comfort women" (*Lolas Kampanyera*), is one of the few Filipina activists who use the term "sex work," refusing to classify these women as simply victims. Interview with Nelia Sancho, Manila, September 27, 2006.
18. Delfin and Enriquez, with Raissa H., eds., *Shifting the Blame,* 9.
19. Aida F. Santos, "Introduction to the 1st Edition: From the Shadows Into the Light," in *Halfway Through the Circle,* ed. Amilbangsa et al., ix–xii.
20. "Challenging and Subverting the System of Prostitution," 7.
21. "Prostitution Profits from Women's Bodies," 19.
22. Aurora Javate de Dios, "Challenging International Instruments to Address Trafficking in Women and Children," 1997, in the archived papers of CATW-AP, Quezon City.
23. Soledad Perpiñan, "The Bought, the Buyer and the Business," from the papers of TW-MAE-W, Quezon City, late 1990s, 2.
24. "Anti-Trafficking Law," Broadcast 157, *XYZone,* May 31, 2003.
25. "Sex Trafficking," *Okay Ka, Mare!* [You are okay, sister!], May 9, 1999.

26. Delfin and Enriquez with Raissa H., eds., *Shifting the Blame,* 22.
27. Santos, "Introduction to the 1st Edition," xi.
28. Montañez with Sicam and Nuqui, eds., *Pains and Gains,* 35 and 44.
29. Nuqui and Montañez, eds., *Moving On.*
30. Amilbangsa et al., eds., *Halfway Through the Circle;* and David, *Nightmare Journeys.*
31. Nuqui and Montañez, eds., *Moving On.*
32. Interview with Carmelita Nuqui, Manila, January 22, 2005.
33. Montañez with Sicam and Nuqui, eds., *Pains and Gains,* 30.
34. Montañez with Sicam and Nuqui, eds., *Pains and Gains.*
35. Ibid., 30.
36. Interview with Nuqui, January 22, 2005.
37. Ballescas, *Filipino Entertainers in Japan.*
38. Ibid., 101–107.
39. Interview with Sancho.
40. Tadiar, *Things Fall Away.*
41. Muldong-Portus, *Streetwalkers of Cubao,* 70.
42. Fabros, Paguntalan, Arches, and Guia-Padilla, "From *Sanas* to *Dapat,* 227–230; Estrada-Claudio, *Rape, Love and Sexuality,* 79–111; and interview with Santos.
43. Cecilia Hofman, "The Pros and Cons of Pink Cards," *Coalition Asia-Pacific Report* 5, no. 1 (January–March 2000), 10–11.
44. www.catwinternational.org/campaigns.php, accessed April 2008; Palermo Protocol, Article 9, www.catwinternational.org/campaigns.php, accessed April 2008.
45. Editorial, "Legitimizing Prostitution as a Sector," *Coalition Asia-Pacific Report* 4, no. 2 (November 1998): 6.
46. Cecilia Hofman, "The Pros and Cons of Pink Cards," *Coalition Asia-Pacific Report* 5, no. 1 (January–March 2000), 11.
47. CATW-AP Chairperson Aurora Javate de Dios discussed the campaign to "break the cycle of prostitution" by unpacking and critiquing society's acceptance of the male prerogative to "buy" women. "Anti-Trafficking Law," Broadcast 157.
48. "Anti-Trafficking Law," Broadcast 157.
49. *Ang babae ay hindi binibili* and *Ang tunay na lalaki ay hindi bumibili ng babae!* Interview with Aurora Javate de Dios, Quezon City, October 6, 2006.
50. "Anti-Trafficking Law," Broadcast 157.
51. "Prostitution," *Tinig,* December 4, 1995.
52. Soledad Perpiñan, "The Bought, the Buyer and the Business," from the papers of TW-MAE-W, Quezon City, late 1990s.
53. "Republic Act No. 9208: An Act to Institute Policies to Eliminate Trafficking in Persons Especially Women and Children, Establishing the Necessary Institutional Mechanisms for the Protection and Support of Trafficked Persons, Providing Penalties for its Violations and for Other Purposes," reprinted in Montañez with Sicam and Nuqui, eds., *Pains and Gains,* 162–173.
54. Interview with Jean Enriquez, CATW-AP, Quezon City, August 11, 2003.

55. Ibid. and interview with de Dios, August 8, 2003.
56. Interview with Enriquez.
57. "Republic Act 9208," 162–173.
58. Chizuko Ueno, *Nationalism and Gender,* Trans Beverley Yamamoto (Melbourne: Trans Pacific Press, 2004), 89.
59. Interview with Enriquez; interview with de Dios August 8, 2003; and interview with Perpiñan, July 28, 2003.
60. See various articles in *Sinag.*
61. "Empowering Survivors and Beijing Plus Ten," *Coalition Asia-Pacific Report* 8, no. 1 (February 2005): 1.

Chapter 3. The Woman as Worker

1. Pingol, *Remaking Masculinities.*
2. See Liza Maza, "Displacement, Commodification and Modern-Day Slavery of Women: The Impact of Imperialist Globalization," in *The Women's Emancipation Movement in the Philippines,* ed. LORENAS, 39–48; Editorial, "Women and the Unions," *Laya Feminist Quarterly* 2, no. 2 (1993): 2–4; Annette Hug, "Women Workers Daily Life: Sexual Harassment in the Industries," *GABRIELA Women's Update* 7, no. 5 (December 1992): 10.
3. Frias, "Women Workers," 5.
4. Parreñas, *Servants of Globalization.*
5. Eviota, *The Political Economy of Gender,* 17, 120; Liza Maza, "Displacement, Commodification and Modern-Day Slavery of Women: The Impact of Imperialist Globalization," in *The Women's Emancipation Movement in the Philippines,* ed. LORENAS, 43; Perlita Lopez, "Women Workers and Trade Unions," Chairperson KMK, presented at GABRIELA WISAP, 1994, in *The Women's Emancipation Movement in the Philippines,* 123.
6. Elisa Tita Lubi with A. Tujan, "Woman Worker," *Laya Feminist Quarterly* 2, no. 2 (1993): 32–33.
7. Frias, "Women Workers," 16–17; Nanette Miranda, "Panayam kay Ka Perlita" [Interview with Comrade Perlita], in *Ugnay-Kababaihan* (KMK newsletter) 1, no. 5 (August 1992): 6.
8. Frias, "Women Workers," 16–17; and interview with Miranda.
9. Interview with Miranda.
10. Ibid.; "The Movement of Women Workers: A Protracted Struggle for Emancipation," *GABRIELA Women's Update* 3, no. 5 (May 1987): 4.
11. Frias, "Women Workers," 17; interview with Miranda.
12. Interview with Miranda. The split that compelled members to choose sides (those who "affirmed" the ideology of founder José Marie Sison [RA] and those who critiqued this [RJ]) resulted in violent purges within the party. See Kathleen Weekly, *The Communist Party of the Philippines 1968–1993: A Story of Its Theory and Practice* (Quezon City: University of the Philippines Press, 2001), 224–257.
13. Interview with Francisco, July 27, 2010; and interview with Anna Leah Sarabia, Makati, July 18, 2010.

14. Interview with Miranda.
15. Lopez, "Women Workers and Trade Unions," 125.
16. Frias, "Women Workers," 9; "Abridged Version of an Interview with Nancy Garcia," *Laya Feminist Quarterly* 2, no. 2 (1993): 57; Mananzan, *The Woman Question in the Philippines,* 22.
17. Nanette Miranda on *Tinig* radio, on women workers, January 29, 1996.
18. "Women Workers Discuss Sexual Violence," GABRIELA Women's Update 8, no. 1 (July 1993): 8; "Have You Ever Been Sexually Harassed?," 1993, 5; and interview with Miranda.
19. CWR, *Kontraktwalisasyon sa Paggawa* [Contractualization of work], 29.
20. Interview with Miranda; and interview with Emmi de Jesus, deputy director of GABRIELA, Quezon City, July 25, 2003.
21. Editorial, "Tungo sa Pagpapanibagong Lakas ng KMK" [Moving toward a new and strong KMK] *Ugnay-Kababaihan* [Linking women] 1, no. 5 (August 1992): 3.
22. Ibid.
23. Eviota, *The Political Economy of Gender,* 108, 120.
24. "Have You Ever Been Sexually Harassed?," 1993, 5; Nanette Miranda on *Tinig;* Annette Hug, "Women Workers Daily Life: Sexual Harassment in the Industries," *GABRIELA Women's Update* 7, no. 5 (December 1992): 9–10; and "Naunsiyaming Pangarap: Ang CALABARZON sa Buhay ng Kababaihan ng Timog Katalugan" [Multiple dreams: The CALABARZON in the life and womanhood of the northern Tagalog region], March 8, no. 4 (1998): 16; and interview with Miranda.
25. Interview with Miranda.
26. "Naunsiyaming Pangarap: Ang CALABARZON sa Buhay ng Kababaihan ng Timog Katalugan" [Multiple dreams: The CALABARZON in the life and womanhood of the northern Tagalog region], March 8, no. 4 (1998): 16.
27. Ibid.
28. Interview with Miranda; and "Have You Ever Been Sexually Harassed?," 1993, 6.
29. "Have You Ever Been Sexually Harassed?," 1993, 5.
30. Interview with Miranda.
31. Ibid.
32. Jean Enriquez (Gab-Youth secretary general in 1993), "A Perversion of Authority: Sexual Harassment in the Campus," *GABRIELA Women's Update* (April–June 1993): 18–19; interview with Jomes Salvador, Gab-Youth secretary general in 2003, Quezon City, August 17, 2003.
33. *Kontraktwalisasyon sa Paggawa,* 36; "Kontraktwalisasyon: Ang Lumalaganap na konsumisyon ni Sion" [Contractualization: Engulfing the suffering of Sion] *Piglas-Diwa* (2000): 29.
34. *Kontraktwalisasyon sa Paggawa,* 13–16.
35. Ibid., 7.
36. Nanette Miranda-Tampico, "Women Workers Organize and Take Action Against Globalization," in *Issues, Challenges, and Strategies,* 21.
37. *Kontraktwalisasyon sa Paggawa,* 25–28.

38. "Kontraktwalisasyon," 29.
39. *Kontraktwalisasyon sa Paggawa,* 27–28.
40. "Mura at Plesibleng Paggawa? Mga Kababaihang Manggagawa sa Ilalim ng Iskemang [Cheap and flexible labor? The women workers under the scheme] Subcontracting at Labor Only Contracting," *Piglas-Diwa* 8, no. 1 (March 1996): 29.
41. "Kontraktwalisasyon," 29.
42. "Mura at Plesibleng Paggawa?" 17.
43. "Kontraktwalisasyon," 22, 34; "Mura at Plesibleng Paggawa?, 31–34; interview with Miranda.
44. *Kontraktwalisasyon sa Paggawa,* 34–36.
45. Interview with Miranda.
46. Nanette Miranda-Tampico, "Women Workers Organize and Take Action Against Globalization," in *Issues, Challenges, and Strategies,* 23.
47. "Buhay at Pakikibaka ng Kababaihang Maggagawa" [The life and struggle of women workers], Ikalawang Bahagi (Part 2), *Marso 8,* 2 (August 1993): 36–37.
48. Nanette Miranda-Tampico, "Women Workers Organize and Take Action Against Globalization," in *Issues, Challenges, and Strategies,* 23–24; and interview with Miranda.
49. Lindio-McGovern, *Filipino Peasant Women,* 86.
50. Ibid.
51. Ibid., 86–95; interview with Estavillo.
52. Ibid.
53. "Land Use Conversion: A Cruel Blow to Peasant Women," *Piglas-Diwa* 10, no. 1 (1999).
54. Daisy Valerio, "Two Types of Rural Women's Organizations: Homemakers and Activists," A Condensation of a Study by Judy Taguiwalo and Virginia A. Miralao, *Laya Feminist Quarterly* 2, no. 4 (1993): 21. See also Lindio-McGovern, *Filipino Peasant Women,* 150–168.
55. Tess Oliveros, "Organizing Peasant Women: Confronting Power Where Power Lies," *Laya Feminist Quarterly* 2, no. 4 (1993): 14–15.
56. Ibid., 15,
57. Daisy Valerio, "Two Types of Rural Women's Organizations: Homemakers and Activists," A Condensation of a Study by Judy Taguiwalo and Virginia A. Miralao, *Laya Feminist Quarterly* 2, no. 4 (1993): 21.
58. Interview with Taguiwalo; and interviews with Tess Vistro, deputy secretary general of Amihan, Quezon City, January 21, 2008, and January 24, 2008.
59. Interviews with Vistro, January 21, 2008, and 24, 2008. Judy Taguiwalo disclosed that membership was always fluid; interview with Taguiwalo.
60. Judy Taguiwalo, "Women as Society's Coping Mechanism," *Laya Feminist Quarterly* 1, no. 4 (1992): 15–21; and interview with Taguiwalo.
61. This point is also made by Lilia Quindoza Santiago writing about the history of feminist poetry. See Santiago, *In the Name of the Mother,* 29.
62. Interview with Estavillo.
63. Judy Taguiwalo, "Women as Society's Coping Mechanism," *Laya Feminist Quarterly* 1, no. 4 (1992).

64. Interview with Vistro, January 24, 2008; "Land Use Conversion," 28.
65. "Kababaihang Biktima ng Militarisasyon" [Women victims of militarization] *Piglas-Diwa* 4, no. 3 (nd).
66. Lindio-McGovern, *Filipino Peasant Women,* 169.
67. Interview with Estavillo.
68. Lindio-McGovern, *Filipino Peasant Women,* 1–4.
69. "The Tortuous Quest for Land," *GABRIELA Women's Update* 8, nos. 3–4 (July–December 1998): 10–13.
70. Ibid., 10.
71. Lindio-McGovern, *Filipino Peasant Women,* 169.
72. Ibid., 171.
73. Interview with Vistro, January 24, 2008.
74. Lindio-McGovern, *Filipino Peasant Women,* 86–95.
75. Interview with Estavillo.
76. Oryentasyon ng SAMAKANA [SAMAKANA orientation] (Quezon City: Samahan ng Malayang Kababaihang Nagkakaisa, nd). See also the *Piglas-Diwa* issue on urban poor women that exhorts these women to organize and unite; and "Urban Development ng Gobyernong Ramos: Paraiso para sa Lokal at Dayuhang Puhunan Ibayong Kahirapan para sa Maralitang Tagalungsod" [Urban development of the Ramos government: Paradise for the local and foreign coffers differs from the hardship for the poor city folk] *Piglas-Diwa* 9, no. 1 (March 1997): 5.
77. "Urban Development ng Gobyernong Ramos," 5.
78. "Women Urban Poor and Peasants Picket to Air Demands," *GABRIELA Women's Update* 3, no. 3 (March 1987): 9–10; Nora O. Gamolo, "Tondo Urban Poor Women Fight for their Housing Rights," *Laya Feminist Quarterly* 3, no. 1 (1994): 19–21; and interview with Nerissa Guerrero "Nanay Neri," secretary general of SAMAKANA, Quezon City, August 27, 2003.
79. "SAMAKANA Chapters Celebrate International Women's Day in the Communities," *GABRIELA Women's Update* 3, no. 3 (March 1987): 10; and interview with Guerrero.
80. Interview with Guerrero.
81. Mary John Mananzan (OSB), "The Babaylan in Me," in *Centennial Crossings,* ed. Mangahas and Llaguno, 141.
82. McKay, "Filipino Sea Men," 63.
83. Mary Lou L. Alcid, "The Impact of the Asian Financial Crisis on International Labor Migration of Filipino Women," in *Carrying the Burden of the World,* ed. Illo and Ofreneo, 86.
84. McKay, "Filipino Sea Men," 63.
85. Tadiar, *Fantasy-Production,* 113–149.
86. This was a title of a book on Filipina overseas domestic helpers. See Parreñas, *Servants of Globalization.*
87. McKay, "Filipino Sea Men," 77.
88. Live-in caregivers provide "in-home care for children, elderly, and disabled people" (definition given by Deirdre McKay, "Filipinas in Canada De-skilling as a Push toward Marriage," in *Wife or Worker? Asian Women*

and Migration, ed. Nicola Piper and Mina Roces (Lanham: Rowman & Littlefield Publishers, Inc., 2003, p. 23.

89. Choy, *Empire of Care Nursing.*

90. Katherine Gibson and Julie Graham, "Situating Migrants in Theory: The Case of Filipino Migrant Contract Construction Workers," in *Filipinos in Global Migrations: At Home in the World,* ed. Filomeno V. Aguilar Jr. (Quezon City: Philippine Migration Research Network and Philippine Social Science Council, 2003), 39–59; Kathleen Weekly, "From Wage Labourers to Investors? Filipino Migrant Domestic Workers and Popular Capitalism," in *Transnational Migration and Work in Asia,* ed. Kevin Hewison and Ken Young (London: Routledge, 2006), 193–212.

91. Robyn Emerton and Carole Petersen, "Filipino Nightclub Hostesses in Hong Kong: Vulnerability to Trafficking and Other Human Rights Abuses," in *Transnational Migration and Work in Asia,* 126–143; Anne Marie Hilsdon, "The Musician, the Masseuse and the Manager: Sexy Mothers in Sabah," in *Working and Mothering in Asia: Images, Ideologies and Identities,* ed. Theresa W. Devasahayan and Brenda S. A. Yeoh (Singapore: NUS Press, 2007), 195–220.

92. McKay, "Filipino Sea Men," 63–83.

93. Eden Corcuera Casareno, "Of Aprons and Bikinis: Filipinas Modern Slaves of the World," *Laya Feminist Quarterly* 2 (1994): 11.

94. A Greek dictionary published by George Babiniotis reads, "Filipineza: a woman from the Philippines, but also a domestic worker from the Philippines; or a person who performs nonessential auxiliary tasks." Quoted in Ma. Odine de Guzman, "Testimonial Narratives: Memory and Self-Representation in Letters by Women Migrant Workers," in *Women and Gender Relations in the Philippines,* Vol. 1, ed. Illo, 29.

95. See Parreñas, *Servants of Globalization;* Nicole Constable, *Maid to Order in Hong Kong* (Ithaca, NY: Cornell University Press, 1997); Lan Pei-Chia, *Global Cinderellas: Migrant Domestics and Newly Rich Taiwanese Employers* (Durham, NC: Duke University Press, 2006); Filomeno V. Aguilar Jr. ed., *Filipinos in Global Migrations,* Quezon City: Philippine Migration Research Network and Philippine Social Science Council, 2003); K. A. Chang and J. M. Groves, "Neither Saints nor Prostitutes: Sexual Discourse in the Filipina Domestic Worker Community in Hong Kong," *Women's Studies International Forum* 23, no. 1 (2000): 73–87; Pe-Pua, "Wife, Mother and Maid," 157–180; and Lisa Law, "Defying Disappearance: Filipino Labour Migrants and Public Space in Hong Kong, *Urban Studies* 39, no. 9 (2002): 1625–1645.

96. See Filomeno V. Aguilar Jr., "Beyond Stereotypes: Human Subjectivity in the Structuring of Global Migrations," in *Filipinos in Global Migrations,* ed. Filomeno V. Aguilar Jr. (Quezon City: Philippine Migration Research Network and Philippine Social Science Council, 2003), 1–36; Lisa Law, Katherine Gibson, and Deirdre McKay, "Beyond Heroes and Victims: Filipina Contract Migrants, Economic Activism and Class Transformations," *International Feminist Journal of Politics* 3, no. 3 (2001): 365–386.

97. Rochelle Ball and Nicola Piper, "Trading Labour-Trading Rights

Recognition for Migrant Workers in the Asia-Pacific," in *Transnational Migration and Work in Asia,* 213–233.

98. Interview with Ellene Sana and Rhordora Abano, Center for Migrant Advocacy, Quezon City, January 28, 2008.

99. Kanlungan Centre Foundation Inc., http://ww.kanlungan.ngo.ph/About_us.htm 1–2 (accessed December 2007).

100. *T.N.T.* no. 8 (January 1995): 10.

101. Interview with Helen Dabu, Research and Advocacy Officer, Kanlungan Centre Foundation Inc., Quezon City, September 22, 2006; and Kanlungan website http://www.kanlungan.ngo.ph (accessed December 2007).

102. *T.N.T.,* Occasional Issue 1 (December 1991): 1.

103. Interview with Dabu.

104. "Kanlungan Goes On and Off the Air," *T.N.T.* no. 6 (January March 1994): 5.

105. See, for example, "Sound the Alarm," *T.N.T.* no. 17 (April–June 1997): 20–21; "Kababaihan Migrante at ang Pamahalaan" [Women migrants and the government] *Kanlungan ng Migrante* 5 [Refuge of migrants], no. 1 (October, 1995): 10–12; Doris, Case Update, "S.O.S from Singapore," *T.N.T.* no. 3 (July 1992): np; Gina, Case Update "What's in Store for Kanlungan in 1992?," *T.N.T* no. 2 (April 1992): 1; Nena Gajudo, "Waiting for Justice," Case Update, *T.N.T.* (First Quarter 1996): 25–26; Nena Gajudo and Merceditas Cruz, "Turning Back the Night for Women Migrant Workers," *T.N.T,* no. 13 (April–June 1996): 3; "Kanlungan's 2004 Report," *T.N.T.* no. 37 (October–December 2004): 9; and Aubrey Bautista, "Hulma's Flight to Freedom," *T.N.T.* no. 26 (November 27–December 11, 2001): 3.

106. See http://www.kanlungan.ngo.ph/Caseupdates.htm (accessed December 27, 2007).

107. Eden Corcuera Casareno, "Of Aprons and Bikinis: Filipinas, Modern Slaves of the World," *Laya Feminist Quarterly* 2 (1994): 11–17.

108. Editorial, "Foreign Policy and Overseas Employment Program: A Twin-Bill to Disaster," *T.N.T.* no. 7 (May–June 1994): 10.

109. "Sound the Alarm," *T.N.T* no. 17 (April June 1997): 20.

110. Editorial, "Foreign Policy and Overseas Employment Program," 10.

111. "An Open Letter to President Fidel V. Ramos:" *T.N.T.* no. 17 (April–June 1997): 25.

112. Joecon Lee, "Bidahang Overseas," *T.N.T.* 2, nos. 3–4 (January–June 1992): 15.

113. "Anna Liza Malaki: With a Big Brave Heart for Migrants," *T.N.T.* 6 (January–March 1994): 10; "OFW's Tale of Hellish Life in Malaysia," *T.N.T.* 2, no. 24 (October 2000–January 2001): 15; and "Bibian Magadang: A Survivor, an Advocate," *T.N.T.,* no. 35 (April–June, 2004): 11.

114. "Migrants Unite Against World Trade Organization," *T.N.T.* 19, no. 40 (July–September 2005): 1; Maria Helen Dabu, "Women Fight Today's Worst Enemies—Poverty and Globalisation," *T.N.T.* no. 40 (July–September 2005): 5.

115. Maya Bans Cortina, "Kapit sa Patalim" [Grasp the blade], *T.N.T.,* no. 26 (November 27–December 11, 2001): 5.

116. Interview with Dabu.
117. Interview with Wowie Lumibao, Kanlungan Migrant Center, Quezon City, July 22, 2010.
118. Pingol, *Remaking Masculinities;* Pe-Pua, "Wife, Mother and Maid," 157–180; and Rhacel Parrenas, *Children of Globalization Transnational Families and Gendered Woes* (Stanford, CA: Stanford University Press, 2005).
119. Emerton and Petersen, "Filipino Nightclub Hostesses," 126; and McKay, "Filipino Sea Men," 63.
120. *GABRIELA Women's Update* 8, no. 1 (January–March, 1998): 1.
121. McKay, "Filipino Sea Men," 70, 71.
122. Pe-Pua, "Wife, Mother, and Maid," 176.
123. Pingol, *Remaking Masculinities.*
124. Parreñas, *Children of Global Migration.*

Chapter 4. Indigenous Women: Women of the Cordillera

1. Jennifer C. Josef, "Women of the Highlands and Survival in the Margins," in *Carrying the Burden of the World,* ed. Illo and Ofreneo, 141.
2. Bernice Aquino-See, "Organizing Indigenous Women in the Cordillera," *Chaneg* 6, no. 1 (January–April 1995): 26.
3. Jacqueline K. Carino, "Women as Victims of Violence at Work," *Chaneg* 5, no. 1 (January–April 1997): 24–25.
4. Vernie Yocogan-Diano, "Imperialist Globalization: Making Rural Women More Hungry, More Angry," *Chaneg* 15, no. 1 (March 2006): 5.
5. "The Peasant Women of the Cordillera," *Chaneg* 9, no. 2 (July–December 2000): 4.
6. The highland population is multilingual, and use English, their native languages, and Tagalog.
7. Hilhorst, *The Real World of NGOs,* 29.
8. Interview with Verni Yocogan-Diano, secretary general of Innabuyog, Baguio City, September 5, 2003.
9. Ibid. and Bernadette Resurrección-Sayo, "Women and the Environment: Two Case Studies," in *Women's Studies Reader,* 223–225.
10. Interview with Yocogan-Diano.
11. Resurrección, *Transforming Nature, Redefining Selves,* 132.
12. Mary John Manangan (OSB), "Building Women's Unity and Solidarity Against Globalization," in *Building Women's Unity and Solidarity Against Globalization,* 14.
13. Cariño and Villanueva, *Dumaloy ang Ilog Chico* [And so the Chico River flows].
14. Ibid.
15. Hilhorst, *The Real World of NGOs,* 18–19.
16. "Tales of Courage Rage On," *Chaneg* 9, no.1 (January–July 2002): 4–5 and 22.
17. See Hilhorst, *The Real World of NGOs,* 18–22.
18. Vernie Yocogan, "Or Cordillera Day 2000 and Victims of the Labor Export Policy," *Chaneg* 9, no. 1 (January–June 2000): 8–13.

19. Tauli-Corpuz, "Women's Power in the Cordilleras," 9–10.
20. Ibid., 10.
21. Ibid.
22. Ibid., 11; and interview with Yocogan-Diano. "Innabuyog" is a Kalinga and Tinguian term referring to practices of labor exchange, the equivalent of *bayanihan* (cooperative endeavor or labor especially in a community project) in Tagalog.
23. Tauli-Corpuz, "Women's Power in the Cordilleras," 11.
24. "Manang Lourdes and the Making of BEGNAS," *Chaneg* 7, no. 2 (May–August 1998): 23–25.
25. Resurrección, *Transforming Nature, Redefining Selves,* 132.
26. Resurrección, *Transforming Nature, Redefining Selves.*
27. June Prill-Brett, "Gender Relations and Gender Issues on Resource Management in the Central Cordillera, Northern Philippines," *Review of Women's Studies* 14, no.1 (January–June 2004): 11.
28. Remedios Mondiguing, "Analysis, Reflections and Recommendations on Gender and Tourism in Banaue, Ifugao," *Review of Women's Studies* 10, nos. 1 & 2 (January–December 2000): 17.
29. Evelyn Santiago, "Examining Gender Economic Inequality in the Philippines," *Review of Women's Studies* 10, nos. 1 and 2 (January–December 2000): 18; Remedios Mondiguing, "Analysis, Reflections and Recommendations on Gender and Tourism in Banaue, Ifugao," *Review of Women's Studies* 10, nos. 1 & 2 (January–December 2000): 18.
30. Evelyn Santiago, "Examining Gender Economic Inequality in the Philippines," *Review of Women's Studies* 10, nos. 1 and 2 (January–December 2000): 18.
31. June Prill-Brett, "Gender Relations and Gender Issues on Resource Management in the Central Cordillera, Northern Philippines," *Review of Women's Studies* 14, no.1 (January–June 2004): 14.
32. Ibid. and Agnes Kollin, "The Sanctity of Marriage in the Cordillera," *Igorota Magazine* 6, no. 3 (1992): 14.
33. Agnes Kollin, "The Sanctity of Marriage in the Cordillera," *Igorota Magazine* 6, no. 3 (1992): 14.
34. "Dilemmas and Challenges in Addressing Gender Issues Among Indigenous Women," *Chaneg* 6, no. 1 (January–April 1995): 25; and interview with Vicki Tauli Corpuz by David Cayley published as "Why Population Control?" in *Chaneg* 6, no. 1 (January–April 1995): 14–15.
35. June Prill-Brett, "Gender Relations and Gender Issues on Resource Management in the Central Cordillera, Northern Philippines," *Review of Women's Studies* 14, no.1 (January–June 2004): 18.
36. Agnes Kollin, "The Sanctity of Marriage in the Cordillera," *Igorota Magazine* 6, no. 3 (1992): 14; "Guardians of Peace: Domination as Violence," *Igorota* 7, no. 3 (nd): 4–5.
37. "Dilemmas & Challenges in Addressing Gender Issues Among Indigenous Women," *Chaneg* 6, no. 1 (January–April 1995): 24.
38. "Innabuyog Condemns Rape of a 17-year old Lass by a Soldier," *Chaneg* 10, no. 2 (July–December 2001): 21. See also Tauli-Corpuz, "Women's Power in the Cordilleras," 12.

39. Dandan, "Women's Lives in an Ethnic Community," 11.
40. Resurrección, *Transforming Nature, Redefining Selves,* Chap. 5 "Industrious Women," 131–169; and Resurrección, "From Resource Managers to Secondary Farm Hands," 195.
41. Ibid.
42. Resurrección, *Transforming Nature, Redefining Selves,* 139.
43. Ibid., 159.
44. "Peasant Women of the Cordillera," *Chaneg* 9, no. 2 (July–December 2000): 7–8.
45. Melinda Madew, "The Historical and Cultural Context of Igorot Women's Struggle for Human Rights," *Igorota Magazine* 6, no. 3 (1992): 5–6.
46. Dandan, "Women's Lives in an Ethnic Community," 13.
47. Tauli-Corpuz, "Women's Power in the Cordilleras, 12.
48. "MP Elders" Conference on Tribal Wars and Conflict Resolution," *Chaneg* 9, no. 1 (January–July 2002): 15.
49. See, in particular, Ian Tyrrell, *Woman's World, Woman's Empire: The Woman's Christian Temperance Union in International Perspective 1880–1930* (Chapel Hill: University of North Carolina Press, 1991). See, in particular, Edwards and Roces, "Introduction: Orienting the Global Women's Suffrage Movement," *Women's Suffrage in Asia,* ed. Edwards and Roces, 1–23.
50. Testimony of "Maria Balabag" quoted in Jennifer C. Josef, "Women of the Highlands and Survival in the Margins," in *Carrying the Burden of the World Women,* ed. Illo and Ofreneo, 153.
51. Tauli-Corpuz, "Women's Power in the Cordilleras" 12–13; and interview with Yocogan-Diano.
52. "People Power in the Cordilleras," *Igorota Magazine* 3, no. 2 (1989): 8, "Pan-Cordillera Women's Network for Peace and Development," *Igorota Magazine* 9, no. 1 (January–March 1995): 13; Melinda Madew, "The Historical and Cultural Context of Igorot Women's Struggle for Human Rights," *Igorota Magazine* 6, no. 3 (1992): 5.
53. Interview with Yocogan-Diano.
54. *Igorota Magazine* I, no. 5 (1990).
55. "Contractualization: A Look Inside the Garments Factory of the Philippine Export Processing Zone in Baguio City," *Kali* Vol. 2, no. 1 (June 2001): 22–42; Jacqueline K. Cariño, "Women as Victims of Violence at Work," *Chaneg* 5, no. 1 (January–April 1997): 24–25; and Gigi Sarfati, "Women Workers in Baguio Export Processing Zone Decry Unfair Company Policies," *Chaneg* 6, no. 3 (September–December 1997): 21–23. See also special issue on Medium Term Development Plan (MTDP) and Women, *Chaneg* 5, no. 1 (January–April 1994), particularly the article "Charging Against the MTDP . . . Why Women Must": 12–16.
56. Rosella Camte-Bahni, "Mega-Tourism and Women," *Igorota Magazine* 8, no. 1, (1994): 14–16.
57. "Igorota Holds Women's Sectorial Consultation on Club John Hay Conversion to Foreign Controlled Recreation Complex," *Igorota Magazine* 7, no. 3 (nd): 16–19; and Leonora San Agustin, "Club John Hay, What Now?" *Igorota Magazine* 2, no. 4 (nd): 4–9.

58. GABRIELA-Youth, Metro-Baguio, "Tuition Fee Increase: An Added Burden for Women Students," *Chaneg* 9, no. 1 (January–June 2000): 6–7, and "Resolution Against 'Prostituition,'" *Chaneg* 14, no. 1 (June 2005): 17.

59. *Chaneg* and GABRIELA used similar national-democratic language.

60. "The Peasant Women of the Cordillera," *Chaneg* 9, no. 2 (July–December 2000); "The Globalization of Mining and Its Impact and Challenges for Women," *Chaneg* 5, no. 1 (January–April 1997); "Impact of Globalization-Sars-MTPDP: Impoverishment, Displacement, Prostitution and Modern-Day Slavery of Women," *Chaneg* 6, no. 2 (May–August 1997); "Globalization: Its Impact on Workers and the Issue of Social Causes," *Chaneg* 7, no. 2 (August 1998); and "Women and Globalization," *Chaneg* 15, no. 1 (March 2006).

61. Jill Cariño and Cornelia Ag-agwa, "The Situation of Mining in the Cordillera Region, Philippines and Its Impact on Land Rights and Indigenous Women," *Chaneg* 9, no. 2 (July December 2000): 31.

62. Jennifer C. Josef, "Women of the Highlands and Survival in the Margins," in *Carrying the Burden of the World,* ed. Illo and Ofreneo, 142.

63. Ibid., 144.

64. Ibid.

65. Ibid., 143.

66. Sarfati, "Women Workers in Baguio Export Processing Zone," 21–23; and Cariño, "Globalization: Its Impact on Workers," 7–9. Jill K. Cariño, "Globalization: Its Impact on Workers and the Issue of Social Causes," *Chaneg,* Vol. VII, No. 2, May–August 1998, 7–9.

67. Jennifer C. Josef, "Women of the Highlands and Survival in the Margins," in *Carrying the Burden of the World,* ed. Illo and Ofreneo, 148.

68. "A Resolution Asking the Philippine Government to Protect the Interests, Rights and Welfare of Overseas Filipino Workers and Their Families," *Chaneg* 14, no. 1 (June 2005): 19.

69. Yocogan, "Of Cordillera Day 2000 and Victims of the Labor Export Policy," 9–10.

70. The retail selling of secondhand clothing is called *wag-wag* or *ukay-ukay.* Jennifer C. Josef, "From Vegetable Vendors to *Wagwageras:* Cordillera Women in Baguio City Four Years into the Crisis," in *Carrying the Burden of the World,* ed. Illo and Ofreneo, 155–163.

71. Ibid., 159–160.

72. Milgram, "Ukay-Ukay Chic," 135.

73. *Chaneg* has several themed issues on the women's movement in the region. See *Chaneg* 7, no. 1 (January–June 1999) on IWWD (International Working Women's Day); *Chaneg* 6, no. 3 (September–December 1997) on past struggles; *Chaneg* 11, no. 1 (January–July 2002) on women in the making of history; *Chaneg* 10, no. 2 (July–December 2001) on asserting women's rights in the Cordillera; and *Chaneg* 9, no. 1 (January–June 2000), a themed issue on the women's movement in the Cordillera.

74. *Chaneg* 7, no. 3 (September–December 1998), special issue on Metro-Baguio.

75. "Lesbians and Gays in Baguio Commemorate Stonewall Uprising," in *Chaneg* 11, no. 1 (January–July 2002): 12, 26; "Rampage Towards a Liberated Gay Future," in *Chaneg* 11, no. 1 (January–July 2002): 13; and "National Lesbian Day Celebrated," in *Chaneg* 15, no. 1 (March 2006): 33.
76. "Pan-Cordillera Women's Network for Peace and Development," *Igorota Magazine* 9, no. 1 (1995): 13–14.
77. See the special issues on Women's Education, *Igorota Magazine* 5, no. 1 (1991), and *Igorota Magazine* 5, no. 3 (1991).
78. "Dilemmas & Challenges in Addressing Gender Issues Among Indigenous Women," *Chaneg* 6, no. 1 (January–April 1995): 23–25.
79. Editorial, "Globalization and the Basic Human Right to Life," *Chaneg* 15, no. 1 (March 2006): 3.
80. "Celebrating International Women's Day," *Chaneg* 8, no. 1 (January–June 1999): 3, 6–10.
81. Ibid., 6.
82. Photo montage, *Igorota Magazine* 9, no. 1 (January–March 1995): 19.
83. Mary John Mananzan (OSB), "Building Women's Unity and Solidarity Against Globalization" in *Building Women's Unity and Solidarity Against Globalization,* 14.

Chapter 5. "There Is No Need to Endure": Women's Health Movements

1. Interview with Anna Leah Sarabia, Manila, January 4, 2008.
2. Interview with Estrada-Claudio, September 18, 2006.
3. KALAKASAN, *Sa Akin Pa Rin ang Bukas* [The future is still mine], 3.
4. Interview with Estrada-Claudio, September 18, 2006; and interview with Nemenzo.
5. Sunny Lansang, "Gender Issues in Revolutionary Praxis," *Philippine Left Review* 1 (September 1991): 41–52 (Sunny/Nikki Lansang was Sylvia Estrada-Claudio's pseudonym); Junice L. Demetrio-Melgar, "Raising Sexuality as a Political Issue in the Philippines," in *Sexuality, Gender and Rights Exploring Theory and Practice in South and Southeast Asia,* ed. Geetanjali Misra and Radhika Chandiramani (New Delhi: Sage, 2005), 150–168; and interview with Estrada-Claudio, September 18, 2006.
6. Sunny Lansang, "Gender Issues in Revolutionary Praxis," *Philippine Left Review* 1 (September 1991): 41–52; and "Sunny/Nikki in Her Own Words," in Patricio N. Abinales, *Love, Sex and the Filipino Communist or Hinggil sa Pagpipigil ng Panggigigil* (Manila: Anvil Publishing, 2004), 86–87.
7. See the excellent chapter by de Dios, "Hidden No More," 152–173.
8. Ibid., 156–157.
9. Julita A. Nery, "Pagod na ang Puso" [The heart is tired] in KALAKASAN, *Sa Akin Pa Rin ang Bukas,* 28.
10. "Si Lorna, si Winnie, Atbp, Mga Kuwento ng Kapaitan at Tagumpay" [Lorna, Winnie, and others: Stories of bitterness and triumph] in KALAKASAN, *Sa Akin Pa Rin ang Bukas,* 75.

11. "Magbago Pa Kaya?" [Will it change?] in KALAKASAN, *Sa Akin Pa Rin ang Bukas,* 90.
12. "Dapat Ba Akong Magtiis" [Should I endure?] in KALAKASAN, *Sa Akin Pa Rin ang Bukas,* 100.
13. *Baka naman hindi binigyan ng lambing ni misis.* Quoted by Sonia Carpio, guest speaker, "Women in Radio," *Tinig,* June 17, 1996.
14. Ma. Ligaya A. Lasam, "Pangkulturang Pananaw sa Karahasan sa Tahanan" [Cultural viewpoints on rape in the home] in KALAKASAN, *Pambubugbog ng Asawa* [Spouse beating, who is at fault?], 28.
15. Raquel Edralin-Tiglao, "Why Are You Being Battered?," in KALAKASAN, *Pambubugbog ng Asawa,* 15.
16. According to KALAKASAN: "One adult hitting another is a crime against the state."Jocelyn M. Rosario, "What Keeps a Woman From Leaving," in KALAKASAN, *Pambubugbog ng Asawa,* 53.
17. de Dios, "Hidden No More," 167; KALAKASAN, *Pambubugbog ng Asawa,* 78–80; and "Pulis! Saklolo!," Mga Tala ni Ate Divi [Police! Help! Notes of older sister Divi], in KALAKASAN, *Sa Akin Pa Rin ang Bukas,* 87.
18. KALAKASAN, *Sa Akin Pa Rin ang Bukas,* 3; and KALAKASAN, *Pambubugbog ng Asawa,* iii.
19. *Tapos na ang lahat ng katangahan at kamartiran ko.* Jocelyn M. Rosario, "Sa Akin Pa Rin ang Bukas," in KALAKASAN, *Sa Akin Pa Rin ang Bukas,* 15.
20. KALAKASAN, *Sa Akin Pa Rin ang Bukas.*
21. Women's Legal Bureau, Inc. for SIBOL, *A Legislative Advocacy Manual for Women,* front cover jacket.
22. Interview with Maureen Pagaduan and Evelyn Ursua, WLB, Quezon City, January 24, 2008.
23. *Women's Journal on Law & Culture* 1, no. 1 (July–December 2001): back cover.
24. Ruiz-Austria and Cruz, *Girls in Law.*
25. Women's Legal Bureau, Inc. for SIBOL, *A Legislative Advocacy Manual for Women,* 58–60; and interview with Pagaduan and Ursua.
26. Women's Legal Bureau, Inc. for SIBOL, *A Legislative Advocacy Manual for Women,* 62.
27. Ibid., 61.
28. Ibid., 63.
29. According to Maureen Pagaduan, the bill was written in 1992 and passed in 1997; interview with Pagaduan and Ursua.
30. Carolina S. Ruiz-Austria, "Sex, Sexuality and the Law: Sexuality and Gender Roles in the Philippine Legal System," *Women's Journal on Law & Culture* 1, no. 1 (July–December 2001): 37–44.
31. Women's Legal Bureau, Inc., "Sexual Violence as a Medico-Legal Issue: An Overview of International and Philippine Laws," *Review of Women's Studies* 14, no. 2 (July to December 2004): 56–60.
32. de Dios, "Hidden No More," 157.
33. Estrada-Claudio, *Rape, Love and Sexuality,* 1–31, but esp. 20–21.
34. de Dios, "Hidden No More," 157.
35. Estrada-Claudio, *Rape, Love and Sexuality,* 1–31, but esp. 21.

36. See the history of SIBOL's attempt to get the Anti-Rape Bill passed, in Women's Legal Bureau, Inc. for SIBOL, *A Legislative Advocacy Manual for Women*, 63–78.
37. Emily V. Sanchez, J.D., LL.M., *The Filipina and the Law: A Tribute to Women's Rights* (Quezon City: Central Book Supply Inc., 2008), 154.
38. Interview with Sarabia, July 24, 2010.
39. Ibid. and Emily V. Sanchez, J.D., LL.M., *The Filipina and the Law: A Tribute to Women's Rights* (Quezon City: Central Book Supply Inc., 2008), 154–173.
40. Quoted in Emily V. Sanchez, J.D., LL.M., *The Filipina and the Law: A Tribute to Women's Rights* (Quezon City: Central Book Supply Inc., 2008), 157–158.
41. Ibid., 166–167.
42. de Dios, "Hidden No More," 167.
43. *No More Sabado Nights,* Philippine Center for Investigative Journalism 1996 (written by Luz Rimban and produced by Sheila Coronel).
44. Ibid.
45. de Dios, "Hidden No More," 167.
46. Viado, *Reproductive Health Politics,* 9.
47. "Executive Summary," in *State of Filipino Women's Reproductive Rights,* 9.
48. Guerrero, ed., *Gender-Sensitive and Feminist Methodologies.*
49. de Dios et al., eds., *Bodytalk,* Vol. 2, 75.
50. Interview with Nemenzo.
51. Interview with Estrada-Claudio, October 6, 2006.
52. Florence L. Macagba Tadiar, "Improving Health Care Services in the Philippines," in *Body Politics Essays on Cultural Representations of Women's Bodies,* ed. Odine de Guzman (Quezon City: University Center for Women's Studies, University of the Philippines, 2002), 97–110.
53. de Dios et al., eds., *Bodytalk,* Vol. 2, ix.
54. "Amour Propio" [Proper love], *XYZ Young Women's Television,* February 3, 2000.
55. Estrada-Claudio left because GABRIELA's national democratic ideology prevented it from accepting aid from abroad, a practical policy to which she was not averse. Interview with Sylvia Estrada-Claudio, Quezon City, January 7, 2008.
56. Interview with Joy Salgado, Joy Pacete (Likhaan staff), Geraldine Teriserio, and Lina Bacalando (community health worker and then president of PiLaKK), Quezon City, September 27, 2006.
57. Interview with Salgado, September 27, 2006.
58. Interview with Bacalando, Salgado, and Pacete, September 27, 2006.
59. Ibid. and interview with Estrada-Claudio, January 7, 2008.
60. Estrada-Claudio, *Rape, Love and Sexuality,* 20.
61. Sylvia Estrada-Claudio, "Isang Panimulang Pagsisiyasat sa Konstruksyon ng Pagkababae sa Kulturang Pilipino" [A first inquiry on the construction of womanhood in Filipino culture] unpublished PhD dissertation University of the Philippines, quoted in Torres, *Love in the Time of Ina Morata,* 138; Narzalina Lim in Garcellano et al., eds., *Sisterhood Is Global,* 26.

62. Estrada-Claudio, "Isang Panimulang Pagsisiyasat" [A first inquiry] quoted in Torres, *Love in the Time of Ina Morata,* 9.
63. See Pingol, *Remaking Masculinities;* and McKay, "Filipino Sea Men, 63–83.
64. Torres, *Love in the Time of Ina Morata,* 41.
65. For an in-depth discussion of this, see Roces, *Women, Power and Kinship Politics,* Chap. 5.
66. Mary John Mananzan (OSB), "The Catholic Church and the Gender Issue," unpublished manuscript, 2; Mary John Mananzan (OSB), "Woman, Religion and Language." Speech presented at San Beda College, March 5, 2001, personal papers, 10; and Mary John Mananzan (OSB), "Benedictine Values and the Woman Question," in *Challenges to the Inner Room,* ed. Mananzan, 59.
67. Dios et al., eds., Vol. 2, *Bodytalk,* Vol. 2, 49.
68. Quoted in Santos Maranan, "Towards a Theory of Feminism, 62.
69. Garcellano et al., eds., *Sisterhood Is Global,* 157, 175.
70. Interview with Sarabia, January 4, 2008.
71. Interview with Josefa Francisco, July 26, 2010.
72. Fabros et al., "From *Sanas* to *Dapat,* 229.
73. *On Our Terms;* Anna Leah Sarabia, *Tibok: The Heartbeat of the Filipino Lesbian* (Pasig City: Anvil Publishing & Circle Books, 1998).
74. *On Our Terms,* inside back cover.
75. Ibid.
76. Ibid.
77. Interview with Estrada Claudio, September 18, 2006, and October 6, 2006; and interview with Salgado and Pacete, January 8, 2008.
78. Interview with Estrada-Claudio, September 18, 2006.
79. Interview with Margarita Holmes, Quezon City, January 23, 2008.
80. See "When Feminists Seek Pleasure," Estrada-Claudio, *Rape, Love and Sexuality,* Chap. 3, 79–111.
81. Ibid., 79–111.
82. Ibid., 97, 106.
83. Interview with Estrada-Claudio, January 7, 2008.
84. Quoted in "When Feminists Seek Pleasure," Chapter 3 of Estrada-Claudio, *Rape, Love and Sexuality,* 85.
85. Torres, *Love in the Time of Ina Morata,* 80.
86. Interview with Salgado, September 27, 2006.

Chapter 6. Women's Studies on the Air: Radio, Television, and Women's Movements

1. The *Womanwatch* byline was "a show by women, about women, for women and produced by women."
2. "Women in Radio," *Tinig,* June 17, 1996.
3. Interview with Anna Leah Sarabia, Manila, September 21, 2006, and September 25, 2006; and interview with Lily Malasa, WMC, Manila, September 21, 2006.

4. Interview with Sarabia, January 4, 2008.

5. *Womanwatch* recorded episodes on Betacam format making it impossible to view them unless the Herculean task of transposing them into DVD format was carried out. WMC kindly transposed their signature two-part program "From Priestess to President: The Story of Women's Struggle in the Philippines," *Womanwatch,* Women's Media Circle, 1986, and their closing episode *The Best of Womanwatch* for me. They also transposed three episodes of *XYZ* to DVD format and a series of feminist plugs or commercials they produced so I could view them.

6. Elizabeth Ramona R. Sanchez, "Womanwatch" on Television: A Case Study," BA thesis, University of the Philippines, 1991.

7. Interview with Lily Malasa, anchor *XYZone,* Manila, September 25, 2006.

8. Interview with Janice Monte, anchor for *Okay Ka,* Quezon City, January 19, 2005.

9. *Okay Ka Mare!,* June 20, 1999, June 27, 1999.

10. "Amour Propio," *XYZ Young Women's Television,* February 13, 2000; *Babae Ka,* January 15, 2005; "Body Talk" in "Back to Basics," *XYZ Young Women's Television,* April 23, 2000; "There Is Life After Breast Cancer," *XYZone,* Episode 25, October 28, 2000; "Breast Cancer Prevention," *XYZone,* Episode 126, October 19, 2002; "Breast Cancer Awareness," *XYZone,* Episode 127, October 26, 2002.

11. "Abuse of Women in an Intimate Relationship," *Kape,* October 6, 2003.

12. *Kape,* October 2, 2003; *Tinig,* November 20, 1995.

13. "Partner Infidelity," *Kape,* October 13, 2002.

14. "Women's Sexuality," *Tinig,* June 9, 1997.

15. Ibid.

16. "Women's Rights, Lesbian Rights," Broadcast 44, *XYZone,* March 10, 2001.

17. Ibid., "Lesbianism: A Matter of Choice?," *XYZone,* Broadcast 4, May 20, 2000; "Homosexuality," *XYZone,* Broadcast 7, June 17, 2000; "Lesbianism: Is it a Choice? Part 2," *XYZone,* Broadcast 22, October 7, 2000; "Lesbianism at the Workplace," *XYZone,* Broadcast 24, October 21, 2000; "Single Mom," *XYZone,* Broadcast 54, May 26, 2001; and "Lesbian Counseling," *XYZone,* Broadcast 65, August 11, 2001.

18. "Dapat Bang Makialam ang Simbahan sa RH Issue?" [Should the Church interfere in the issue of reproductive health?] *XYZone,* November 16, 2002.

19. *Babae Ka,* January 8, 2005.

20. "Family Code Separation and Annulment," *Tinig,* February 3, 1997.

21. "Dapat Bang Makialam ang Simbahan sa RH Issue?"

22. *Tinig,* November 6, 1995; *Tinig,* October 16, 1995.

23. "Babaylan and Women in the Pre-Colonial Period," *Tinig,* August 24, 1997; "Women During the Spanish Period," *Tinig,* August 31, 1997; "KAANAK and Women During the Spanish Period," *Tinig,* September 7, 1997; "Testimonies of Relatives of Women Heroes During the Spanish Period," *Tinig,* September 14, 1997; "Women During the American

Period," *Tinig,* September 21, 1997; "Women During the Japanese
Period," *Tinig,* September 28, 1997; "Japanese Invasion and Comfort
Women," *Tinig,* October 5, 1997; "Comfort Women," *Tinig,* January
8, 1996; "Introduction to Women in the Resistance Movement," *Tinig,*
August 17, 1997; "Hukbalahap Movement," *Tinig,* October 12, 1997;
"Women During the 70s and 80s," *Tinig,* October 26, 1997; "Summing up
of Women in the Resistance Series," *Tinig,* November 9, 1997.
24. "Socializing Forces," *Tinig,* April 15, 1996; "Gender Fair Education," *Tinig,* April 22, 1996; "Critique of Mainstream Education," *Tinig,* April 15,
1996; *Tinig,* October 9, 1995; *Tinig,* October 16, 1995. See also "Filipino-
American War," *Okay Ka,* February 7, 1999; "Martial Law," *Okay Ka,*
September 29, 1998; "Pagbabalik-tanaw, Part 1 [Looking back in history];
Okay Ka, December 27, 1998, "End of Word War 2," *Okay Ka,* August 12,
2000; "Araw ng Kalayaan, History ng Paglaban ng mga Muslim/Moro
para sa Kanilang Kalayaan" [Independence day, history of the Muslims'
fight for their independence], *Okay Ka,* June 11, 2000; and "Filipino-
American War and Balikatan 2002," *Okay Ka,* February 3, 2002.
25. "Women in the Holy Week," *Tinig,* April 1, 1996; "Women in the Old
Testament," *Tinig,* April 29, 1996; "Women in the New Testament,"
Tinig, May 6, 1996; "Women in Church History," *Tinig,* May 13, 1996;
"Women in Philippine Church History," *Tinig,* May 20, 1996; and
"Women in Church Today," *Tinig,* June 3, 1996.
26. "The Women's Movement," *Womanwatch,* Episode 26, September 1, 1987;
"Women's Health Movement," feature in "Peace," *Womanwatch,* Episode
29, October 6, 1987; "From Priestess to President: The Women's Struggle
in the Philippines," Part 1, *Womanwatch,* Episode 38, December 23, 1987;
"From Priestess to President: The Women's Struggle in the Philippines,"
Part 2, *Womanwatch,* Episode 39, December 30, 1987; "Feminism in the
Philippines," *Womanwatch,* Episode 69, November 2, 1988; "Alay sa Mga
Filipina Suffragists," *XYZone,* Broadcast 57, June 16, 2001; "To the Young
Women of Malolos," *XYZone,* Broadcast 58, June 23, 2001; "Ten Years of
KALAKASAN/Women Against Violence," *XYZone,* Broadcast 62, July
14, 2001; "Women's Role in History," *XYZone,* Broadcast 160, June 21,
2003; and "Women's Movement in the Philippines," *Tinig,* March 4, 1996.
27. "Trailblazers: Mga Babaeng Nanguna" [Trailblazers: Pioneering women],
XYZone, Broadcast 120, September 7, 2002.
28. "From Priestess to President: The Women's Struggle in the Philippines,"
Part 1, *Womanwatch,* December 23, 1987; and "From Priestess to President: The Women's Struggle in the Philippines," Part 2, *Womanwatch,*
December 30, 1987.
29. "Women Migrant Workers," *Womanwatch,* Episode 47, February 24,
1988; "Migrante: Filipina Maids in Hong Kong," *Womanwatch,* Episode
57, no telecast date, probably first two weeks in July 1988 (filmed entirely
in Hong Kong); "Ang Pinay sa Saudi" [Filipina worker in Saudi Arabia],
Womanwatch, Episode 64, September 7, 1988; "Maids in Hong Kong,"
Womanwatch, Episode 70, November 9, 1988; "Filipinos in Germany,"
Womanwatch, Episode 90, April 9, 1989; España con Amor" (Spain 1),

Womanwatch, Episode 109, October 25, 2989; "Viva España" *Womanwatch* (Spain 2), Episode 110, "Bella Italia," *Womanwatch,* Episode 113, November 29, 1989; "La Dolce Vita," *Womanwatch,* Episode 114, December 6, 1989; "Escape from Kuwait," *Womanwatch,* Episode 147, October 3, 1990; "*Atsay ng Mundo*" [Maid of the world], *Womanwatch,* Episode 225, nd, probably October 1992; "Buhay ng Pinay sa Hong Kong I," [The lives of Filipinas in Hong Kong], *Womanwatch,* Episode 232, nd, possibly end of December 1992; "Buhay Pinay sa Hong Kong Part 2" [The life of Filipino women in Hong Kong Part 2] *Womanwatch,* Episode 234, January 20,1993; and "DH sa Kuwait" [DH (Domestic helper) in Kuwait]," *Womanwatch,* Episode 247, July 28, 1993. See also "Maids," *Womanwatch,* Episode 36, December 2, 1987 (although focusing on maids in the Philippines, it had as one of the guests or resource persons Mary Lou Alcid, the regional coordinator of Asia Pacific Mission for Migrant Workers).

30. "Women Migrant Workers," *Womanwatch,* Episode 47, February 24, 1988 had as one guest Peachy Robles, an ex-dancer/entertainer in Japan; and "Maids," *Womanwatch,* Episode 36 had a feature on "Maids in the Philippines," December 2, 1987.

31. "Overseas Contract Workers," *Tinig,* December 18, 1995. *Okay Ka* also featured episodes on these topics: "Overseas Filipinos Particularly Domestic Helpers," *Okay Ka,* April 4, 1999; "Migrante, KMP," *Okay Ka,* June 6, 1999; "Migrante and Special Registration," *Okay Ka,* March 18, 2001.

32. "Kalusugan sa Karagatan" [Seafarer's health], *XYZone,* Broadcast 36, January 13, 2001; "Seafarers, Medical Side," *XYZone,* Broadcast 18, January 27, 2001; "Seafarers, Research Side," *XYZone,* Broadcast 39, February 3, 1001; "Seafarers, Training and Education," *XYZone,* Broadcast 40, February 10, 2001; and "Pasalubong" [Gifts from abroad], a sixty-second plug by WMC for the Department of Health, in "Hindi Kailangang Magtiis [There is no need to endure]: An IEC Campaign on Women's Health and Safe Motherhood," developed by the WMC for the Department of Health, CD-Rom, WMC, nd.

33. "Overseas Contract Workers," *Tinig,* December 18, 1995.

34. "Abortion: Illegal but Real," *XYZone,* Broadcast 48, April 7, 2001.

35. See Stella Gonzalez, "Hospitals Slam Doors on 'A' Cases," Inquirer News Service, September 3, 2004, in *Women's Studies Reader,* 183–186; Stella Gonzalez, "Doctors, Nurses Lack Basic Skill to Handle 'A' Cases," Inquirer News Service, September 4, 2004, in *Women's Studies Reader,* 187–189; Stella Gonzalez, "Abuse Not Unusual for 'A' Patients," Inquirer News Service, September 3, 2004, in *Women's Studies Reader,* 192–193; Yolanda Sotelo-Fuentes, "The Pangasinan 'A' Experience," Inquirer News Service, September 4, 2004, in *Women's Studies Reader,* 194–195;

36. Abortion was also featured in three episodes of *Womanwatch:* "CNN Special-Abortion," *Womanwatch,* September 13, 1989; "Abortion," *Womanwatch,* Episode 254, November 17, 1993; and "Abortion Stories From North and South," *Womanwatch,* Episode 272, June 15, 1994.

37. "Women's Rights, Lesbian Rights," Broadcast 44, *XYZone,* March 10, 2001.

38. Interview with Sarabia, January 4, 2008.

39. "Family Code, Separation and Annulment," *Tinig,* February 3, 1997.
40. "Single Mom," *XYZone,* Broadcast 54, May 26, 2001; and "Single Parenthood," *Kape,* October 20, 2002.
41. "Condoms, Nakakatulong ba?," [Condoms, do they help?], *XYZone,* Broadcast 30, December 2, 2000.
42. "Dapat Bang Makialam ang Simbahan sa RH Issue?"
43. Melchora Aquino or Tandang Sora was one of the heroines of the Philippine Revolution against Spain, *Babae Ka,* January 15, 2005; *Babae Ka,* January 29, 2005.
44. *Tinig,* November 6, 1995.
45. "Internet Trafficking," *XYZone,* Broadcast 95, March 9, 2002.
46. *Babae Ka,* January 8, 2005; interview with Katrina Legarda.
47. Interview with Sarabia, September 21, 2006; interview with Monte.
48. Interview with Anna Leah Sarabia, Makati City, August 12, 2003.
49. Interview with Sarabia, January 4, 2008.
50. Interview with Sarabia, September 21, 2006.
51. *Dito lahat tayo celebrity, kuwento ko, kuwento mo, mahalaga.*
52. Interview with Sarabia, January 4, 2008.
53. Interview with Sancho; and Henson, *Comfort Woman.*
54. Interview with Sarabia, January 4, 2008.
55. Sonia Capio, "Women on Primetime Radio," in *Who Calls the Shots? Proceedings of the 1991 International Conference on Women, Media and Advertising,* ed. Rosario A. Garcellano (WMC, 1991), 176.
56. Mary Grino, sometimes called Sister Mayang, in "Teaching Sexuality in the Home: Women Sexuality Education," *Tinig,* June 16, 1997.
57. "Pro-Gay Rights of Gay," *Okay Ka,* June 27, 1999; "Rights of Gays," *Womanwatch,* Episode 251, October 13, 1993; "Women's Rights, Lesbian Rights," Broadcast 44, *XYZone,* March 10, 2001; "Lesbianism: A Matter of Choice?," "Sexuality, Choices and Options," *XYZone,* Broadcast 6, June 10, 2000; "Homosexuality," "Lesbianism, Is it a Choice? 2," "Lesbianism at the Workplace," "Images of Gay and Lesbians in Media," *XYZone,* Broadcast 31, December 9, 2000; "Lesbian Counseling," and "Transgendered Persons," *XYZone,* Broadcast 167, August 9, 2003.
58. "Dapat Bang Makialam ang Simbahan sa RH Issue?"
59. Interview with Sarabia, September 21, 2006 and September 25, 2006.
60. The list of awards was provided by Sinag de Leon, WMC. Interview with Malasa, September 25, 2006.
61. List of *XYZone* episodes, Philippine WMC Archives.
62. "Women in Radio," *Tinig,* June 17, 1996; "Women in Television," *Tinig,* June 24, 1996; "Women in Advertising," *Tinig,* July 1, 1996, "Summary of Women in Media Series," *Tinig,* July 15, 1996; "Women in Media," *Womanwatch,* Episode 18, June 10, 1987; and "Women in Advertising," *Womanwatch,* Episode 176, June 5, 1991.
63. This inspired one academic to use the commercial as a metaphor about Philippine patriarchy. See Payonggayong, "Nakatikim ka ba ng Kinse Anyos?," 89–106.
64. Penny Azarcon de la Cruz, in Garcellano et al., eds., *Sisterhood Is Global,* 56.

Chapter 7. Fashioning Women through Activism, Ritual, and Dress

1. The term "comfort women" has had a controversial history in the politics of naming. I've used the term in quotation marks because I am reproducing how it was used by the women's organizations in the Philippines, including Lila-Pilipina and Lolas Kampanyeras. See also Sidonie Smith's footnote explaining why she also used this same representation. Sidonie Smith, "Belated Narrating: "Grandmothers" Telling Stories of Forced Sexual Servitude During World War II," in *Just Advocacy? Women's Human Rights, Transnational Feminisms;* and *The Politics of Representation,* ed. Wendy S. Hesford and Wendy Kozol (New Brunswick, NJ: Rutgers University Press, 2005), 141.
2. The eleven years refers to the length of time that her organization Lila Pilipina has been lobbying the Japanese government.
3. Interview with Sancho.
4. See David, *Nightmare Journeys;* Amilbangsa et al., eds., *Halfway Through the Circle;* and Nuqui and Montañez, eds., *Moving On.*
5. Mary Soledad Perpiñan, "Preventing Trafficking and Rescuing the Trafficked," Personal Papers of Mary Soledad Perpiñan (TW-MAE-W Office, Quezon City, nd, circa 1990s). See also David, *Nightmare Journeys;* and Amilbangsa et al., eds., *Halfway Through the Circle.*
6. The Peace Boat is an NGO that organizes cruises where NGOs deliver lectures. Mary Joy Barcelona delivered her testimony on life as a former entertainer in Japan during the Workshop on Promoting Human Security to Prevent Exploitative Migration in Africa with Special Emphasis on Trafficking in Women and Children in Durban, South Africa, and at the Public Hearing of Migrant Workers. Both were part of the NGO forum in the World Conference Against Racism, Racial Discrimination, Xenophobia and Related Intolerance held at South Africa. "Year Ender: Highlights of 2001 A Rewarding Year for DAWN," *Sinag* 6, no. 4 (October–December 2001): 8. The complete transcript of her testimony was published as Barcelona, "Unable to Find a Customer," 6–7, in Nuqui and Montañez, eds., *Moving On,* 145–164.
7. "UN Special Rapporteur Gabriela Rodriguez Meets the DAWN Family," *Sinag* 7, no. 2 (April–June 2002): 5.
8. Nuqui and Montañez, eds., *Moving On;* "Iba't Ibang Mukha ni Misty" [The different faces of Misty]. Script published in Nuqui and Montañez, eds., *Moving On,* 263–279.
9. "Coalition Holds Prostitution and Sexual Exploitation Symposium at UN CSW," *Coalition Asia-Pacific Report* 4, no. 1 (April 1998): 9. See also "Experts Group Meeting," January 26, 1999, Morning Plenary session, in the CATW Asia Pacific Papers, CAT-W office, Manila; Vida Subingsubing, "CATW-AP Launches Radio Program," *Coalition Asia-Pacific Report* 5, no. 1 (January–March 2000): 7; Jean Enriquez, "Fighting it Out in the Philippine Congress," *Coalition Asia-Pacific Report* 5, no. 1 (January–March 2000): 6.
10. Nuqui and Montañez, eds., *Moving On.*

11. Sikhay was the business arm of DAWN where women were taught to weave and sew products sold in the Philippines and overseas.
12. Nuqui and Montañez, eds., *Moving On,* 224.
13. Ibid., 241.
14. Interview with PETA Women's Theater Program (WTP) Director, Maribel Legarda, Quezon City, October 9, 2006.
15. DAWN brochure, 2005. See also "DAWN Recharges, Holds Team-Building Workshop at Villa de Oro, Tagaytay," *Sinag* (April–June 1999): 12; "'Misty' Play Reveals Life, Dreams of Japan-Bound Entertainers," *Sinag* (July–September 2000): 6.
16. 1998 Year-End Report, *Sinag* (January–December 1998): 8–9.
17. Interview with Nuqui, January 22, 2005.
18. DAWN brochure.
19. See issues of *Sinag* from 1997 to 2005.
20. From the reports of the DAWN activities in *Sinag,* I identified four plays by Japanese-Filipino children. In 1997, "Fujiwara Junko: JFC" performed to Peace Boat Participants; in 1998, "Sana, Isang Kuwento ng Pangarap" [I wish: A story of dreams] (also performed in Japan); in 2001, "The Ugly Duckling"; in 2002, "Pagsilay ng Bagong Pag-Asa" [The dawning of a new hope] and in 2004, "Ang Maskara: A Glimpse of the Joys and Pains of the Japanese-Filipino Children."
21. "Advocacy Through Theater Arts: Teatro Akebono Goes on Tour," *Sinag* 9, no. 4 (October–December 2004): 4.
22. Mary Soledad Perpiñan, "Preventing Trafficking and Rescuing the Trafficked" (Personal papers of Mary Soledad Perpiñan, nd); and Mary Soledad Perpiñan (TW-MAE-W Office, Quezon City, nd, circa 1990s); and Mary Soledad Perpiñan, "Empowering Marginalized Women" (Personal Papers of Mary Soledad Perpiñan, TW-MAE-W Office, Quezon City, nd circa 1990s).
23. Mary Soledad Perpiñan, "Preventing Trafficking and Rescuing the Trafficked" (Personal papers of Mary Soledad Perpiñan, nd).
24. Script of the play "They Are So Sweet, Sir," in Mary Soledad Perpiñan, "Preventing Trafficking and Rescuing the Trafficked" (Personal papers of Mary Soledad Perpiñan, nd).
25. Ibid.
26. Mary Soledad Perpiñan, "Empowering Marginalized Women" (Personal papers of Mary Soledad Perpiñan, TW-MAE-W Office, Quezon City, nd circa 1990s).
27. Quoted in Espallardo, "The Stage, the Body," 62.
28. *The PETA Journey Towards a Home* (Manila: Philippine Educational Theater Association, 2006), 26.
29. Barrameda, *Breaking Silence,* 29.
30. Espallardo, "The Stage, the Body," 56.
31. Barrameda, *Breaking Silence,* 36.
32. Ibid; No author, *Libby Manaoag Files Ang Paghahanap sa Puertas Princessas* [The search for the doors to the princess], *Discussion Guide* (Manila: PETA and NCCA), 3.

33. Barrameda, *Breaking Silence,* 30–32.
34. Ibid., 33.
35. Ibid., 75.
36. Legarda, "Imagined Communities," 343–347.
37. *Libby Manaoag Files,* VHS.
38. *Libby Manaoag Files,* Discussion Guide, 19–26.
39. Ibid., 62.
40. *Libby Manaoag Files,* VHS.
41. Barrameda, *Breaking Silence;* and *Birthings.*
42. Espallardo, "The Stage, the Body," 59–60
43. *Birthings,* 127–134.
44. *Libby Manaoag Files,* VHS; and interview with Maribel Legarda.
45. Interview with C. B. Garrucho, Quezon City, October 6, 2006.
46. *Libby Manaoag Files,* VHS.
47. Neferti Xina M. Tadiar, "Filipinas: Living in a Time of War," in *Body Politics: Essays on Cultural Representations of Women's Bodies,* ed. Odine de Guzman (Quezon City: University Center for Women's Studies, University of the Philippines, 2002), 15.
48. "Soap," in *Sining Lila,* GABRIELA, CD, 2002.
49. "O Maria, O Maria," "Bagong Maria," "Bangon Maria," and "Maria," in *Sining Lila,* GABRIELA, CD, 2002.
50. *Kali* 3, no. 1 (July 2003).
51. *Libby Manaoag Files,* VHS.
52. "Hindi Kailangang Magtiis."
53. "Maria," published in *Chaneg* 9, no.1 (January–June 2000): 35; and "Maria," published in *GABRIELA Convention Proceedings* (Quezon City: Mount Carmel Community Center, March 2–3, 1985), 51.
54. "Maria," published in GABRIELA Convention Proceedings, 51.
55. Teresa Magbanua was another prominent heroine of the revolution who rose to the rank of general in the army. See "Maria," published in *Chaneg* 9, no.1 (January–June 2000): 35.
56. "Maria," words published in *Kali* 3, no. 1 (July 2003): 122.
57. "Gumising Ka, Babae!" [Wake up, woman!], music by Julie Palaganas, lyrics by Luchie Maranan, *Chaneg* 11, no. 1 (January–June 2002): 31; "Awit ay Diringgin/Abante, Babae" [Pay attention to the song: Go forward, woman], by Kalantog (lyrics by Joi Barrios, music by Rica Palis), *Chaneg* 14, no. 1 (June 2005): 39; "Maria," published in *Chaneg* 9, no.1 (January–June 2000): 35; and "Maria," published in GABRIELA Convention Proceedings, 51. Some of the songs were written and composed by men such as Mon Ayco, while others such as "Hindi Kailangan Magtiis," was composed by a man (Diwa de Leon) with lyrics by three women (composed by Diwa de Leon, and lyrics by Ani S. de Leon, Sinag Amado, and Anna Leah Sarabia).
58. "Atsay ng Mundo."
59. "Martsa ng Kababaihan" [March of women], in *Kali* 3, no. 1 (July 2003): 125–126.
60. "Hindi Kailangang Magtiis."

61. Interview with Mary John Mananzan (OSB), Manila, July 20, 1995.
62. Interview with de Jesus.
63. Interview with de Dios, August 8, 2003.
64. Transcribed field notes tape recorded at the protest in Quezon City, January 19, 2005.
65. Interview with Rechilda Extremadura, director of Lila-Pilipina, Quezon City, August 26, 2003.
66. *Babae Ka,* January 15, 2005.
67. See *Gabriela Update* newsletters from the 1990s.
68. See Roces, "Gender, Nation and the Politics of Dress," 354–377.
69. Sarabia's grandmother Natividad Almeda Lopez was the first woman judge and a suffragist. Interview with Sarabia, September 21, 2006.
70. Interview with Extremadura.
71. Interview with Sancho.
72. Interview with de Dios, August 8, 2003.
73. Ibid. and interview with Enriquez.
74. Susan O. Michelman, "Fashion and Identity of Women Religious," in *Religion, Dress and the Body,* ed. Linda B. Arthur (Oxford: Berg, 1999), 135.
75. Interview with Gertrude Borres (RA), Makati City January 21, 2002.
76. Interview with Mananzan, July 17, 2003; interview with Graham.
77. Interview with Borres.
78. Interview with Dimaranan.
79. Ibid.
80. Interview with Perpiñan, August 28, 2003.
81. Interview with Mananzan, July 17, 2003.

Chapter 8. Women's Movements in Transnational Spaces

1. See *Kontraktwalisasyon sa Paggawa,* 36.
2. Ian Tyrrell, *Transnational Nation: United States History in Global Perspective Since 1789* (New York: Palgrave Macmillan, 2007), 3.
3. Akira Iriye and Pierre-Yves Saunier, "Introduction: The Professor and the Madman," in *The Palgrave Dictionary of Transnational History From the Mid-19th Century to the Present Day,* ed. Akira Iriye and Pierre-Yves Saunier (New York: Palgrave Macmillan, 2009), xviii.
4. Ellen Carol DuBois, "Women's Movements," entry in *The Palgrave Dictionary of Transnational History From the Mid-19th Century to the Present Day,* ed. Akira Iriye and Pierre-Yves Saunier (New York: Palgrave Macmillan, 2009), 1120; see Tyrrell, *Transnational Nation.*
5. Interview with Maitet Ledesma, Amsterdam, July 31, 2006.
6. Interview with Enriquez; interview with de Dios, August 8, 2003; and interview with Perpiñan, July 28, 2003; interview with Extremadura; interview with Lola Asiang Cortes and Lola Viginia Guillermi, August 9, 2003.
7. "Women's International Solidarity Affair in the Philippines 1989," x.
8. Interview with Amelia Vazquez (RSCJ), Quezon City, August 19, 2003.

9. Ibid.
10. Interview with Soledad Perpiñan (RGS), Quezon City, April 20, 1996.
11. Primer on TW-MAE-W, archives of TW-MAE-W, Quezon City, Philippines, 6.
12. Ibid.
13. See, for example, "Third World Movement Against the Exploitation of Women: Statement Given to the Commission on the Status of Women Beijing PrepCom," March 15 to April 4, 1995, United Nations New York (Personal papers, Soledad Perpiñan, Quezon City); and "TW-MAE-W Statement for the Preparatory Committee for the International Conference on Population and Development United Nations," April 4–22, 1994 (Personal papers, Soledad Perpiñan, Quezon City).
14. Interview with Sarabia, September 25, 2006.
15. Garcellano et al., eds., *Sisterhood Is Global,* 266.
16. "Women's International Solidarity Affair in the Philippines 1989," x.
17. Ibid.
18. Ibid., 158–159.
19. Ibid., 21.
20. Proceedings of the Sixth International Women and Health Meeting, Philippines Organizing Committee.
21. Interview with Ledesma.
22. Margaret E. Keck and Kathryn Sikkink, *Activists Beyond Borders Advocacy Networks in International Politics* (Ithaca, NY: Cornell University Press, 1998), 171–183.
23. "Purple Rising" was the code name for the anti-violence against women campaign launched by GABRIELA for the international chapters. *GABRIELA Women's Update* 9, no. 1 (January–March 1999): 23; and flier, Pinay sa Holland, published in *Chaneg* 7, no. 2 (July–December 1999): 6–7.
24. *GABRIELA Women's Update,* 23.
25. Ibid.
26. Interview with Cahilog.
27. Fiona Seiger, "Meet Fiona from Vienna," *Sinag* 13, no. 3 (July–September 2008): 9.
28. Sikhay is part of the NGO DAWN. Since the NGO is helping former entertainers in Japan and is against further overseas work in Japan, they have to give these women jobs in the Philippines with salaries that enable them to live above the poverty line at the very least. DAWN pays the tuition for the former entertainers to learn new job skills including sewing and weaving for the Sikhay business. Visitors are welcome in Sikhay because they are potential buyers for Sikhay products.
29. Interview with Nuqui, January 22, 2005.
30. Ibid.
31. Ibid.
32. Margaret E. Keck and Kathryn Sikkink, *Activists Beyond Borders: Advocacy Networks in International Politics* (Ithaca, NY: Cornell University Press, 1998), 181–183.

33. Interviews with Estrada-Claudio, September 18, 2006, October 6, 2006, and January 7, 2008.
34. Anna Leah Sarabia's note in "Evaluation and Sharing," Garcellano et al., eds., *Sisterhood Is Global,* 293.
35. Ibid., 296–300. The quote is by Robin Morgan, on p. 300.
36. Marilyn Waring in ibid., 303.
37. Robin Morgan in ibid., 301.
38. Interview with Nuqui, January 22, 2005.
39. Interview with de Dios, August 8, 2003, and January 26, 2008.
40. Interview with Cahilog.
41. Interviews with Sarabia, September 21, 2006, September 25, 2006, and January 4, 2008.
42. Interview with Patricia Licuanan, Quezon City, July 23, 2003; interview with Aurora Javate de Dios, Quezon City, July 23, 2003; interview with Francisco, July 23, 2003; interview with Illo; and interview with Enriquez.
43. Interview with Enriquez; interview with Illo.
44. Helen Benitez (CSW vice chair, 1964–1966, CSW chair, 1966–1970), Leticia Shahani (CSW vice chair 1973–1973, CSW chair 1974–1975), Rosario Manalo (CSW chair 1984–1985), and Patricia Licuanan (1994–1996) revealed that each decade since the 1960s could boast of one Filipina chair. Shahani was the secretary general of the Third World Conference on Women, Nairobi, 1985, and was a member of the group that drafted the CEDAW. Manalo also served as CEDAW expert in 1999–2006 and CEDAW committee chair in 2005–2006. Two other women, Aurora Javate de Dios and Teresita Quintos-Deles, also served as CEDAW experts. Although these women were in these positions as government representatives rather than as women activists, some of them actually wore several hats as academics and as activists. See Olivia H. Tripon, ed., *Shaping the Women's Global Agenda: Filipino Women in the United Nations Commission on the Status of Women/CEDAW Committee* (Manila: National Commission on the Role of Filipino Women, 2006).
45. Interview with Patricia Licuanan, July 23, 2003.
46. Interview with Patricia Licuanan, Quezon City, January 18, 2008.

Chapter 9. Women's Movements in Liminal Spaces:
Abortion as a Reproductive Right

1. Poster, The Women and Development 210 class, "Abortion as a Reproductive Right: Women's Perpectives," A Symposium with speakers from Likhaan, WCC, Family Planning Organization of the Philippines, Education Forum, WomenLead, and GABRIELA, October 9, 2006, College of Social Work and Community Development, The University of the Philippines, Quezon City.
2. Sylvia Estrada-Claudio, MD, PhD, associate professor of Women and Development Studies, University of the Philippines, and chair of the board of directors, Likhaan, "Message Delivered at the International Meeting

on Amnesty International's Sexual and Reproductive Rights Policy,"
London, June 10–12, 2005, 8.

3. Quoted in Carolina S. Ruiz-Austria, Flordeliza C. Vargas, Amy A. Avellano, Clara Rita A. Padilla, Rowena V. Legaspi, and Abigail V. Acuba,
"From Mortal Sin to Human Rights: Redefining the Philippine Policy
on Abortion," *Women's Journal on Law & Culture,* 1 no. 1 (July–December
2001): 90–105.
4. See Andrea Whittaker, *Abortion, Sin and the State in Thailand* (London:
Routledge/Curzon, 2004).
5. Singh et al., "Addressing Abortion as a Public Health Concern and Social
Problem," in *Unintended Pregnancy,* ed. Singh et al., 4, 28, 29; Dañguilan,
Making Choices in Good Faith, 47; Sharon Cabusao, "Shadows in the Abortion Debate," *Laya Feminist Quarterly* 3 (1992), 26; and "Soiree on Abortion," *Womenews* 8, no. 3 (July–September 1991): 3.
6. Singh et al., eds., *Unintended Pregnancy,* 4.
7. Ibid., 5.
8. Quoted in Carolina S. Ruiz-Austria, Flordeliza C. Vargas, Amy A. Avellano, Clara Rita A. Padilla, Rowena V. Legaspi, and Abigail V. Acuba,
"From Mortal Sin to Human Rights: Redefining the Philippine Policy
on Abortion," *Women's Journal on Law & Culture,* 1 no. 1 (July–December
2001): 90.
9. Ibid., 90–93.
10. Hearings on the Committee on Revision of Laws, Batasan, Quezon City,
September 20, 2006.
11. Quoted in Singh et al., eds., *Unintended Pregnancy,* 8.
12. Carolina S. Ruiz-Austria, Flordeliza C. Vargas, Amy A. Avellano, Clara
Rita A. Padilla, Rowena V. Legaspi, and Abigail V. Acuba, "From Mortal
Sin to Human Rights: Redefining the Philippine Policy on Abortion,"
Women's Journal on Law & Culture, 1 no. 1 (July–December 2001): 92;
Dañguilan, *Making Choices in Good Faith,* 96.
13. Cabiling, *Erika;* Cabiling, *Serena;* Cabiling, *Angelika;* Bautista, *Hugot sa
Sinapupunan* [Taken from the womb]; Bautista, *Desisyon*; Bautista, *Ang
Kabilang Panig.*
14. Jurilla, *Tagalog Bestsellers;* and interviews with Joy Salgado, Quezon City,
September 27, 2006 and January 8, 2008.
15. Information on publication particulars of the pocketbooks came from an
e-mail correspondence with Joy Salgado, Likhaan Office, October 2, 2007.
16. Bautista, *Ang Kabilang Panig,* 110, 135.
17. Bautista, *Hugot sa Sinapupunan,* 78.
18. Bautista, *Ang Kabilang Panig,* 95; Cabiling, *Serena,* 42.
19. Bautista, *Desisyon,* 135.
20. Bautista, *Ang Kabilang Panig,* 52.
21. Lualhati Bautista in the prologue to *Buhay Namin, Isang Dula Tungkol
sa Aborsyon,* [Our lives: A play about abortion], Likhaan, nd (circa
2004). Written by Lualhati Bautista, directed by Raffy Tejada, PETA
production.
22. The Tagalog word "*dakila*" was used to describe national heroes or iconic

figures in history or myth. Sylvia Estrada-Claudio, in the prologue to
Buhay Namin. Written by Lualhati Bautista, Directed by Raffy Tejada,
PETA production.
23. Ibid.
24. Cabiling, *Angelika,* 4, 112.
25. Ibid., 68, 108, 111.
26. *Nabuntis ka, magtiis ka.*
27. *Buhay Namin.* Written by Lualhati Bautista, Directed by Raffy Tejada,
PETA production.
28. http://prolife.org.ph/home/index.php/about-us/the-foundation,
accessed February 2010.
29. Interview with Estavillo.
30. Interview with Francisco, July 27, 2010.
31. Interview with Nemenzo.
32. *Birthings,* 51–55.
33. Ibid., 55.

Conclusion

1. Pingol, *Remaking Masculinities.*
2. See the chapter on polygamy in Susan Blackburn, *Women and the State in Modern Indonesia* (Cambridge, UK: Cambridge University Press, 2004), 11–137
3. Interview with Minerva Quintela and Claire Lucson, WomenLead, Quezon City, January 11, 2008.
4. Interview with Miranda; Mananzan, "The Babaylan in Me," 141; "Profiles of the POC Member Organizations," in *Proceedings,* Sixth IWHM, November 3–9, 1990 (Quezon City: Philippines Organizing Committee, 1992), 205; interview with Vistro, January 24, 2008; and interview with Taguiwalo.
5. Monica Lindberg-Falk, "Feminism, Buddhism and Transnational Women's Movements in Thailand," in *Women's Movements in Asia: Feminisms and Transnational Activism,* ed. Mina Roces and Louise Edwards (London: Routledge, 2010), 110–123.

Selected Bibliography

This bibliography is not the complete record of all the works and sources I have used as primary and secondary research materials for this book. I have chosen to select here the most important primary sources including the published works of the feminist nuns, the periodicals (listed here to include the years I've consulted inclusively rather than an individual list of articles cited as is protocol for historians), as well as the most important books and printed material published by women's organizations discussed in this book. In addition, I list the interviews I conducted with prominent members of women's organizations and feminist activists and politicians. Only a small number of secondary sources consulted are included here since complete references are available in the relevant footnotes of each chapter. I have not included the list of radio, DVDs, and television shows I watched, most of which are referenced in Chapters 7 and 8, or the songs analyzed in Chapter 8.

Archives

Battung, Mary Rosario (RGS). Papers. Good Shepherd Convent, Quezon City.
CATW-AP. Papers. CATW-AP Office, Quezon City.
Fabella,Virginia (MM). Papers. Maryknoll Convent, Quezon City.
Mananzan, Mary John (OSB). Papers. Nursia, Manila.
Perpiñan, Soledad (RGS). Papers. TW-MAE-W Office, Quezon City.
Women's Media Circle (WMC). Papers and radio programs. Manila.

Published Sources

Aguilar, Delia. *The Feminist Challenge. Initial Working Principles Toward Reconceptualizing the Feminist Movement in the Philippines.* Manila: Asian Social Institute, 1988.

———. *Toward a Nationalist Feminism*. Quezon City: Giraffe Books, 1998.

Angeles, Leonora. "Feminism and Nationalism: The Discourse on the Woman Question and Politics of the Women's Movement in the Philippines." MA thesis, University of the Philippines, 1989.

Apuan, Victoria Narciso, Mary Rosario B. Battung (RGS), Liberato C. Bautista, eds. *Witness and Hope Amid Struggle: Towards a Theology and Spirituality of Struggle Book II*. Manila: Ecumenical Bishops Forum, Forum for Interdisciplinary Endeavors and Studies (FIDES), and Socio-Pastoral Institute, 1992.

Arriola, Fe Capellan. *Si Maria, Nena, Gabriela Atbp* [Maria, Nena, Gabriela and others]. Manila: GABRIELA, and Institute of Women's Studies, St. Scholastica, 1989.

"Asian Peasant Women Conference on Landrights and Globalization." Conference Proceedings, June 28–30, 2004, Diliman, Quezon City. Quezon City: Amihan, PWLD, Asian Peasant Women Network, 2004.

Asian Rural Women Study Session on CEDAW and Poverty Proceedings, November 17–21, 2005, Bayview Park Hotel, Manila. Quezon City: Amihan, 2006.

Ballescas, Ma. Rosario. *Filipino Entertainers in Japan: An Introduction*. Quezon City: Foundation for Nationalist Studies, 1992.

Barrameda, Teresita V., with contributions from Lea Espallardo. *Breaking Silence: A Nationwide Informance Tour for the Prevention of Violence Against Women in the Family*. Quezon City: PETA and UNIFEM, 2000.

Battung, Mary Rosario (RGS), Liberato C. Bautista, Ma. Sophia Lizares-Bodegon, Alice G. Guillermo, eds. *Religion and Society: Towards a Theology of Struggle, Book 1*. Manila: Forum for Interdisciplinary Endeavors and Studies (FIDES), 1988.

Bautista, Lualhati. *Ang Kabilang Panig ng Bakod* [The other side of the fence]. Quezon City: Likhaan, 2005.

———. *Desisyon* [Decision]. Quezon City: Likhaan, 2005.

———. *Hugot sa Sinapupunan* [Taken from the womb]. Quezon City: Likhaan, 2004.

Birthings: A Journal of Shared Lives. Quezon City: Philippine Educational Theater Association (PETA), 2002.

Brewer, Carolyn. *Shamanism, Catholicism and Gender Relations in Colonial Philippines, 1521–1685*. Aldershot, VT: Ashgate, 2004.

Building Women's Unity and Solidarity Against Globalization. WISAP '98 Women's International Solidarity Affair in the Philippines, August 19–21, 1998. Villa Julia Resort, Silang, Cavite. Metro-Manila: GABRIELA, 1998.

Caagusan, Flor, ed. *Halfway Through the Circle: The Lives of Eight Filipino Survivors of Prostitution and Sex Trafficking*. Manila: WEDPRO Inc, 2001.

Cabiling, Carmen. *Angelika* [Angelica]. Quezon City: Likhaan, 2006.

———. *Erika* [Erica]. Quezon City: Likhaan, 2004.

———. *Serena* [Serena]. Quezon City: Likhaan, 2005.

Cariño, Judy and Rene Villanueva. *Dumaloy ang Ilog Chico* [And so the Chico River flows]. Metro Manila: GABRIELA, 1995.

"Challenging and Subverting the System of Prostitution: A Policy Paper."
Quezon City: Women's Legal Bureau, Inc., 1999.

Chant, Sylvia, and Cathy McIlwaine. *Women of a Lesser Cost: Female Labour, Foreign Exchange and Philippine Development.* Quezon City: Ateneo de Manila University, 1995.

Cheung, Fanny et al., eds. *Breaking the Silence: Violence Against Women in Asia.* Hong Kong: UNESCO, 1999.

Choy, Catherine Ceniza. *Empire of Care Nursing and Migration in Filipino American History.* Quezon City: Ateneo de Manila University Press, 2003.

Claussen, Heather. *Unconventional Sisterhood Feminist Catholic Nuns in the Philippines.* Ann Arbor: The University of Michigan Press, 2001.

Constable, Nicole. *Romance on a Global Scale: Pen Pals, Virtual Ethnography and "Mail-Order" Marriages.* Berkeley: The University of California Press, 2003.

Culture of Foreign Domination: Women's Issues, Alternatives and Initiatives, Women's International Solidarity Affair in the Philippines '91 conference proceedings, August 23-September 6, 1991. Metro-Manila: GABRIELA, 1991.

Dandan, Virginia B. "Women's Lives in an Ethnic Community: A Profile of the Samoki." *Review of Women's Studies* 1, no.1 (1990): 2–14.

Dañguilan, Marilen J. *Making Choices in Good Faith: A Challenge to the Catholic Church's Teachings on Sexuality and Contraception.* Quezon City: Woman-Health Philippines, Inc., 1993.

David, Rina. *Nightmare Journeys: Filipina Sojourns Through the World of Trafficking.* Manila: Milflores Publishing, 2002.

de Dios, Aurora Javate. "Participation of Women's Groups in the Anti-Dictatorship Struggle: Genesis of a Movement." In *Women's Role in Philippine History,* no editor, 141–168. Quezon City: University Center for Women's Studies, The University of the Philippines, 1996.

———. "Hidden No More: Violence Against Women in the Philippines," in *Breaking the Silence: Violence Against Women in Asia,* eds. Fanny M. Cheung, Malavika Karlekar, Aurora de Dios, Juree Vichit-Vadakan, Lourdes R. Quisumbing (Hong Kong: Equal Opportunities Commission, Women in Asian Development & UNESCO National Commission of the Philippines, 1999).

de Dios, Stella G. et al. with Mary Ann Asico, Anna Leah Sarabia, and Virata Gillian Joyce, eds. *Bodytalk: The XYZ Guide to Young Women's Health and Body,* Vol. 1 and Vol. 2. Manila: The Women's Media Circle, 1999, 2001.

Delfin, Lynn P., and Jean C. Enriquez with Jajurie Raissa H., eds. *Shifting the Blame: A Primer on Prostitution Policies.* Manila: SALIGAN and CATW-PHILS, 2002.

Demeterio-Melgar, Junice L. "Raising Sexuality as a Political Issue in the Catholic Philippines." In *Sexuality, Gender and Rights Exploring Theory and Practice in South and Southeast Asia,* edited by Geetanjalii Misra and Radhika Chandiramani, 152–253. New Delhi: Sage Publications, 2005.

Edwards, Louise, and Mina Roces, eds. *Women's Suffrage in Asia: Gender, Nationalism and Democracy.* London: Routledge/Curzon, 2004.

"Empowering Women in a Situation of Crisis." Congress Proceedings, GABRIELA 5th National Congress, March 10–12, 1989, Baguio City. Metro-Manila: GABRIELA 1989.

Encanto, Georgina Reyes. *Constructing the Filipina: A History of Women's Magazines (1891–2002).* Quezon City: The University of the Philippines Press, 2004.

Espallardo, Lea Lastrilla. "The Stage, the Body: The Sites for Women's Dissent A Case of Engendering the Praxis of Theatre in the Philippines." In *Sexuality, Gender and Rights Exploring Theory and Practice in South and Southeast Asia,* edited by Geetanjali Misra and Radhika Chandiramani, 47–66. New Delhi: Sage Publications, 2005.

Estrada-Claudio, Sylvia, "The Psychology of the Filipino Woman." In *Women and Gender Relations in the Philippines: Selected Readings in Women's Studies,* Vol. 1, edited by Jeanne Frances I. Illo, 183–192. Quezon City: Women's Studies Association of the Philippines and Center for Women's Studies, 1999.

———. *Rape, Love and Sexuality: The Construction of Woman in Discourse.* Quezon City: The University of the Philippines Press, 2002.

Eviota, Elizabeth U., ed. *Sex and Gender in Philippine Society.* Manila: NCRFW, 1994.

———. *The Political Economy of Gender: Women and the Sexual Division of Labour in the Philippines.* London: Zed, 1992 and Manila: Institute of Women's Studies, 1993.

Fabella, Virginia (MM). "Christology from an Asian Perspective," in *We Dare to Dream: Doing Theology as Asian Women,* ed. Virginia Fabella and Sun Ai Lee Park, 3–13. Hong Kong: Asian Women's Resource Centre for Culture and Theology, 1989.

———, ed. *Asia's Struggle for Full Humanity: Toward a Relevant Theology.* Papers from the Asian Theological Conference, January 7–20, 1979, Wennappuwa, Sri Lanka. Maryknoll, NY: Orbis Books, 1980.

———. "Inculturating the Gospel: The Philippine Experience." *The Way, Review of Contemporary Christian Spirituality* 39, no. 2 (1999): 118–128.

———. "Mission of Women in the Church in Asia: Role and Position." In *Essays on Women,* edited by Mary John Mananzan (OSB), 159–170. Manila: Institute of Women's Studies, 1987, 1991 Edition.

———. "The Roman Catholic Church in the Asian Ecumenical Movement," in *A History of the Ecumenical Movement in Asia,* Vol. II, edited by Nina Koshy, 115–138. Hong Kong: World Student Christian Federation Asia-Pacific Region, Asia and Pacific Alliance of YMCAs and Christian Conference of Asia, 2004.

———. *Beyond Bonding: A Third World Women's Theological Journey.* Manila: Ecumenical Association of Third World Theologians and Institute of Women's Studies, 1993.

Fabella, Virginia, Peter K. H. Lee, David Kwang-sun Suh, eds. *Asian Christian Spirituality Reclaiming Traditions.* Maryknoll, NY: Orbis Books, 1992.

Fabella, Virginia, and Sun Ai Lee Park, eds. *We Dare to Dream: Doing Theology as Asian Women.* Hong Kong: Asian Women's Center for Culture and Theology and EATWOT Women's Commission in Asia, 1989.

Fabella, Virginia M. M., and R. S. Sugirtharaja, eds., *Dictionary of Third World Theologies*. Maryknoll, NY: Orbis Books, 2000.

Fabella, Virginia, and Sergio Torres, eds. *Doing Theology in a Divided World, Papers from the Sixth International Conference of the Ecumenical Association of Third World Theologians,* January 5–12, 1983, Geneva, Switzerland. Maryknoll, NY: Orbis Books, 1985.

———, eds. "Irruption of the Third World Challenge to Theology." Papers to the Fifth International Conference of the Ecumenical Association of Third World Theologians, August 17–29, 1981, New Delhi, India. Maryknoll, NY: Orbis Books, 1983.

Fabros, Mercedes Lactao, Aileen May C Paguntalan, Lourdes L. Arches, and Maria Teresa Guia-Padilla. "From *Sanas* to *Dapat:* Negotiating Entitlement in Reproductive Decision-Making in the Philippines." In *Negotiating Reproductive Rights: Women's Perspectives Across Countries and Cultures,* edited by Rosalind P. Petchesky and Karen Judd, 217–255. London: Zed Books, 1998.

Francisco, Josefa. *Gaining Ground? Southeast Asian Women in Politics and Decision-Making, Ten Years After Beijing, A Compilation of Five Country Reports.* Pasig City: Friedrich Ebert Stiftung, 2004.

———. *Women's Participation and Advocacy in the Party List Election.* Quezon City: The Center for Legislative Development, Occasional Paper, No. 3, 1998.

Frias, Eileen. "Women Workers: Life and Struggle," *Laya Feminist Quarterly* 2, no. 2 (1993).

GABRIELA Conference Proceedings. Metro-Manila: GABRIELA. March 2–3, 1985.

Gaerlan, Kristina, ed. *Women Religious Now: Impact of the Second Vatican Council on Women Religious in the Philippines.* Manila: Institute of Women's Studies, 1993.

Gaining Ground Building Strength: Advancing Grassroots Women's Struggles for Liberation, WISAP '94 Women's International Solidarity Affair in the Philippines, October 20–28, 1994, Antipolo, Rizal, Metro-Manila: GABRIELA, 1994.

Garcellano, Rosario A. "Who Calls the Shots?" Proceedings of the 1991 International Conference of Women, Media and Advertising. Manila: The Women's Media Circle Foundation Inc., 1991.

Garcellano, Rosario, Elizabeth Lolarga, and Anna Leah Sarabia, eds. *Sisterhood Is Global: Dialogues in the Philippines.* Quezon City: Circle Publications, 1992.

Guerrero, Milagros C., "The Babaylan in Colonial Times: Bodies Desecrated." In *Gender/Bodies/Religions,* edited by Sylvia Marcos, 167–178. Mexico: ALER Publication, 2000.

Guerrero, Sylvia, ed. *Gender-Sensitive and Feminist Methodologies: A Handbook for Health and Social Researchers.* Quezon City: The University of the Philippines Press, 2002 edition.

Henson, Maria Rosa. *Comfort Woman: Slave of Destiny.* Manila: Philippine Center for Investigative Journalism, 1996, reprinted by Rowman and Littlefield, 2001.

Hilhorst, Dorothea. *The Real World of NGOs: Discourses, Diversity and Environment.* Quezon City: Ateneo de Manila University Press, 2003.

Hilsdon, Anne Marie. "Introduction: Reconsidering Agency—Feminist Anthropologies in Asia." *The Australian Journal of Anthropology* 18, no. 2 (2007): 127–137.

Illo, Jeanne Frances I. "Speaking in Different Voices: An Introduction." In *Women and Gender Relations in the Philippines: Selected Readings in Women's Studies,* Vol. 1, edited by Jeanne Frances I. Illo, 1–8. Quezon City: Women's Studies Association of the Philippines, 1999.

Illo, Jeanne Frances I., and Rosalinda Pineda Ofreneo, eds. *Carrying the Burden of the World: Women Reflecting on the Effects of the Crisis on Women and Girls.* Quezon City: University of the Philippines Center for Integrative and Development Studies, 1999.

Issues, Challenges, and Strategies: Selected Speeches and Articles on Globalization. Metro-Manila: GABRIELA, March 8, 1999.

KALAKASAN, *Pambubugbog ng Asawa, Sino Ang May Sala? Tigil Bugbog Action Pack* Vol 2. [Spouse beating, who is at fault? Stop beating action pack]. Manila: Circle Publications, 1994.

KALAKASAN. *Sa Akin Pa Rin Ang Bukas at Iba Pang Kuwento, Tigil Bugbog Action Pack,* Vol 1. [The future is still mine and other stories, stop beating action pack]. Manila: Circle Publications, 1994.

Law, Lisa. "A Matter of 'Choice': Discourses on Prostitution in the Philippines." In *Sites of Desire: Economies of Pleasure,* edited by Lenore Manderson and Margaret Jolly, 233–261. Chicago: The University of Chicago Press, 1997.

Legarda, Maribel. "Imagined Communities PETA's Community, Culture and Development Experience." In *Community, Culture and Globalization,* edited by Don Adams Arlene Goldbard, 335–351. New York: The Rockefeller Foundation, 2002.

Libby Manaoag Files: Ang Paghahanap sa Puwertas Princesas [The search for the doors to the princess], *A Nationwide Informance Tour on Women's Health and Reproductive Rights.* Quezon City, PETA, 2002. VHS.

Lindio-McGovern, Ligaya. *Filipino Peasant Women: Exploitation and Resistance.* Philadelphia: The University of Pennyslvania Press, 1997.

LORENAS. "Impact of Imperialist Globalization" People's Conference Against Imperialist Globalization, 23 November 1996. In *The Women's Emancipation Movement in the Philippines, An Anthology,* no editor (np, nd, circa 2000).

Mananzan, Mary John (OSB), ed. *Essays on Women.* Manila: Institute of Women's Studies, 1987, rev. ed., 1991.

———. *Woman, Religion and Spirituality in Asia.* Pasig City: Anvil Publishing, 2004.

———. "Redefining Religious Commitment in the Philippine Context," in *We Dare to Dream,* ed. Fabella and Park, 101–114.

———. "Redefining Religious Commitment Today: Being Woman Religious in a Third World Country," in *Challenges to the Inner Room, Selected Essays and Speeches on Women by Mary John Mananzan OSB,* Mary John Mananzan (Manila: Institute of Women's Studies, 1998).

———. "Suprema Isabel Suarez," in *Gendering the Spirit Women, Religion and the Post-Colonial Response,* edited by Durre S. Ahmed, 129–135. London: Zed Books, 2002.

———. *Challenges to the Inner Room: Selected Essays and Speeches on Women by Sr. Mary John Mananzan (OSB).* Manila: The Institute of Women's Studies, 1998.

———. *The Woman Question in the Philippines.* Manila: Institute of Women's Studies, 1997.

———. "Theological Perspectives of a Religious Woman Today—Four Trends of Emerging Spirituality," in *Feminist Theology in the Third World,* edited by Ursula King, 340–349. New York: Orbis Press, 1994.

Mangahas, Fe B., and Jenny R. Llaguno, eds. *Centennial Crossings: Readings on Babaylan Feminism in the Philippines.* Quezon City: C & E Publishing, 2006.

McKay, Steven C. "Filipino Sea Men: Identity, Masculinity in a Global Labor Niche." In *Asian Diasporas: New Formations, New Conceptions,* edited by Rhacel Parreñas and Lok C.D. Siu, 63–83. Stanford: Stanford University Press, 2007.

Milgram, B. Lynne. "Ukay-Ukay Chic: Tales of Second Hand Clothing: Fashion and Trade in the Philippine Cordillera." In *Old Clothes, New Looks, Second-Hand Fashion,* edited by Alexandra Palmer and Hazel Clark, 135–153. London: Berg, 2005.

Montañez, Jannis T., with Paulynn P. Sicam and Carmelita G. Nuqui, eds. *Pains and Gains: A Study of Overseas Performing Artists in Japan—from Pre-Departure to Reintegration.* Manila: DAWN, 2003.

Moreno, J. *Philippine Costume.* Manila: J. Moreno Foundation, 1995.

Muldong-Portus, Lourdes A. *Streetwalkers of Cubao.* Manila: Giraffe Books, 2005.

Muñez, Marles. Can Reforms Withstand Guns-and-Gold Politics?." In *Gaining Ground? Southeast Asian Women in Politics and Decision-Making, Ten Years After Beijing, A Compilation of Five Country Reports,* no editor, 143–202. Pasig City: Friedrich Ebert Stiftung, 2004.

Nakpil, Carmen Guerrero. *Woman Enough and Other Essays.* Manila: Vidal Publishing, 1964.

Nuqui, Carmelita G., and Jannis T. Montañez, eds. *Moving On: Stories of DAWN Women Survivors.* Manila: DAWN, 2004.

On Our Terms: A Lesbian Primer. Manila: Can't Live in the Closet (CLIC) Inc., 1999.

On the Wings of a Dove: We Shall No Longer Be Silent! Overcoming Violence Against Women and Children. Manila: Board of Women's Work-United Methodist Church, Association of Women in Theology (AWIT), Women's Desk—National Council of Churches in the Philippines, November 25 to December 10, 2004.

Parreñas, Rhacel Salazar. *Children of Global Migration: Transnational Families and Gendered Woes.* Quezon City: Ateneo de Manila University Press, 2006. Originally published by Stanford California Press, 2005.

———. *Servants of Globalization: Women, Migration and Domestic Work.* Stanford,

CA: Stanford University Press 2001, and Quezon City: Ateneo de Manila University Press, 2003.

———. "Transgressing the Nation-State: The Partial Citizenship and Imagined (Global) Community of Migrant Filipino Domestic Workers," *Signs* 26, 4 (Summer 2001): 1129–1154.

Payonggayong, Ma. Theresa T. "Nakatikim ka ba ng Kinse Anyos?" [Have you tasted a 15 year old?]. The Philippine Experience of Patriarchy." In *Quilted Sightings: A Women and Gender Studies Reader,* edited by Marilen Abesamis and Josefa Francisco 89–106. Quezon City: Miriam College, 2006.

Pe-Pua, Rogelia. "Wife, Mother and Maid: The Triple Role of Filipino Domestic Workers in Spain and Italy." In *Wife or Worker? Asian Women and Migration,* edited by Nicola Piper and Mina Roces, 157–180. Boulder: Rowman and Littlefield, 2003.

Philippines Organizing Committee. Proceedings of the Sixth International Women and Health Meeting. November 3–9, 1990. Quezon City: The Philippines Organizing Committee, CWR, GABRIELA, KABAPA, PILIPINA, SAMAKANA, WomanHealth, WRRC, 1990.

Pingol, Alicia Tadeo. *Remaking Masculinities: Identity, Power and Gender Dynamics in Families with Migrant Wives and Househusbands.* Quezon City: UP Center for Women's Studies, 2001.

Purcell, Francesca B. *Coming of Age: Women's Colleges in the Philippines During the Post-Marcos Era.* New York and London: Routledge, 2005.

Quimpo, Nathan Gilbert. "The Left, Elections, and the Political Party System in the Philippines," *Critical Asian Studies* 37, no.1 (2005): 3–28.

Resurrección, Bernadette. "From Resource Managers to Secondary Farm Hands: Changing Gender Divisions of Labour in a Philippine Upland Village." In *Labour in Southeast Asia: Local Processes in a Globalised World,* edited by Rebecca Elmhirst and Ratna Saptari, 187–214. London: RoutledgeCurzon, 2004.

———. *Transforming Nature, Redefining Selves: Gender and Ethnic Relations, Resource Use, and Environmental Change in the Philippine Uplands.* Maastricht, Germany: Shaker Publishing, 1999.

Rizal, José. *Noli Me Tangere,* trans. Charles E. Derbyshire as *The Social Cancer.* Manila: Philippine Education Company, 1912, 1976.

Roces, Mina and Louise Edwards, "Women in Asia as a Distinct Research Field." In *Major Works on Women in Asia,* Vol. 1, edited by Louise Edwards and Mina Roces, 1–18. London: Routledge, 2009.

Roces, Mina, "Is the Suffragist an American Colonial Construct? Defining 'the Filipino Woman' in Colonial Philippines." In *Women's Suffrage in Asia: Gender, Nationalism and Democracy,* edited by Louise Edwards and Mina Roces, 24–58. London: Routledge, 2004.

———. "Gender, Nation and the Politics of Dress in Twentieth Century Philippines." *Gender and History* 17, no. 2 (August 2005): 354–377.

———. *Women, Power and Kinship Politics: Female Power in Post-War Philippines.* Westport, CT: Praeger, 1998.

Ruiz-Austria, Carolina S., and Venus Cruz. *Girls in Law: Laws Affecting Young Women.* Quezon City: WomenLead, 2005.

————, ed. *Heresy.* Quezon City: WomenLead, 2005.

Salazar, Zeus A. "Ang Babaylan sa Kasaysayan ng Pilipinas" [The priestess or *babaylan* in Philippine history]. In *Women's Role in Philippine History: Selected Essays,* 52–72. Quezon City: University Center for Women's Studies, 1996.

Santiago, Lilia Quindoza. "Ang Salaysay ng Babae, Pagkababae at Kababaihan sa Rebolusyon ng 1896" [The discussion on woman, womanhood and the women in the revolution of 1896]. In *Kumperensya '93, Ang Papel ng Kababaihan at Katutubo sa Rebolusyong 1896* [Conference '93: The role of women and ethnic minorities in the revolution of 1896] no editor, Baguio and Benguet: University of the Philippines Kolehiyo sa Baguio and Benguet State University, 1995.

————. *In the Name of the Mother: 100 Years of Philippine Feminist Poetry.* Quezon City: University of the Philippines Press, 2002.

Santiago, Luciano P. R. *To Love and to Suffer: The Development of the Religious Congregations for Women in the Spanish Philippines, 1565–1898.* Quezon City: Ateneo de Manila University Press, 2005.

Santos Maranan, Aida F. "Towards a Theory of Feminism: Preliminary Discussions on the Woman Question in the Philippines." Unpublished manuscript, University of the Philippines, CSWCD Library, 1985.

Singh, Susheela, Fatima Juarez, Josefina Cabigon, Haley Ball, Rubina Hussain, and Jennifer Nadeau, eds. *Unintended Pregnancy and Induced Abortion in the Philippines: Causes and Consquences.* Washington, DC: Guttmacher Institute, 2006.

Sobritchea, Carolyn I. "Women's Movement in the Philippines and the Politics of Critical Collaboration with the State." In *Civil Society in Southeast Asia,* edited by Lee Hock Guan, 102–121. Singapore and Copenhagen: ISEAS and NIAS Press, 2004.

State of Filipino Women's Reproductive Rights: 10 Years Post-Cairo Shadow Report. Quezon City: Likhaan and Arrow, 2004. No author.

Tadiar, Neferti Xina M. *Fantasy-Production: Sexual Economies and Other Philippine Consequences for the New World Order.* Quezon City: Ateneo de Manila University Press, 2004.

————. *Things Fall Away: Philippine Literatures, Historical Experience and Tangential Makings of Globality.* Durham, NC: Duke University Press, 2009.

Tancangco, Luzviminda G. "Voters, Candidates, and Organizers: Women and Politics in Contemporary Philippines." In *Filipino Women and Public Policy,* edited by Proserpina Domingo Tapales, 59–95. Manila: Kalikasan Press, 1992.

Tapales, Proserpina Domingo, ed. *Filipino Women and Public Policy.* Manila: Kalikasan Press, 1992.

Tauli-Corpuz, Victoria. "Women's Power in the Cordilleras: A Herstory of Resistance," *Laya Feminist Quarterly* 2, (1992): 9–10.

Torres, Amaryllis Tiglao. "The Filipina Looks at Herself: A Review of Women's Studies." In *The Filipino Woman in Focus: A Book of Readings,* edited by Amaryllis T. Torres, 1–27. Quezon City: The UP Office of Research Coordination and the UP Press, 1995.

———. *Love in the Time of Ina Morata.* Quezon City: University Center for Women's Studies, 2002.

Tripon, Olivia H., ed. *Shaping the Women's Global Agenda: Filipino Women in the United Nations Commission on the Status of Women /CEDAW Committee.* Manila: NCRFW, 2007.

Ursua, Evalyn G. *Women's Health and the Law.* Quezon City: Women's Legal Bureau Inc., for SIBOL, 1997.

Veneracion-Rallonza, Lourdes, "Women and the Democracy Project: A Feminist Take on Women's Political Participation in the Philippines." In *Women's Political Participation and Representation in Asia: Obstacles and Challenges,* edited by Kazuki Iwanaga, 210–252. Copenhagen: NIAS Press, 2008.

Viado, Lalaine. *Reproductive Health Politics, Health Sector Reforms and Religious Conservatism in the Philippines (1964–2004).* Calabar, Cross River State, Nigeria: Development Alternatives with Women for a New Era, 2005.

Women's International Solidarity Affair in the Philippines 1989, Conference Proceedings, April 8–21, 1989.

Women's Legal Bureau, Inc. for SIBOL. *A Legislative Manual for Women.* Quezon City: Women's Legal Bureau, 2001.

Women's Studies Reader. Manila: Institute of Women's Studies, 2004. No editor.

Author's Interviews

Bacalando, Lina. Quezon City, September 27, 2006.

Barcelona, Joy. Manila, January 22, 2005.

Battung, Rosario (RGS). Quezon City, January 23, 2005.

Bermisa, Leonila V. (MM). Quezon City, July 20, 2003.

Borres, Gertrude, RA. Makati City, January 21, 2002.

Cahilog, Emily. Quezon City, August 18, 2003.

Cortes, Lola Asiang. Quezon City, August 9, 2003.

Dabu, Helen. Quezon City, September 22, 2006.

David, Rina. PILIPINA, Quezon City, September 26, 2006.

de Dios, Aurora Javate. Quezon City, July 23, 2003, August 8, 2003, October 6, 2006, and January 26, 2008.

de Jesus, Emmi. Quezon City, July 25, 2003.

de Leon, Sinag. Manila, September 25, 2006.

Dimaranan, Mariani SFIC. Quezon City, February 3, 1995.

Enriquez, Jean. Quezon City, August 11, 2003.

Estavillo, Cathy. Quezon City, August 23, 2003.

Estrada-Claudio, Sylvia. Quezon City, September 18, 2006, October 6, 2006, January 7, 2008, and July 6, 2010.

Extremadura, Rechilda. Quezon City, August 26, 2003.

Fabella, Virginia (MM). Pasig City, Metro-Manila, January 18, 2005.

Francisco, Josefa. Quezon City, January 23, 2003, July 23, 2003, October 6, 2006, January 8, 2008, July 26, 2010, July 27, 2010, and July 28, 2010.

Garrucho, C. B. Quezon City, October 6, 2006.

Graham, Helen (MM). Quezon City, August 1, 2003.

Guerrero, Nerissa. Quezon City, August 27, 2003.
Guillermi, Lola Virginia. Quezon City, August 9, 2003.
Holmes, Margarita, Quezon City, January 23, 2008.
Hontiveros-Baraquiel, Ana Theresia (Risa). Quezon City, October 5, 2006.
Illo, Jeanne Francis. Quezon City, August 7, 2003.
Ledesma, Maitet. Amsterdam, July 31, 2006.
Legarda, Katrina. Makati City, January 20, 2005.
Legarda, Maribel, She Maala, and Cecile B. Garrucho. Quezon City, October 9, 2006.
Licuanan, Patricia, de Dios, Aurora Javate, and Francisco, Josefa. Miriam College, Quezon City, July 23, 2003.
Licuanan, Patricia. Quezon City, January 18, 2008.
Lubi, Elisa Tita. Quezon City, January 17, 2005.
Lucson, Claire, and Quintela, Minerva. Quezon City, January 11, 2008.
Lumibao, Wowie (Kanlungan). Quezon City, July 22, 2010.
Magat, Josefina (RA). Makati City, Febuary 1, 2002.
Malasa, Lily. Manila, September 21, 2006, September 25, 2006.
Mananzan, Mary John (OSB). Manila, July 20, 1995, and July 17, 2003.
Mangahas, Fe. Manila, February 1, 2005.
Maza, Liza. Quezon City, January 19, 2005.
Miranda, Nanette. Quezon City, August 26, 2003.
Monte, Janice. Quezon City, January 19, 2005.
Nemenzo, Ana Maria "Princess." Quezon City, October 10, 2006.
Nuqui, Carmelita G. Manila, January 22, 2005, and July 19, 2010.
Pagaduan, Maureen, and Ursua, Evelyn. Quezon City, January 24, 2008.
Perpiñan, Soledad (RGS). Quezon City, April 20, 1996, July 28, 2003, August 28, 2003.
Punzalan, Sonia. (Cenacle Sisters). Quezon City, September 8, 2003.
Quintela, Minerva, and Cruz, Venus. Quezon City, October 10, 2006.
Salgado, Joy, and Pacete, Joy. Quezon City, September 27, 2006, and January 8, 2008.
Salvador, Jomes. Quezon City, August 17, 2003.
Sana, Ellene and Abano, Rhordora. Quezon City, January 28, 2008.
Sancho, Nelia. Manila, September 27, 2006.
Santos, Aida Maranan. Makati City, October 11, 2006.
Sarabia, Anna Leah. Makati City, August 12, 2003, and Manila, September 21, 2006, September 25, 2006, January 4, 2008, July 18, 2010, and July 24, 2010.
Sarenas, Patricia. Makati City, January 18, 2008.
Taguiwalo, Judy. Quezon City, January 7, 2008.
Tan, Christine (RGS). Malate, February 7, 1995.
Valeria, Chit, (RVM). Quezon City, August 25, 2003.
Vasquez, Amelia (RCSJ). Quezon City, August 19, 2003.
Villegas, Emelina (ICM). Quezon City, January 10, 2005.
Vistro, Tess. Quezon City, January 21, 2008, January 23, 2008, and January 24, 2008.
Yocogan-Diano, Verni. Baguio City, September 5, 2003.

Periodicals

"Ang Programang Pabahay ng Gobyernong Arroyo: Isang Pinagtagpi-tagping Pangako" [The housing allowance program of the Arroyo government: A patchwork of promises], 2002.

Chaneg, 1994-2006. Newsletter/magazine published by the organization CWERC.

Coalition Asia-Pacific Report (incomplete), Vol 1. 1995–Vol 6. 2002.

Gabriela Women's Update, September 1985–August 2007. Newsletter published by GABRIELA.

Igorota Magazine, 1989–1995.

IMA, Vol. IV no. 11, April–June 2000. Newsletter.

In God's Image, December 1982–2004. Journal.

Kali, Voice of Cordillera Women, Vol. 1–3, 2000–2003. Journal.

Kanlungan ng Migrante [Kanlungan Migrant Center], 1990–2005.

Kontraktwalisasyon sa Paggawa [Contractualization of work], 2002. Center for Women's Resources in Quezon City.

Laya Feminist Quarterly, 1992–1994. Newsletter.

Lola's Bulletin, Japanese-Military Sexual Slavery in the Philippines. Annual bulletin of AWHRC Lolas Kampanyeras, 2002.

Marso 8, Nos. 2–5, 1993–1998. Regular journal of the CWR.

Piglas-Diwa, Issues and Trends About Women in the Philippines, 1992–1999. English version of *Piglas Diwa.* "Piglas-Diwa is a Pilipino term which means a spirit/idea trying to break free. Piglas-Diwa, the publication is an attempt to contribute to the liberation of Filipino women from economic, political and socio-cultural bondage. Through the discussion of issues and trends on women, we hope to be able to contribute to this cause."

Piglas-Diwa, Isyu't Tunguhin sa Pakikibaka ng Kababaihan [Piglas Diwa, Issues and Trends on the Women's Struggle], 1988–2000.

Sinag, January 1998–June 2010. Newsletter.

The Review of Women's Studies, 1990–2008. Journal.

T.N.T. (Trends, News, Tidbits), December 1991–December 2005. Newsletter.

Ugnay-Kababaihan, April–June 1992, and August 1992. Newsletter.

Women's Journal on Law and Culture, WomenLead Foundation Inc., July–December 2001.

WomenLead Monograph Series, Vol. 1, Issues 1–4, 2005. Series published by WomenLead.

Index

Note: Page references in bold type indicate the most detailed discussion of the topic.

abortion, 185; "comfort women,"
146; Cordillera women, 87, 90–92,
96, 100–102; demonstrations, **158–
63,** 165; health movements, 110,
112, 115, 119, 122; history, 8, 26,
48; media, 127–28, 130, 136; membership, 201; official history book
(Si Maria, Nena, Gabriela Atbp),
17–18, 21, 24, 157; performing
group, 155, 168; politics, 10–11,
41; publications, 157; rituals, 168;
transnationalism, 28, 174, 177–82,
236n55, 246n23; women workers,
66–68, 70–71, 73–79, 82, 84–85
GABRIELA Circle of Friends, 112,
165–67, 169
GABRIELA-USA, 28, 178
GABRIELA Women's Party, 141–42,
161, 163
GABRIELA-Youth, 66, 71, 161, 163
gambling, 95
Garcia, Fanny, 59
Garrucho, Cecile B., 20, 155, 164
Gates, Christina, 57–58
GATT, 66, 83–84
gay men, 112, 116, 120, 122
gender issues: abortion, 193; Catholic
Church, 35; "comfort women,"
146; discrimination and equality,
4, 74, 87, 110, 121, 127, 152, 193;
indigenous women, 87, 92–93, 97,
102; media, 127; peasant women,
74; roles, 2, 86, 93; theater as advocacy, 152; women workers, 110;
women's movements, 121. *See also*
women's rights
globalization: indigenous women, 88–89,
92–93, 97–99, 101–3; overseas
contract workers, 80, 83; peasant
women, 76; prostitution and, 55;
women workers, 66–67, 71–73, 77,
85, 201; women's movements, 9,
13–14, 178
GLOW (Gloria's League of Women), 10
GO-NGO network, 11
government: abortion, 187, 190–93;
church and, 23; "comfort women"
and, 146–47; family and, 187;
feminist nuns and, 36, 49, 167;
indigenous women and, 89, 97,
100–102; media productions,
139; overseas contract workers,
79–81, 83, 85, 135; prostitution
and, 55–57, 59, 62, 64; theater as

advocacy, 153; transnational lobbying, 173; women workers and, 77,
84; women's health, 104–5, 108–9,
113–15, 128, 135, 141; women's
movements and, 5, 11–13, 16, 144,
198, 203
Graham, Helen (MM), 37, 42
grassroots women, 17, 40, 67, 110, 116,
128, 201
Guerrero, Milagros, 20, 27
Guerrero, Nerissa, 78
guest workers. *See* overseas contract
workers
Guidote, Cecile, 152
HASIK (Harnessing Self-Reliant Initiatives and Knowledge, Inc.), 113
The Haven, 109
health. *See* information and services;
reproductive rights & health;
women's health
Henson, Maria Rosa, 140
Hilao, Liliosa, 24–25, 158
Hilhorst, Dorothea, 91
HIV/AIDS, 63, 131, 135, 153, 159
Holmes, Margarita, 122, 140
homosexuals. *See* gay men; lesbianism
Hong Kong, 80, 99, 134, 173, 191
Hontiveros-Baraquiel, Risa, 129, 142,
154
human rights: abortion, 131; "comfort
women," 146; indigenous women,
89; lesbians, 121; Marcos regime,
38; media, 131; oral testimony,
149; overseas contract workers,
79, 82; prostitution, 53–54, 59–60;
theater as advocacy, 150, 153;
transnational activism, 179–80;
violence against women, 111;
women workers, 72, 85; women's
movements, 200
Human Rights Commission, 76
Human Rights Day, 54
Igorota Foundation, 48, 87–88, 92
Igorots, 88–89, 95–97, 100, 102
Ilagan, Luzviminda Calolot "Luz," 10
Illo, Jeanne Frances, 182
incest, 48, 63, 129, 131, 199
indigenous women (Cordillera region),
87–103; dress, 90–91, 102, 163;
feminist nuns and, 38, 41, 47–48,
92; Filipino women and, 96–101;
International Working Women's
Day, 101–2; media productions,
89, 134, 139; resistance to Marcos

About the Author

MINA ROCES received her PhD from the University of Michigan and is presently associate professor in the School of History and Philosophy at the University of New South Wales in Sydney, Australia. She is the author of two previous books, *Women, Power and Kinship Politics: Female Power in Post-War Philippines* (1998) and *Kinship Politics in Postwar Philippines: The Lopez Family, 1946-2000* (2001), and has co-edited several volumes on women in Asia, most recently with Louise Edwards (*Women's Movements in Asia: Feminisms and Transnational Activism,* 2010, and *The Politics of Dress in Asia and the Americas,* 2007). Her articles have been published in *Gender & History, Women's History Review, Women's Studies International Forum*, and *Modern Asian Studies.* She is the editor for the Sussex Library of Asian Studies series and regional editor for Southeast Asia for the *Asian Studies Review.*